IF MY
PEOPLE

IF MY PEOPLE

Repairing the Breach

Jabez Abraham

All Scripture quotations are taken from the
King James Version (KJV) – *public domain.*

Cover illustration: Sonia Bennett

Paperback ISBN-13: 979-8-218-97684-2

Published by: Jabez Abraham | Desiring Revival Ministries

Thou art worthy, O Lord, to receive glory and honour and power: for thou hast created all things, and for thy pleasure they are and were created. – Rev. 4:11

Contents

Introduction

In 2000 I was staying in Santa Cruz, California, with my cousin, and one evening we were walking around the city and came across a gay parade. I had no idea what "gay" was and saw it more as a spectacle that happens in America. On a Sunday night, my cousin and I went to the evening service at a church I had never been to. But it was not the traditional church setting. I entered the church, and the place was dark, and large curtains surrounded the auditorium; the place had stage lights, and musicians played it up with "Christian rock" music that was part of their Christian worship service. During my time in America, I spent many years in Bible-believing fundamental Baptist churches, attended multi-denominational conferences, and visited churches in many parts of the land. After over two decades of being actively involved in church programs, leading youth programs, bus ministry, and everything else under heaven as a layperson that would have made me seem like a "great" Christian in the eyes of those around me, I found myself doubting everything I was confident about regarding Christianity, from when I came from India. Sharing my journey has been done in obedience to Christ. It is a burden that has not been shared in haste or in a desire to usurp authority or be unkind; neither has the book been for generating a response toward me, but rather something that would be for one's searchings' with God. Why must this be considered? Is this about being critical? The answer to that, I believe, is the difference between critical and analytical. Critical is to tear down, being jealous of something contrary to what one believes in a negative way; analytical, on the other hand, is to evaluate with an honest view so change can be applied positively. The desire here is the analytical viewpoint with a hope that truth would be clarified, and God would revive His work, in wrath remember mercy (Hab. 3:2).

This has been captured as my personal faith journey and God's revelation of the need we have in our beloved land. Written here is an updated version of what was published in an earlier book titled "American pseudo-Christianity." Crucial clarifications and additions needed to be made, thus this publishing as a new book has been warranted. In recording this, the recount is from the various events from over two decades of what God has led me through in many seasons of prayers, frustrations, tears, barrenness, and His healing. I stand on no foundation of my own but on the sole authority of the word of God, and the truths that He has graciously brought me to.

With the awareness that the American church has jaded appetites, where it makes folks skim through deeply consequential truths, my humble request is that you read it in its entirety with purposeful intent before you make your conclusions before God. The truths presented are just as relevant to someone who has been faithful in the ministry but seems to be going through a spell of barrenness and not seeing a tangible move of God in their local congregation. "For we must all appear before the judgment seat of Christ; that every one may receive the things done in his body, according to that he hath done, whether it be good or bad" – 2 Cor. 5:10. What is said is just as true for me to examine in my own life and take into serious consideration where I have need of.

To get started, we need to go back to when I met Christ.

Who Am I?

I need to begin with the event where I encountered Christ and received new life through Him, what Jesus stated as being born again (John 3:5-7). My name is Jabez Abraham, and I was born in South India. I was born into a culture that contained a myriad of religions and was convinced that each religion had its own path to truth. My life was filled with the faith of my parents: Christianity. We went to church, read the Bible, and prayed. By the time I was in college, I knew a lot about the Bible and could teach others its teaching and stories. I even passed out gospel tracts, taught Vacation Bible School, and went to other churches for special events and competitions.

During my junior year in school, I started getting involved in what you could call "living it up." I lied to my parents, and when I was caught, I would lie without hesitation that I did not commit the act; it was natural to me; I was of my father the devil (John 8:44); used foul language, was in bondage to the lusts of the flesh, cheated, and drank with my buddies during my college years. This was what I thought living life was all about. For me, this was the balance between life and religion; you live it up and then do good to others by following your religion; even an atheist could do some charitable works and help their fellow man. After all, what is the purpose of life? Why are we here on planet Earth and what happens after we die? These are questions that everyone is confronted with, and so was I.

In 1996, at 21 years of age, I continued faithfully attending church and reading my Bible. I believed what it said. I brushed off anyone who wanted to talk to me about anything more than what I already knew about religion. After all, in my mind, the Bible was just a religious book of history with enjoyable stories. It didn't mean anything more than that to me. On April 7th, after going about my routine of attending the Easter Sunday service at my church, I came home and started watching an animated story about the crucifixion of Christ. I had seen similar movies all my life, but something was different this time.

Suddenly I came under a profound realization of what happened during that familiar history of Christ's Crucifixion, and I ran into my parents' bedroom. It was revealed to me that the main reason Jesus came was for my sin, not just as a historical figure or as the leader of Christianity. It was a supernatural revelation that Jesus was God in human flesh. I was brought to the vision of the cross and what happened there. Not, as it were, an impression of truth, but visibly seeing Him hanging there for me. The true nature of my sin was suddenly made real to me, and I was brought under deep conviction of sin. I had broken God's law and, in turn, offended Him when I lied and lusted after forbidden things, among many others. When I realized this, I understood that Jesus had taken MY sin upon that cross. He was not crucified because of the Romans but because of the penalty of my sin that I owed: "the wages of sin is death" – Rom. 6:23. I cried out to God and said, "God, why, why did you go through such suffering and agony when you didn't have to?" Then I heard His voice, "Because I love you." That was the defining moment in my life. I realized that my sin put Him on that cross, and I said, "Lord, I am sorry," amidst my tears.

It was a Divine exchange when God saved me and took my guilt of sin away. I rose from my knees and could tell things were now different. It was not an intellectual "decision" I made, for I loved my sin and would have continued in it; instead, it was all of Christ who conquered me unto Himself. My dramatic conversion brought new desires, victories, and a different outlook on life. I immediately made restitution with my brother, went and confessed the evil I had participated to those needed, and gave up all my worldly music (in cassette tapes) to be erased and reused for transcription for the blind, things which I used to enjoy were now vile in my sight. This change came without anyone telling me what is to be expected of a Christian; it was a radical change of having been given a new heart and the Spirit of God residing in me, a sensitivity to sin and repentance which continues to this day; though, it has its ebb and flow.

My burden of sin was gone, which had such an impact at that time that I felt lighter when I walked outside my parents' bedroom after what had happened; I had a sense of being clean, a heart of joy, a love for Him, and a thought that I could never sin against God anymore; my relationship to God, who created all things, was restored and I knew it. I was going one way, ignorant of God's righteousness, and suddenly, supernaturally, was turned around and sent the other way by God. Others could tell that something had happened, where once I had a contentious spirit of pride, but now a heart that was willing to ask for forgiveness; where once I thought that being "confirmed" in the church was the way that one becomes a serious Christian, but now I realized that it was this matter of being born again and not what man can do, that no one is born a Christian. It was not that I was seeking after God; instead, it was God seeking after me and drawing me unto Himself. It was not about any good works I could do, about being religious or getting baptized. I realized that Christ came to restore our relationship with God, the living God. The Scriptures made sense now; I could see why we have the problems around us, what the only hope for this world is, and for life that is to come after we die. I could see that religion was manmade and that Christ did not come to start a religion. Looking back, it has been many decades since that glorious day, and I can tell from personal experience and seeing God's providential care the reality of what began that day.

That was in 1996, and in the year 2000, I arrived in the US to work as a Computer Professional, landing in Dallas, Texas, and then moved to the Bay Area, California.

THE REVEALING

Americanized Christianity

Apart from the many churches that I went to, from Salvation Army church services and Christian churches to Baptist churches, Christianity was at the pinnacle of what I was supposed to experience, or so I thought. Of course, seeing American churches through the eyes of television back in India when I was growing up seemed so lively and genuine. The ornate Cathedrals, large crusades, large crowds, people coming forward after a service, people falling to the ground under the "power of God," and so forth were all amazing. From the outside world, America was considered a beacon of truth in Christendom; it was a "Christian" nation.

Coming to America and attending churches was a dream come true for this young Christian convert. The great music, crowds, large buildings, famous preachers, energetic preachers thumping the pulpits to programs for kids to adults. Then I moved to the Bible Belt because of my work in Nashville, Tennessee, in 2002, with churches on every corner. I remained faithful to Sunday morning, Sunday night, Wednesday evening, Saturday visitation, fellowships, ministry outreaches, etc. Biblical truths were embraced, which showed the false belief systems of what goes under the general guise of Christendom in learning the fundamentals of the faith and so forth. But they were all out there and given over to false teachings, but I was faithfully taught the Bible. Years went by, and then the doubts began to appear.

Much Activity, No Progress

At this point, I need to clarify what I mean by Americanized Christianity for the context of the topics being addressed. These would be those who would call themselves evangelicals, fundamentalists who strictly adhere to the fundamentals of the faith, believing the Bible from cover to cover and proclaiming it. It could be Arminian doctrine, following Reformed theology, or called by any other name who pride themselves on following the word of God without compromise.

At first, it was just a concern here and there, there was much talk of God working and moving, but it seemed empty words. There was nothing where I could relate to what I read in New Testament Christianity in the book of Acts. Yes, God specifically worked in my life on occasions, but it was not consistent in the long run and evidenced by increasing my faith, bringing me to holiness, and such. I was struggling in certain areas of my life in not being watchful against the things of the flesh, and the victorious Christian living seemed to be a pipedream. I could sing in the choir and hear sermons but still have no sense of the fear of God to keep me from evil. There was much talk about special efforts during Christmas, Easter, and such to bring visitors so they could hear the "gospel," many did come, but the church did not increase with new converts desiring to be fed from the word. People were baptized but didn't show up or fell away shortly. Or those who came never seem to stay or show spiritual maturity after years of instruction, church services, and fellowships. The kindness was there, but it seemed to be more and more of a social club than an encounter with the living God of the Bible.

Shallow Roots, Shallow Results

When hearing of people being "saved," there were a lot of "amens," but looking back, there did not seem to be much interest in seeing what happened to them after the decisions were counted and the "amens" died out. And no one seemed to care, to take serious consideration of why. The word of God was preached, and emphasis was given to the word, but you never came from the service having met the God of the word. Instead, you were just instructed like you would at a lecture in a college on some topics. There was nothing supernatural in it. In the morning, I would go to the "altar" and make a decision; in the evening, I would feel "impressed" with an opposite decision than what I went forward for in the morning. You hear phrases like "The Bible says it, and that settles it" without any reason of "Why?" We had many youth and church events. Monster Truck crushing cars for Jesus, old-fashioned Sunday, swallowing goldfish, outdoor tent meetings, human dunk tanks and dressing in costumes, etc. I thought it was all part of the great activities for getting the gospel out, and I was actively and sincerely participating and leading in many of the efforts.

During this time, doubts about what the Americanized version of salvation produced was confirmed when I gave a survey to our church teen group with some simple questions such as When did you get saved? What happened? What changed? For many years in the summer, we had "decision cards" from a particular ministry during their summer marketplace evangelism. In following them up, not one of them showed any interest in even coming to church, let alone joining it. In another instance, I witnessed an evangelist who had those who were saved raise their hand and those that didn't want to get saved (in an earlier invitation) look up and tell them to go back to get saved. The shallowness did not stop when I witnessed a seasoned preacher (Who pastors a church and teaches at a Bible college) who convinced a young child with arguments when dealing with supernatural matters. This is how the conversation went when he conversed with her about eternal salvation. Preacher: *Do you believe in Jesus?* Child: Yes. Preacher: *What does the Bible say if you believe?* Child: *You will be saved?* Preacher: *Does God lie?* Child: *No.* Preacher: *So, what are you now?* Child: *Saved?* And he went on to plan to have her baptized. In another instance, I watched in disbelief when one of my coworkers, who claimed to be a Christian, grabbed a bottle of beer and took a swing at it. When asked, he brushed it off as nothing to give any thought into, though he bore the name of "Christ" in his claim of being a Christian. I heard it stated emphatically that "we have the answer that the world needs," but the more I saw the "answer" that had no power to change a life but was content to call them children of God, the more the "answer" became of lesser value.

I have regretted many of the cookie-cutter methods that I had learned and participated in (from what I was taught and seen done in church services) and led people into an intellectual belief of the gospel, where they lacked that true life of Christ in them, and called them as Christians, having their blood upon my hands, unable to go back now and correct my mistakes.

The Grand Assumptions

Growing up in that environment, some lesser results were genuine but seemed grossly disproportionate to what was being promised, with "souls saved, and lives changed." We realize that talk is cheap, but to show it in lives that have been radically transformed by the power of God and living it is to prove the reality of it. We read in 1 Thess. 5:21 to "Prove all things." There was no lack of Bible knowledge or sincerity in the ministers, programs, and events. In India, even as a lost person, I saw churches holding all-night prayer meetings, hearing of periods of fasting and prayer, New Year's Eve services that last over three hours starting at 11:30 pm, Good Friday services that last over three hours, early dawn service at 5:30 am for Easter and such. Coming to America and seeing time-conscious members (in a one-hour church service) and apologetic Pastors when they went a few minutes over the allotted time were becoming a common sight. I started hearing a common thread of verses being used. God is always with us, and there is nothing more to be prayed for, using the verse, "For where two or three are gathered together in my name, there am I in the midst of them." – Matt. 18:20. The verse, "I will never leave thee, nor forsake thee." – Heb. 13:5 used in all circumstances. Soon the purposes of God in the lives of His people became more for man's best interest rather than the glory of God that shone through a changed life. I saw salvation presentation's that put man in the driver's seat with an impotent God waiting patiently for him *(and the lost man likes that since his old Adamic nature wants to have face and control)*.

Americanized Christianity stopped asking for change when people said they got "saved." They stopped requiring communities to be transformed when an evangelist came and conducted a "revival." They started finding ways to allow God to fit into our busy schedules while assuring that we are following God and that He is what it is all about. While many parts of the world were going through intense persecution for their faith, being martyred, facing starvation, and giving up all they had for the cause of Christ, the American church was busy pursuing the American dream, shouting for the rapture, and seeing how we can get out of here before it gets too hot. American spirituality was reduced to making movies where one sheds a few tears, drama, and music concerts to show that you love Jesus with face paintings, t-shirts, stickers, and wristbands.

I was taught how to "win souls" and have them make a "decision" for Christ. Looking back on those years, the more I "led others to Christ" or saw others lead someone to Christ, the more I saw it as one-sided and unnecessary for the Holy Spirit to do anything. We were to explain the gospel, make sure they understood what was being said, use the "Roman's Road," have them raise their hand, or pray a sinner's prayer that goes like "Dear Jesus, I know I am a sinner. I believe that you died for my sin. The best I know how I now place my trust in you to save me and take me to heaven when I die. Thank you for saving me." And the sinner was told to claim it and write it on a piece of paper with a Bible verse like John 3:16 since he has prayed that prayer and believed on Jesus. It was always one-sided, where Jesus did His part two thousand years ago, and man can choose to accept or reject;

whether in a card that had the four steps and "pray this prayer," in their seats repeating after the preacher, or in a sermon to pray and trust Christ; without any implication of what part the Spirit plays, what it means to repent, godly sorrow, or the evidential change that God works in us at the point of regeneration.

"Believe" was just intellectual assent that the sinner had within himself; sincerity was praised, and repentance was not expected or pushed aside as the same as "believe" or just as a change of mind that has no consequence on any change of action. Where regeneration was historically seen as this inflow of new life and infusion of new desires, it was now aggressively promoted to not depend on the experiential witness of the transaction but rather the intellectual agreement of truths. *Sidenote:* One can convince someone by reasoning where they are convinced in the mind of its validity, even by using the law (Rom. 3:20, 1 John 3:4), but the Spirit who takes it to the sinner's heart produces "felt" conviction by Divine illumination where "believe" is from the heart and not the mind alone (Rom. 10:9-10). Though we realize that feelings can mislead us, and we always look to the Source, we know that God has made us with characteristics that make us human with desires, emotions, intuition, etc.

Faith was portrayed as something you have in you already, and you can use the example of getting into an Airplane as having faith in the Airplane to get you to your destination, and salvation was nothing more than putting that same trust in Jesus. No submission to the authority of Christ was expected. There was an emphasis on the method to get the message across more than the Person of salvation. Almost a salesmanship way of asking if they were 90% or 100% sure that they were on their way to heaven. A person having doubts regarding their salvation were told to think back to when they decided to trust Christ and get a verse from the Bible for assurance and write it down. If they were unsure, they were told to go ahead and pray and write that date down, quoting 1 John 5:13, not realizing that that verse was given to believers to exhort them

15

to persevere. It was in man's control whenever he wanted to make a decision that suited him rather than telling them to seek the Lord through the word to see if that doubt was from the blessed Spirit of God convicting an unregenerate soul.

I saw the glorious message of salvation with its profound implication of the Spirit bringing the law of God on the self-righteousness of man, the cost of following Christ, the need for Biblical repentance that bringeth forth life, and such were mentioned as a simple hurried statement sandwiched into a general sermon. *Sidenote:* We need to realize the gross Biblical illiteracy we face in America and the assumptions of specific words that may mean a world of difference, including the cults that have a semblance of believing in Jesus. Everyone in America believes in "jesus," but the jesus that Americanized Christianity has produced is a long-haired, sentimental, feminine-looking god and country jesus, who is nothing but a figment of our imagination and not the God of the Bible. The Mormons sing "Amazing Grace," though they lack that very grace that they sing about. The Jews in Jesus' day who were under the tyranny of Rome wanted a god who could fix their problem with Rome; in similarity, our prayer for revival is nothing more than wanting this god to come and fix our problems, keep us from persecution, and make us look good in the process. Our Lord, who knows the weakness of His followers (Heb. 4:15, Psa. 103:14), does not warrant the follower to use it as an excuse for continuing to accommodate their weakness. Instead, it is for the follower to look to the strength of His Lord and fight the good fight of faith (1 Tim. 6:11-13), knowing that the victory has already been won by their Lord (2 Tim. 4:7-8). There is nothing sentimental about it; it is a call to persevere, a call to battle, to endure hardness as a good soldier of Jesus Christ. The need we have, whether with visitors who attend a worship service or even members who have been going to church for decades, is on the existence of God, the God of the Bible. It may mean that we may have one or many sermons just on what it means to be born again, where each sermon may last for over an hour, so the people are brought to the reality of phrases and what it accurately means.

I saw that as folks came to join the church, they were to make sure they only "believe" and not "believe + baptized" before they could be part of the church family. Transfer of membership from other churches was allowed, to join by a letter from the church they left, instead of sharing any credible evidence of regeneration. Invitation systems that were well rehearsed to greet someone and lead them through some pre-canned verses from the Bible during the songs that were being played, the noise of those coming and going, and distractions; there is an expectation that you can get this lost person to be born again before the invitation song ends. A teenager gave testimony that she was saved as a kindergartener because she was given a certificate in the school upon her decision to trust Christ. I saw that people were led to Christ and had no interest in coming to church to grow in their supposedly newfound Christ, yet the decision was announced, and the church rejoiced that someone got "saved." There were great numbers reported, but for the most part, there was no interest in a prayer meeting on the weekends, no interest in laboring in the ministry, and no desire for spiritual growth. They were easily offended, though, having been in the same church for many years. In essence, spiritual birth was conferred to sons and daughters of devils who had no spiritual experience of being born again by the Spirit of God.

I saw more and more of the elevation of men instead of being broken before God in humility. Young people rushed to have their Bibles signed by great preachers, calling out accolades of how great they were in "soul-winning," giving standing ovations when they came to the pulpit, and so forth. I saw denominational arrogance in putting oneself above others and that they were purebred amidst a pariah of others. At the same time, the need within the church to address gaping holes was being ignored. "Revivals" were scheduled but were forgotten within a week, and the community remained untouched. I am getting tired of hearing how "churches out there" need to or are missing out etc. What about "in our church"? We are good at slinging dirt at others while we stink in our own vomit. With the elevation of man came pride. Pride that we are the greatest nation on earth, the pride that our lawyers can stop any legislation we don't like from passing, the pride that we are the only ones who are the beacon of genuine Christian truth, pride of the past, the pride that we are the most capable in our military, and so on. And when a famous athlete says something nice about Jesus and blows kisses to heaven, Americanized Christianity rushes to showcase them as a model for the Christian witness. If America is the beacon of truth and hope from a Biblical standpoint, why is she at the forefront of leading the world to evil by promoting what the Biblical God calls an abomination? From rainbow flags to PRIDE month, that keeps sin at the forefront of the nation to make it the norm and acceptable. It is not the fault of the politicians, media, or entertainment; instead, it is the fruit of the weakness of evangelism that Americanized Christianity has produced. A strong delusion has overtaken the land and her churches, where what was known as "normal" for over six thousand years in gender and marriage is being questioned, and perversions are promoted and embraced as "normal." "Woe unto them that call evil good, and good evil; that put darkness for light, and light for darkness; that put bitter for sweet, and sweet for bitter!" – Isa. 5:20.

Slowly my faith was being eroded from what I had experienced in my new birth experience of this **relationship-based enjoyment of God to a man-centered theory-based instruction about God**. Preaching became teaching where in teaching, you may take an event or passage from the Scriptures, set the context of the event and maybe some background around it, bring out some application of that truth or convey other truths from that text and context. It brings the responsibility to the audience to see the gaps and to align or apply those truths in their lives and leave having potentially learned something new. I see little difference between this and what you do in a classroom or learning how to fix a car. Conviction of sin by the Spirit, where the sinner is bowed down, realizing the absolute holiness of God and the wretched sinfulness of sin by an external force, was reduced to convincing of truth, which is well within the realm of the individual who has been trained to do so in their system of education. I saw cults flourishing, wickedness not being restrained by the Spirit of the Lord who is to lift up a standard against the enemy, a church that has lost its voice, and the world asking her, "Where is now their God?"

I started seeing a trend of where once messages were preached on hell, but now only silence; where contending for the faith was once part of the church's duty to guard the sheep, now the "gay" agenda was picking up in full steam, and the church remained silent for the most part. During covid-19 viral outbreak in 2020, the government was allowed to call the shots if the church was to function as God intended in "assembling of ourselves together." Instead of praying for God's heart and taking a stand, most American churches followed suit. It folded up, obeying man rather than God. Americanized Christianity quickly finds a logical way out when inconvenienced. We are crippled by our self-preservation to make sure we don't face liability issues, though what we are asked to do, is what God would have us to do. We want the power of Pentecost, but we don't want to take the risk of having that power and getting sued or thrown in jail. There was much talk of losing the next generation and young people with poll results which concerned many leaders, but there seemed to be an unwillingness to examine if what was being preached had God's hand upon it. I was beginning to ask, where was the supernatural in any of this? There was a rejection of exhortation to "examine yourselves, whether ye be in the faith." There were a lot of churches, blogs, sermons, podcasts, prayers, "revivals," programs, and conferences, **but where was God?** We sing a lot of energizing songs, such as God on the throne, nothing can stop Him, we are more than conquerors, and such, while the reality is evil has been given a free course to plunder the land. The American church today is a thermometer telling how hot or warm the conditions are; the church in the New Testament was a thermostat that regulated the temperature around her with the power of God. We are just running on fumes. If the church does not impact the community radically to the point where the world stops and takes notice or persecutes it, then they have failed to be the salt and light but has become a social club. Truth does not care about political parties based on who accepts it or not; it flows from the eternal and unchanging God Himself.

There was much talk of the large number of "decisions" for Christ year after year, with almost a passion for reporting the numbers. Still, continually we see a nation that has been speedily plunging into deeper depravities of sin and unbelief, the moral declension of basic morality, the things that were done in secret now displayed on billboards and promoted on entertainment and social media, and regular stream of news of Pastors and "Christian" leaders living in sin or being caught in acts of perversions that are even detested by the world. While America was burning to the ground around me, I found myself amid a mindset that went like this, "as long as we have good politicians and we elect the right person in the office, we can legislate holiness, and all will be well." It became more and more evident that Americanized Christianity was more about guns and glory, personal preferences, 2nd amendment rights, having a form, and so forth. But where was the God of the word? *Sidenote:* God has ordained the government as a divine institution to uphold the moral code set by God, and the church has been ordained for spiritual health and to proclaim the truth. The government is subject to the law of God, so must she help the true church to uphold truth so that her subjects can be benefitted from it "that we may lead a quiet and peaceable life in all godliness and honesty." – 1 Tim. 2:2.

The gospel did not impact lives in the way that it was promised by God, in pulling down strongholds (2 Cor. 10:4), sinners crying out for mercy during the preaching (Acts 2:37), to the point where it caused the world to stop and take notice (Acts 4:13, 17:6); instead, sinners remain un-awakened to their need week after week, the church not having greater works or fruit that remain (John 14:12, 15:16). We exist as a church and do not alarm the enemy in attacking his dominion, in rescuing souls from perishing, where our progress threatens Satan, and so he leaves us alone. On the contrary, the disciples of Jesus Christ who met in the upper room, around a hundred and twenty of them, had to reckon with the military power (The Romans), the intellectual dominance (The Greeks), and the religious monopoly (The Pharisees and the Sadducees). They had no money, no New Testament, no influence, no internet, no blogs, no newsletters, and no social status. Many of the teachings were propagated to anyone from slaves of Rome to kings, uneducated fishermen, and women. Yet, they turned the world upside down and reached the whole world in a single generation (Acts 17:6, Col. 1:23). Something or someone was missing.

A Concerned Christian Layman

God started seeding a burden in 2005 for genuine revival and a Christian witness that was, as seen in the book of Acts and church history, God in the midst of His people, similar to times of true moving's of God in the past as what we call revival. While it was said that revival is just a new dedication of the Lord's people and not expecting anything more than a renewed vigor of religion or an alignment to the Scriptures, I was brought to the realization that revival is to **make alive where there was death, to create life**. We see this in these two instances where the word "revived" is referenced, where the child who was dead came to life (1 Kings 17:22), and the man who had died and was to be buried came alive again (2 Kings 13:21). Think about this declaration from that widow at Zarephath in 1 Kings 17, "And the woman said to Elijah, Now by this I know that thou art a man of God, and that the word of the Lord in thy mouth is truth" (v24). Here is the prophet who has shut up heaven, performed the miracle of the meal and the cruise of oil which was to sustain them until the famine was over, but still, she recognizes something far greater where he was able to raise the dead and says, "by this I know that thou art a man of God." There is a vast difference between a "godly man" and a "man of God." Saying that a backslidden Christian needs to be revived is one thing that emphasizes the pews, but to expect life to flow where there is death is to emphasize the pulpit (Eze. 37); we see this in history where when anointed men of fire came and preached, churches were revived that bled into whole communities that were affected, and sin in the community was arrested. This power of the Spirit gives authority where preaching or witnessing becomes the "ability to do," whereas teaching is the "ability to inform." It does not validate their theology in its entirety, though there is fundamental adherence to proper doctrine such as repentance, faith, being born of the Spirit, etc. But it validates the truth of "Not by might, nor by power, but by my spirit, saith the Lord of hosts." – Zech. 4:6. We see this again and again in the book of Acts. We see the Spirit outpoured, which was on select individuals in the Old Testament, but the prophecy of Joel 2:28-29 was fulfilled at Pentecost (Acts 2:17-18) and was poured "upon all flesh," in that upper room (Acts 2:1-4); and continued with subsequent fillings similar to Pentecost in Acts 4:8, 31, 10:44-45, 13:9, 52, 19:6. We see this enduement of power for service in times of revival across the centuries where God pours out His Spirit in a greater measure and communities are transformed by the power of God.

To summarize a few key features that are seen in the Scriptures and church history, during times of revival/spiritual awakening and seasons of refreshing, we see that there are:

1. The manifest presence of God and love toward God (Psa. 85:6)
   - Response of the people in stillness, awe, nearness of Christ, bowing down in worship and adoration, prostration, suddenly God comes down.
2. Deep conviction of sin, fear of God, and repentance in the church (Isa. 6:5)

3. Obedience unto holiness among God's people (Isa. 6:6-7)
4. The glory of God fills His temple (2 Chr. 7:1-2)
5. It brings an awareness of God to the community (Isa. 64:1)
6. It cannot be scheduled or organized by human means (2 Chr. 7:14, John 3:8)
   - It cannot be restricted to a denomination
7. The Spirit and the word of God go as a flood in saving power (Isa. 55:11, 59:19)
   - Community is affected, there is a restraint on sin, and the world takes notice.

In 2008, A thousand Audio CDs attached with a letter of "A Call to Prayer" were mailed out regarding genuine revival. The CD had a brief recording from a local Pastor and a sermon regarding the 1904 revival in Wales. These were sent to fundamental, Bible-believing, separated churches and Organizations in America. Fewer responses, less than five or so, showed some interest by responding.

During this time, being alarmed at the gradual erosion of what seemed to be a solid foundation into a veneer that was quickly fading away where we wist not that the Lord was departed from us, God burdened me to write the book, "ICHABOD, The Condition of American Christianity in the 21st Century" under the name of A. C. Clayman, which stood for "A Concerned Christian Layman." — published in 2014 and republished in 2020.

Quarterly newsletters began to be published beginning in 2015 on the Desiring Revival Ministries website. The desire was to personally help keep historic truths alive as long as the Lord allowed, with a vision that Christ might be known to all generations and to all nations.

Seeing a need to confront the false perceptions of what is followed in the church by what was preached against what is scriptural, God moved me to pen the book "Here I Stand." A pattern was seen where when we don't desire the supernatural, we will be left with the superficial — published in 2016.

In response to Christ's warning, "because iniquity shall abound, the love of many shall wax cold." In Matt. 24:12 and Christ, after His resurrection, asked Peter, "Simon, son of Jonas, lovest thou me?" and the coldness that was beginning to settle in my own heart, God gave me a burden to write the book, "Lovest Thou Me?" — published in 2017.

The grief of seeing a skewed way that Americanized Christianity was polarized to extremes such as elevating the sovereignty of God that nullifies the responsibility of man, or the other extreme of the responsibility of man that overruled God's sovereignty, the book "The Sovereignty of God and the Responsibility of Man" was written — published in 2019.

The growing concern about the work of the Holy Spirit that was being pushed aside or reduced to someone we only say in phraseology but never showed in our practice in desiring His definitive work in our midst in prayer and supplication was beginning to weigh heavily upon my heart, where the book "The Sovereignty of the Holy Spirit" was written — published in 2020.

From 2020 to 2021, there were outbursts of God's truth in my journey of rediscovering the God of the Bible, which led to publishing the yearly devotional "Still Waters for Shallow Shores" under my given name — published in 2021.

In 2021 another "Call to Prayer" were mailed to all 50 states to churches that will hear and heed the call, with resources on practical ways to have a corporate prayer meeting. There was no response from those who received it.

Other efforts were made throughout this time as the Lord led using various avenues.

The reason for sharing all the avenues that I feel God led is **not to showcase the work done**, but rather the desperate place that we are in America in the place of apathy, of spiritual coldness which seems to have settled in our beloved land, and the years of comfort that we have become accustomed to without seeing a genuine work of God in our midst. I am just a sinner saved by grace with feet of clay and but by the grace of God there go I; it is Christ who is to be the focus. I realize that we cannot schedule a Divine intervention; instead, it must be sent from God. The idea that we can have a revival as long as we have human means to produce it is antithetical to the ways of God that He has revealed in the Scriptures. Have you seen any of the movements of the Spirit in the book of Acts that were planned by men? It was sudden, it was prayed for and sought after, but God sent it in His own way, and it was unpredictable (Acts 2:1-4, 4:31, 8:26, 10:44). We see that a heaven-sent revival is heaven-sent and cannot be ordered or organized but must be prayed down as God prepares the hearts of His people to receive it. "the Lord, whom ye seek, shall suddenly come to his temple" – Mal. 3:1. In those grand Psalms of revival, the call is made, but it is not a conditional call that God must come according to man's organized schedule and at certain times during a week of services. "quicken us, and we will call upon thy name. Turn us again, O Lord God of hosts, cause thy face to shine; and we shall be saved." – Psa. 80:18-19. "Wilt thou not revive us again: that thy people may rejoice in thee?" – Psalm 85:6. God does come, but it is always according to His ways. While a focus on the "topic of revival" and desiring God to work can be beneficial, equating what only God can send with what we have organized is to be presumptuous.

God, in His infinite mercy, continued the work of purging and cleansing in my own life, though, at times, it was hidden as streams that flow while hidden from plain sight, nevertheless continue to flow.

Why was there such prevailing darkness sweeping the land? Why were there many who seemed to have given up on seeking

25

after God? Churches exist to have a name, but the manifest presence of God (which we will see later under the topic of God in the Midst) has not been experienced in decades. We have become like the children of Israel in Judges 2 that "knew not the Lord, nor yet the works which he had done for Israel" (v10). A generation that speaks about the revivals of the past but has never experienced it personally, in a state of smug contentment and an unwillingness to examine oneself. A Pharisaism that exalts how they look, dress, and act, as above others who may not look like them, smell like them, or act like them. It is one of the most abominable characteristics of a dead church, a stench in God's nostrils.

Maybe your faith has been slowly eroded, like mine was, into believing another "god" and another "gospel" that brings frustration and breeds unbelief. Could it be because of an unseen erosion of faith similar to what I went through? But the revealing moment regarding my own heart that was being affected unbeknownst to me by the winds of Americanized Christianity was to come shortly in 2021 when my dad passed into eternity.

THE BREAKING

Wake-Up Call

In October of 2021, my dad, a man of faith who proved it through his life in India, went home to be with his Savior, whom he loved. He was born again during his college years in India and received assurance from God when hearing Corrie ten Boom during her visit to India after the War. As an example of His faithfulness to God, living in India as a believer, he **never once** gave or received a bribe (in a nation that is riddled with taking bribes from the policeman on the street to government officials), but through prayer and the love of Christ was able to live, excel and be a faithful witness being a successful Veterinary Doctor. After his passing, I went to India for the memorial service, and while staying at my sister's house, I had the following incident transpire.

We had a Pastor from another denomination come to visit us with his family. During the visit, he spoke of God's hand in what happened to a large Hindu temple encroachment into their church property, which was illegal. He spoke regarding the various obstacles they met. Over the course of calling their people to pray for seventy-one days of fasting (one fast per day) and prayer, seeking God's hand to overrule, favor with the officials, and such. They saw an impossible deliverance of the local authorities destroying (physically) the established large temple, which was by the church. So much so was the witness of God's hand that the lawyer who fought for them (a Hindu) converted to Christianity when seeing the authenticity and reality of the God of the Bible, who was a living God and not a figure of the past.

During the time this was testified, my heart was struggling to believe God's greatness and the proofs of external eyewitnesses in media and police reports, etc., who attested to the work. That night was one of the defining moments where I struggled to grasp this hidden but deadly sin of unbelief that had reared its true colors. Unable to believe the truth. I was alarmed at what I experienced; I had come to a point unknowingly, living in America for over twenty Years, embracing Americanized Christianity as the authentic religion of the Bible, had, in essence, created a heart of unbelief. **I was horrified to see what I had become**. It was a struggle that I had to seek the face of God, and I eventually saw God bring me to the place of victory over a course of time. I realized that though there is a very small remnant in America (not seen in popular Christendom), **America has come to embrace a god of their own making**. I once saw a man buying idols in a store, and he was carrying two of them in his hand to the cashier, and this thought came to me; we are willing to worship or submit to a "god" as long as we can manage him, keep him in a box; in essence, we have become our own god. This was the temptation of Satan to Eve "ye shall be as gods," and Americanized Christianity has fallen hook, line, and sinker to it. A god who changes to adapt to the culture he finds himself in. She is found serving an UNKNOWN GOD, singing songs to a "Christian" god who does not exist, except in sentimental words and pictures that evoke warm feelings. A god who "yearns" for the favors and approval of his subjects. A gospel that is catered to and made acceptable to the world, where anyone can come and leave un-offended and happy, shaking the preachers' hand, whether they live in sin or be lost on their way to hell. They embrace Christ for all the good He can do for them, including taking them to heaven, and are never asked to consider the cost of following Him.

The Long and Lonely Road to Recovery

The truth hit me like a ton of bricks; what has become of me? Instead of faith being this vibrant lifestyle of life in Christ that flows from within, it had become a whack-a-mole game of keeping our heads up and serving with a smile. So, where do I go from here? God, as my loving heavenly Father, had to guide me, who does not let His children stray too far. He had already been putting seeds of truth into my life. In addition to God bringing me to the truth of the Scriptures, I had been reading books from historical authors who had gone before us, hearing some of their messages, and slowly, God started opening my understanding to getting to know this God of the Bible. Seeing many of the topics discussed in stark contradiction to what was being followed, the Spirit was bearing witness in my heart to the truth of what I read or heard from those who have gone before us. I was driven to God's word and to hear and read from those whom God had used in the past, such as Leonard Ravenhill, A. W. Tozer, Dr. Martyn Lloyd-Jones, and many others. Though this unbelief had surfaced, and God used this poor lisping sinner during various times, God continued to teach me to see my frailty in this lifelong journey with Him. None of us have "arrived" while on earth ("But by the grace of God I am what I am" – 1 Cor. 15:10), but we must ensure we are on the proper foundation or end up in unbelief. We will begin to question the very foundational truths of being born again, assurance, and, if left unchecked, the very existence of God Himself.

Though one may consider men like Whitefield and Wesley as different in certain theological matters, we must come to the place of realizing that the vein of Christianity was carried by men and women like them where they were able to see the fundamental truths of the high view of God, the Person and work of the Holy Spirit, being born of God, heaven-sent revival, and such. These patterns have the same thread of God's desire on earth, though we understand that it is not an indication of agreement regarding every doctrine. The truths experienced were to be received if they followed the Biblical pattern found in the Old and New Testaments, knowing that the Scriptures are the final source of truth for all we believe in, faith, and practice.

THE REMAKING

Rediscovering Faith

Some would consider my journey as having its beginning when the time I went to my dad's memorial service in India in 2021. Still, I would suggest that it was constantly being kept alive even before then by Christ's mediatorial work. Here is a parallel that I see in the below exchange in Bunyan's Pilgrims Progress at the Interpreter's house.

Excerpt from The Pilgrim's Progress

Then I saw in my dream that the INTERPRETER took CHRISTIAN by the hand, and led him into a place where was a fire burning against a wall, and one standing by it always casting much water upon it to quench it; yet did the fire burn higher and hotter.

Chr. Then said CHRISTIAN, "What means this?"

Inter. The INTERPRETER answered, "This fire is the work of grace that is wrought in the heart; he that casts water upon it to extinguish and put it out, is the devil: but in that thou seest the fire notwithstanding burn higher and hotter, thou shall also see the reason of that." So he had him about to the backside of the wall, where he saw a man with a vessel of oil in his hand, of the which he did also continually cast, but secretly, into the fire.

Chr. Then said CHRISTIAN, "What means this?"

Inter. The INTERPRETER answered, "This is Christ, who continually with the oil of his grace maintains the work already begun in the heart: by the means of which, notwithstanding what the devil can do, the souls of his people prove gracious still.

"And he said unto me, My grace is sufficient for thee: for my strength is made perfect in weakness. Most gladly therefore will I rather glory in my infirmities, that the power of Christ may rest upon me." – 2 Cor. 12:9

And in that thou sawest that the man stood behind the wall to maintain the fire; this is to teach thee, that it is hard for the tempted to see how this work of grace is maintained in the soul."

Public domain

What glorious Christ! Worthy of all my praise and adoration. I worship thee, Oh Lord, for thy name is great, and thy mercies are everlasting, forever and ever thou art God alone, and there is none other.

I join in worship with the writer of the hymn, **O For a Thousand Tongues,** by **Charles Wesley**.

> Oh, for a thousand tongues to sing
> My great Redeemer's praise
> The glories of my God and King
> The triumphs of His grace
>
> To God all glory, praise, and love
> be now and ever given
> by saints below and saints above,
> the Church in earth and heaven.

public domain

Four Consequential Truths

How does one unlearn and recover from decades of being taught a certain way and having to rethink and painfully recover from false thinking that has now been made natural to the mind and accepted as "truth"? The grace of God alone enables us to endeavor on such a costly journey. It is the yearning of God's promise of "Blessed are they which do hunger and thirst after righteousness: for they shall be filled." – Matt. 5:6 and girded by the precious Spirit of God that can bring us through that path.

God brought me to the place of these four consequential truths that were essential in my life to begin this journey of rethinking God.

1. GOD
2. Rejecting teachings that have a skewed output of faith, love, regeneration, etc.
3. Standing outside the camp to seek Him
4. What is my standing before God?

Though these topics are too vast to cover, and God had been dealing with me in some form while writing the earlier mentioned books and newsletters, these truths came as a woven thread for the need that I had, the crossroads that I had come to.

1. GOD

It has been rightly stated that what comes to our mind when we hear the word "God" determines who we are. Having the proper view of God will help us have an appropriate view of who we are, how far we have fallen, and the means for reconciliation. I have relatives who are sincere in their beliefs in a cult that denies the deity of Christ, the Trinity, and such, but they are firm in their faith and fervent in the propagation of their message. They pray for others, follow their leader, are incredibly faithful to their place of attendance, etc. A belief in good works, but the thought comes, why? It is because of a skewed view of God and forming a belief system that emphasizes that a sincere sacrifice or belief of man from himself can suffice to avert God's judgment. Thus, they go about to establish their own righteousness, "For they being ignorant of God's righteousness, and going about to establish their own righteousness, have not submitted themselves unto the righteousness of God." – Rom. 10:3.

I heard sayings like God and the life we live here is like a dance that we join and perform as it were through this journey. On the contrary, I see God's declaration of Himself in the Scriptures as "For thus saith the high and lofty One that inhabiteth eternity, whose name is Holy; I dwell in the high and holy place, with him also that is of a contrite and humble spirit, to revive the spirit of the humble, and to revive the heart of the contrite ones." – Isa. 57:15. "For I am the Lord, I change not; therefore ye sons of Jacob are not consumed." – Mal. 3:6; that He is incomparable, "To whom will ye liken me, and make me equal, and compare me, that we may be like?" – Isa. 46:5; that the greatness of who He is has not even entered into our minds, "For as the heavens are higher than the earth, so are my ways higher than your ways, and my thoughts than your thoughts." – Isa. 55:9; that He never needed any counsel and is perfect in self-existence without needing man or the angels to add to anything He lacks, "With whom took he counsel, and who instructed him, and taught him in the path of judgment, and taught him knowledge, and shewed to him the way of understanding? Behold, the nations are as a drop of a bucket, and are counted as the small dust of the balance: behold, he taketh up the isles as a very little thing. All nations before him are as nothing; and they are counted to him less than nothing, and vanity. To whom then will ye liken God? or what likeness will ye compare unto him?" – Isa. 40:14-15, 17-18. "I have made the earth, and created man upon it: I, even my hands, have stretched out the heavens, and all their host have I commanded." – Isa. 45:12.

God's holiness is beyond our understanding, that the stars and saints themselves are not pure in His sight, "Behold, he putteth no trust in his saints; yea, the heavens are not clean in his sight." – Job 15:15; that His burning holiness has the seraphims that cry day and night "Holy, holy, holy" and are not even able to look at Him, "In the year that king Uzziah died I saw also the Lord sitting upon a throne, high and lifted up, and his train filled the temple. Above it stood the seraphims: each one had six wings; with twain he covered his face, and with twain he covered his feet, and with twain he did fly. And one cried unto another, and said, Holy, holy, holy, is the Lord of hosts: the whole earth is full of his glory." – Isa. 6:1-3; that He is the same God in the Old Testament and the New Testament, and He judges sin just as much as He did in the past, "I am Alpha and Omega, the beginning and the ending, saith the Lord, which is, and which was, and which is to come, the Almighty." – Rev. 1:8, that the final judgment to the end of the world has been granted to the Second Person of the Triune God (John 5:26-27, Acts 17:31), "And whosoever was not found written in the book of life was cast into the lake of fire." – Rev. 20:15. That Jesus Christ is Lord who rises in authority and power, co-equal with God the Father and God the Holy Spirit, "Therefore let all the house of Israel know assuredly, that God hath made the same Jesus, whom ye have crucified, both Lord and Christ." – Acts 2:36; that all things were made by Christ since the beginning and in Him is all fullness and unending glory, "All things were made by him; and without him was not any thing made that was made." – John 1:3, "For in him dwelleth all the fulness of the Godhead bodily." – Col. 2:9; that He is to have the preeminence, "And he is the head of the body, the church: who is the beginning, the firstborn from the dead; that in all things he might have the preeminence." – Col. 1:18, that all will bow down and worship Him, "That at the name of Jesus every knee should bow, of things in heaven, and things in earth, and things under the earth; And that every tongue should confess that Jesus Christ is Lord, to the glory of God the Father." – Phili. 2:10-11. He is the King of kings, and Lord of lords, who only hath immortality, dwelling in the light which no man can approach (1 Tim. 6:14-16).

When we think about the triune nature of God, God the Father, God the Son, and God the Holy Spirit are all of one substance, GOD. They are three in Persons and one in Almighty, ineffable, eternal, undivided, uncreated, unapproachable, and incomprehensible. One GOD. Unable to comprehend it in our mortal minds, we echo with the author of the hymn, **Immortal, Invisible, God Only Wise,** by **Walter C. Smith**, who captures glimpses of this glorious Being.

> Immortal, invisible, God only wise,
> in light inaccessible hid from our eyes,
> most blessed, most glorious, the Ancient of Days,
> Almighty, victorious, thy great name we praise.
>
> Unresting, unhasting, and silent as light,
> nor wanting, nor wasting, thou rulest in might;
> thy justice like mountains high soaring above
> thy clouds, which are fountains of goodness and love.
>
> To all life thou givest, to both great and small;
> in all life thou livest, the true life of all;
> we blossom and flourish as leaves on the tree,
> and wither and perish but naught changeth thee.
>
> Great Father of glory, pure Father of light,
> thine angels adore thee, all veiling their sight;
> all praise we would render, O help us to see
> 'tis only the splendor of light hideth thee.
>
> All laud we would render; O help us to see,
> 'tis only the splendour of light hideth thee;
> and so let thy glory Almighty impart,
> through Christ in the story, thy Christ to the heart.

public domain

2. Rejecting teachings that have a skewed output of faith, love, regeneration, etc.

I heard of teaching to "be yourself" and the "best you," God was there to help sharpen what you already have. That He was after our best interest. On the contrary, I see Paul who, after He was converted, realizes the depravity of His own heart and the battle of the flesh against the Spirit and cries, "O wretched man that I am! who shall deliver me from the body of this death?" – Rom. 7:24. That God declares the heart of man to be wretched and depraved, "The heart is deceitful above all things, and desperately wicked: who can know it?" – Jer. 17:9, that of Paul's most significant achievements and his learning he was gladly willing to consider them as dung, "But what things were gain to me, those I counted loss for Christ. Yea doubtless, and I count all things but loss for the excellency of the knowledge of Christ Jesus my Lord: for whom I have suffered the loss of all things, and do count them but dung, that I may win Christ" – Phili. 3:7-8.

I heard the teaching of "the best life now" and that "God wants you to be rich." But I found the contrary in the Scriptures. I heard Christ declare, "These things I have spoken unto you, that in me ye might have peace. In the world ye shall have tribulation: but be of good cheer; I have overcome the world." – John 16:33 and Jesus further states, "Take heed, and beware of covetousness: for a man's life consisteth not in the abundance of the things which he possesseth." - Luke 12:15, His call was for us to carry our cross daily and follow Him, "Then said Jesus unto his disciples, If any man will come after me, let him deny himself, and take up his cross, and follow me." – Matt. 16:24. Not the picture of having my rights but surrendering my rights so that the life of Christ might be made manifest in my life. Jesus said, "Enter ye in at the strait gate: for wide is the gate, and broad is the way, that leadeth to destruction, and many there be which go in thereat: Because strait is the gate, and narrow is the way, which leadeth unto life, and few there be that find it." – Matt. 7:13-14. Not the life of ease and finding what brings pleasure to me with one foot in the world and one foot in heaven, not the life that does not count the cost of following Christ.

I heard faith as this one-time decision you make for going to heaven and not expecting any difference in what happens in living the Christian life. On the contrary, I saw faith as the nature of it being acted out by its outflow of ongoing obedience to Christ, and you obey because you believed; and you have believed because "flesh and blood hath not revealed it unto thee, but my Father which is in heaven." – Matt. 16:17. In regeneration, we are ushered into a life of faith that acts upon what it believes. And this is a life of obedience to what God has said, realizing the nature of who God is; it was not "blind" belief but the illumination of Divine light from above. Faith is also the ongoing walk of truth. It is not because of what you are told to do but because of what you are compelled to do by the Spirit. When obedience to God goes beyond reason, faith must take place in the form of action that believes in God and what He has said and acts on that belief. We see that in the life of Peter walking on water (Matt. 14:28-29). You act because you believe, and you have believed because you acted (Those who acted upon faith in Heb. 11). Thus, John the Baptist could say, "Bring forth therefore fruits meet for repentance:" – Matt. 3:8. James states that while faith is not by sight, it is proved by sight (James 2:18). And such faith is from a life of looking unto Jesus (Heb. 11:6, 12:2).

I saw that "love" was coming to God on His terms and not on ours, that charity (love) "Rejoiceth not in iniquity, but rejoiceth in the truth;" – 1 Cor. 13:6; that we are to "Follow peace with all men, and holiness, without which no man shall see the Lord:" – Heb. 12:14; that true faith will prove itself by the outflow of works unto holiness, "Being then made free from sin, ye became the servants of righteousness." – Rom. 6:18 and again in v22 "But now being made free from sin, and become servants to God, ye have your fruit unto holiness, and the end everlasting life." We see that faith is not based on assumption. Instead, it is hearing the voice of the Lord and acting upon it that produces good works. Thus, in that chapter on the hall of faith in Hebrews 11, we see that each person who exhibited faith was associated with something they did because of the result of that faith. This outflow of works is not based on external persuasion but rather by the blessed Spirit who indwells us and drives us to action. It will be as "he that doeth the will of my Father which is in heaven." – Matt. 7:21. Those that said, "Lord, Lord, have we not prophesied in thy name? and in thy name have cast out devils? and in thy name done many wonderful works?" (Matt. 7:22) had a faith that was not wrought of God but a natural human faith. Though it produced good works by the flesh, it was rejected. The test of a Christian is not in what he did with Jesus Christ but in what it did to him to live the Christ-life; Christ living His life in me and through me.

I heard that the gospel is good news, and it can be accepted for the betterment of man, who was already doing pretty good in his own eyes. Growing up in India, we had many gods. If you want wealth, you follow one deity; if you like to perform well in your studies, you can take this other god. And so, in a similar fashion, Americanized Christianity has many gods, the god of entertainment, the god of sports, the god of guns, and the god of pride of the nation. So, to add to that, for going to heaven, there was another god provided, the god of one's imagination, an imagined Christ. On the contrary I found that **the true gospel is offensive to the lost man** because it destroys the righteousness of man (Isa. 64:6, James 2:10); it condemns the best that he can offer in his morality (Rom. 3:23, Psa. 14:1-3); it humiliates his pride and puts him in line with drunkards, harlots, and what he considers as the worst of human depravity around him (Job 15:14-16); it judges his sincerity, ability and goodness as filth in the eyes of a holy God (Job 25:4-6); it requires coming on God's terms, requiring submission and lifelong servitude to Christ (Matt. 10:38, 16:24-26); it calls the wisdom of the world as foolishness (Prov. 14:12, 1 Cor. 1:19-23); it hangs his eternal redemption on the pure mercy and absolute pleasure of Almighty God and not of anything that he can offer (Luke 18:13, Rom. 9:15-16, 18-20); it shatters his self-esteem, for the gospel is primarily for the glory of God alone and not for the happiness of man (Col. 1:16-19, Rev. 4:11); it demands the dethronement of his god of self and requires absolute submission to the true God of the Universe (Acts 2:36, 16:31, Rom. 10:9). One vital truth to note. The offense of the gospel destroys the self-righteousness of man not because of what he has done, which makes him a sinner, but because of who he is. Rom. 3:23 and the perfection of the law (Exo. 20) against our imperfection deals with the fruit of what we have done. Psa. 51:5 deals with the source of that fruit, **who we are**, conceived in sin from our original father, Adam. Our seed was in him, and the effect of the fall passed to all his descendants. What we call original sin, sin was imputed to all his descendants just as life was imputed to all his descendants through his seed (Rom. 5:12-14). This fall does not imply that we were made prisoners against our will by this enemy called "sin," passed from one generation to another. Instead, we are dead and willingly desire to continue in it (John 3:19). Since we love our sin, it aligns with why we must ask for fruits meet for repentance (Matt. 3:8) to see if the Spirit has shown the true nature of sin and that we hate it and sorrow over how it has offended a good God (2 Cor. 7:10), it makes sense for calling to submit to the Lordship of Christ to see if we will submit to Christ and come in humility having no strength of our own. Come as a little child instead of a proud rebel.

The cross is a symbol of death, death to self, death to the old ways, and every sinner must face the cross that will put him in submission to Christ and death to what he considers his rights or how he wants to run his life. I am so sick and tired of heaven being our motivation and not Christ, who is our great reward. The only person who came to Jesus asking to go to heaven never made it there (Mark 10:17-22) but was asked to bring forth fruits meet for repentance, for there can never be two Gods.

The true gospel makes a man poor in spirit, where he cries out with Augustus Toplady ...

> Rock of Ages, cleft for me,
> Let me hide myself in Thee;
>
> Not the labor of my hands
> Can fulfill Thy law's demands;
> Could my zeal no respite know,
> Could my tears forever flow,
> All could never sin erase,
> Thou must save, and save by grace.
>
> Nothing in my hands I bring,
> Simply to Thy cross I cling;
> Naked, come to Thee for dress,
> Helpless, look to Thee for grace:
> Foul, I to the fountain fly,
> Wash me, Savior, or I die.

public domain

and God responds in saving grace, for theirs is the kingdom of heaven (Matt. 5:3). And the rest of the Beatitudes (Matt. 5:4-12) follow for those thus redeemed of the Lord. God has no obligation to save you, but it is of His mercy that He saves us. "Not by works of righteousness which we have done, but according to his mercy he saved us, by the washing of regeneration, and renewing of the Holy Ghost; Which he shed on us abundantly through Jesus Christ our Saviour;" – Titus 3:5-6.

I heard prayer as crucial in the life of a Christian and the church, but there was no corporate prayer meeting other than the mid-week prayer for physical needs and Bible study. Prayer was considered as something to fit into a time schedule. Doing it with the attitude "if possible or to fit it into something when it is convenient for us" showed in practice that we are praying because we are expected to pray. It is the same as a heathen throwing some incense to his idol to appease his conscience because he knows it is expected of him. It is a mockery. The overwhelming evidence points to the reality that those who are not interested in prayer or the things of God but come because of their membership or obligation are just goats who think they are sheep. We quote, "And we know that all things work together for good to them that love God, to them who are the called according to his purpose." – Rom. 8:28. In our midweek service, even in praying for the needs of the body, there is no consideration given as to the root cause of the underlying issue in an affliction someone is faced with. There are four reasons affliction can arise that we see in the Scriptures. One, it could be due to the consequences of their sin before God and God's judgment upon them (Prov. 13:15); if so, we must ask for them to repent and make restitution so they might obtain mercy. Secondly, it may be for them to endure hardness as a good soldier of Jesus Christ that they might stand firm in the power of His might to be conformed to the image of God's Son (Eph. 6:12), then we ought to pray that they might find strength in Christ. Thirdly if this affliction is for the furtherance of God's kingdom that they might bear God's burden to see Him glorified in their midst (Dan. 11:32), then we pray that they draw near to Christ. Such was the prayer of Hannah for having a man child, whose womb the Lord had shut up (1 Sam. 1:6-11), and God raised up the mighty prophet Samuel. And finally, if this affliction is due to the normal course of life in dealing with sickness and for them to know and go deeper into their experiential witness of the Spirit by His word that He is a God who hears and answers prayers (John 11:4, Luke 11:9), then it is appropriate to pray for their healing or grace to walk the path that lies ahead (James 5:14-15). Such deeper issues are not dealt with; all we desire are to deal with the surface-level resolutions and not with God, who deals with the roots. There was no agonizing prayer for God to come and awaken sinners, the Spirit to fulfill His exclusive office in bringing them under conviction of sin and regenerating them. Of the many blessings, prayer is essential for the life of a church; prayer is not only a privilege to be able to come to God through Christ but also an absolute necessity if we are to have any move of God in a service. And the quality of prayer and quantity is essential for having the right expectation of God to come. There was no evidence that the church believed in prayer since salvation was just the ability to convince someone of their need, and with the grand assumptions, they expected all was well. On the contrary, I realized that Jesus in the book of Revelation was outside the door of His church, knocking to come in, "Behold, I stand at the door, and knock: if any man hear my voice, and open the door, I will come in to him, and will sup with him, and he with me." – Rev. 3:20. I read that the last command of our Lord to the church was not the Great Commission but "Repent" (Rev. 2 and 3).

I started reevaluating the commonly accepted assumptions, and I realized that in "For where two or three are gathered together in my name, there am I in the midst of them." – Matt. 18:20, that though Jesus was present with others, He was a total stranger to the Jews at large. In Revelation, we see Jesus knocking at the door of His church, standing outside though they were gathered inside "in His name." It was not a matter of mentioning the name of Christ or even having the intent of meeting to worship Him; instead, it was about obedience where He was Lord and Master and what He represented, by being in absolute submission to His authority in all things, and not "Having a form of godliness, but denying the power thereof" – 2 Tim. 3:5. In Mark 4, Christ was in the boat but not in power. However, when the disciples cried out to Him for help, He rebuked the wind to "be still," and the wind obeyed. God is everywhere, even in dens of iniquity, in His essential or inherent presence upholding all things and seeing all things. However, those involved in sin continue in their deeds unhindered by that fact, "Whither shall I go from thy spirit? or whither shall I flee from thy presence? If I ascend up into heaven, thou art there: if I make my bed in hell, behold, thou art there." – Psa. 139:7-8. He declares of Himself, "Can any hide himself in secret places that I shall not see him? saith the Lord. Do not I fill heaven and earth? saith the Lord." – Jer. 23:24.

The other assumption that I stated as being used for all circumstances was found wanting as well, "I will never leave thee, nor forsake thee." – Heb. 13:5. I saw that the reference it pointed to was given to Moses and Joshua, but it was always a conditional promise. We read of when Israel sinned against God in worshipping the golden calf. Judgment was executed in the death of about three thousand men (Exo. 32:28). But immediately after that, we see where Moses removed the Tabernacle that was pitched in the midst of them, representing God in the midst and pitching it far outside the camp. "And Moses took the tabernacle, and pitched it without the camp, afar off from the camp, and called it the Tabernacle of the congregation. And it came to pass, that every one which sought the Lord went out unto the tabernacle of the congregation, which was without the camp." – Exo. 33:7. In Hosea, we see where God has withdrawn His presence from His people. "They shall go with their flocks and with their herds to seek the Lord; but they shall not find him; **he hath withdrawn himself from them**." – Hos. 5:6. We see it again at the end of the chapter, "I will go and return to my place, till they acknowledge their offence, and seek my face: in their affliction they will seek me early." – Hos. 5:15. When confessing his sin against God, David says, "Cast me not away from thy presence" – Psa. 51:11. We see the same implication repeated to Asa by Azariah, "The Lord is with you, while ye be with him; and if ye seek him, he will be found of you; **but if ye forsake him, he will forsake you**." – 2 Chr. 15:2 *(emphasis mine)*. And the sad history of Israel sinning against God and God withdrawing His manifest presence is seen again and again; in 1 Samuel with ICHABOD, spoken of in Jeremiah, Joel, and a host of others. The same God who gave that promise also called them into account for their sin against Him, and when they did not repent, became their enemy, "But they rebelled, and vexed his holy Spirit: therefore he was turned to be their enemy, and he fought against them." – Isa. 63:10. Later in Isaiah 63:17, the prophet identifies God's hand in hardening their hearts with, "O Lord, why hast thou made us to err from thy ways, and hardened our heart from thy fear? Return for thy servants' sake, the tribes of thine inheritance." Have you ever wondered why Jesus said in the Lord's prayer (Matt. 6:13), "lead us not into temptation, but deliver us from evil"? It should awaken us to the need to be right with God and walk in His ways lest our sin blinds us and we are confounded by our own pride, and the Lord leaves us to our own devices (Heb. 3:13). Samson found that the hard way when he played with sin and ended up blind and grinding corn for the enemy.

You hear alarming statements from God such as, "I will no more have mercy upon the house of Israel, ... ye are not my people, I will not be your God" – Hos. 1:6, 9. While we see His promise of restoration, we also see the consequences of their sin in His withdrawal. To Moses, "And the Lord said unto Moses, Behold, thou shalt sleep with thy fathers; and this people will rise up, and go a whoring after the gods of the strangers of the land, whither they go to be among them, and will forsake me, and break my covenant which I have made with them. Then my anger shall be kindled against them in that day, **and I will forsake them, and I will hide my face from them**, and they shall be devoured, and many evils and troubles shall befall them; so that they will say in that day, Are not these evils come upon us, because our God is not among us? And I will surely hide my face in that day for all the evils which they shall have wrought, in that they are turned unto other gods." – Deut. 31:16-18. In Joshua, after they sinned against God in Ai, God declared, "And the Lord said unto Joshua, Get thee up; wherefore liest thou thus upon thy face? Israel hath sinned, and they have also transgressed my covenant which I commanded them: for they have even taken of the accursed thing, and have also stolen, and dissembled also, and they have put it even among their own stuff. Therefore the children of Israel could not stand before their enemies, but turned their backs before their enemies, **because they were accursed: neither will I be with you any more**, except ye destroy the accursed from among you." – Josh. 7:10-12. We see the sad state of Saul, who sought a familiar spirit at Endor and was given the dreadful news, "Wherefore then dost thou ask of me, seeing **the Lord is departed from thee, and is become**

thine enemy?" - 1 Sam. 28:16. We see stern warnings in the New Testament, "Know ye not that ye are the temple of God, and that the Spirit of God dwelleth in you? If any man defile the temple of God, **him shall God destroy**; for the temple of God is holy, which temple ye are." - 1 Cor. 3:16-17 *(emphasis mine)*.

God's said through Jeremiah, "Then shalt thou say unto them, Thus saith the Lord, Behold, **I will fill all the inhabitants of this land**, even the kings that sit upon David's throne, and the priests, and the prophets, and all the inhabitants of Jerusalem, **with drunkenness**. And I will dash them one against another, even the fathers and the sons together, saith the Lord: **I will not pity, nor spare, nor have mercy, but destroy them**." – Jer. 13:13-14. God can be angry with the prayers of His people, "O Lord God of hosts, how long wilt thou be angry against the prayer of thy people?" – Psa. 80:4. "Behold, I am against thee, saith the Lord of hosts" – Nah. 2:13. "It is a fearful thing to fall into the hands of the living God." – Heb. 10:31. We see the dreadful judgment of "Behold, the days come, saith the Lord God, that **I will send** a famine in the land, not a famine of bread, nor a thirst for water, but of hearing the words of the Lord:" – Amos 8:11 *(emphasis mine)*. The famine of hearing anointed preaching. We ought to emphasize that we walk humbly in fear of God, desiring His favor and ensuring sin is dealt with in the individual's life and as a church. Not the fear that brings condemnation "For God hath not given us the spirit of fear; but of power, and of love, and of a sound mind." (2 Tim. 1:7); instead, for us to have the proper response of awe in facing a God who dwells in thick darkness (Exo. 20:21, 2 Chr. 6:1) and the fear of mocking God (Gal. 6:7), even unknowingly by our actions (Psa. 19:13) and grieving His Spirit (Eph. 4:30).

I realized that our view of God, who is portrayed as only desiring man's interest even at the expense of His own holiness by claiming the love of Christ, was far from the truth. It was the justice of God that moved His hand to destroy the whole world in a global flood but save Noah and his family, where God shut the door after mercy had ended (2 Pet. 2:5); it was a fire from the Lord that consumed the two hundred and fifty men that offered incense where the others had been swallowed up earlier into the pit with their women, sons, and their little children (Num. 16); It was God who sent the evil spirit to oppress Saul (1 Sam. 16:14-15). It was God who was seen in that vision of Micaiah (2 Chr. 18:19-22), where he saw the throne room of God, and God asked, "Who shall persuade Ahab, that he may go up and fall at Ramothgilead?" and a lying spirit was sent which entered into all the prophets where they prophesized saying, "Go up to Ramothgilead, and prosper: for the Lord shall deliver it into the king's hand." Is God evil? God forbid, sin will be accounted for, and God will judge sin no matter who does it, for "Be not deceived; God is not mocked: for whatsoever a man soweth, that shall he also reap." – Gal. 6:7, and "He, that being often reproved hardeneth his neck, shall suddenly be destroyed, and that without remedy." – Prov. 29:1. We see a similar response of God in Proverbs where "Then shall they call upon me, but I will not answer; they shall seek me early, but they shall not find me: For that they hated knowledge, and did not choose the fear of the Lord:" – Prov. 1:28-29. When Solomon forsook the living God and went after other gods, "the Lord stirred up an adversary unto Solomon, Hadad the Edomite...And God stirred him up another adversary, Rezon the son of Eliadah" - 1 Kings 11:14, 23. We see this in the epistle to the Thessalonians, where those who received not the love of the truth, that they might be saved, were given over to their delusion. "And for this cause **God shall send them strong delusion, that they should believe a lie:** That they all might be damned who believed not the truth, but had pleasure in unrighteousness." - 2 Thess. 2:11-12 *(emphasis mine)*. God said, "I, even I, am he, and there is no god with me: I kill, and I make alive; I wound, and I heal: neither is there any that can deliver out of my hand." – Deut. 32:39. Our rebellion can cause God to harden our hearts (Rom. 9:18) in judicial judgment.

Similar to how Jesus quoted the word of God in His response to Satan, I was told to write a piece of Scripture and keep it in my pocket. Still, I sinned against God with the Scripture tucked in my pocket, and reciting or sincerely believing it intellectually didn't help me. Have we considered the reality that the devils believe (James 2:19), the devils obey (Luke 4:34-35), the devils submit to Christ (Matt. 8:31-32), and the devil is not a heretic because he knows that everything written in the Bible is true? I realized that Satan quoted the Scripture to Jesus as well (Matt. 4:6), and he knows the Bible better than we do and can quote it better than us. A. W. Tozer stated, "The devil is a better theologian than any of us and is a devil still." In all His responses, Jesus was using the word of God to reveal the nature of the God of the word, and the preeminence the Father had upon His life (Matt. 4:1-11), from provision to protection to worship. It is the sword of the Spirit as wielded by Him that has Satan flee from us. We must realize that Satan never doubts the word of God; he believes every letter of it because he knows it is true; he was there when it all happened, from Creation to the resurrection and so forth, and that is the very reason he works so hard on making us doubt it. I am reminded of the early Christians in the book of Hebrews 11, who did not have the completed canon of Scripture as we do but "Who through faith subdued kingdoms, wrought righteousness, obtained promises, stopped the mouths of lions. Quenched the violence of fire, escaped the edge of the sword, out of weakness were made strong, waxed valiant in fight, turned to flight the armies of the aliens. Women received their dead raised to life again: and others were tortured, not accepting deliverance; that they might obtain a better resurrection:" – Heb. 11:33-35 and onwards. God had absolute preeminence in their lives.

I was told and brought under the teaching that if God is working, you will have a big church. In light of the bigness of many churches but the smallness of their impact on a community, I had to reevaluate that. While in the context of the springs of living waters, the genuine work of God can draw men unto Himself. But numbers are not an indicator of God, for one realizes that the cults have prominent temples made with hands and can grow from a small number to thousands, if not hundreds of thousands, in a short period. We have Pastors living in gross sin but seeing their church grow in number and being "busy" with the Lord's work. Does that mean that God was the one bringing the increase? What could be termed a successful church? The Macedonian church did not think material possessions were the indicator of God's blessing, but they were said to be the recipients of the grace of God; how? "How that in a great trial of affliction the abundance of their joy and their deep poverty abounded unto the riches of their liberality." - 2 Cor. 8:2. Deep poverty and affliction, but it produced something; the abundance of joy, giving out of an overflowing heart. This is unknown in our culture, and we think we are blessed because we have money. Instead of numbers, financial growth, decisions, and such, here are a few indicators that a church is healthy. **The true church will be identified by** its members that desire holiness of heart (1 Peter 1:15), a place of concerted nights of prayer (Acts 2:42) and the ministry of the word (Acts 6:4), in singleness of heart (Acts 2:44-46), in its humility and piety to have a broken spirit and a contrite heart (Psa. 51:17), the genuine work of the Holy Spirit in regeneration (John 1:12-13), in worship that reflects the character of God (Psa. 96:9, John 4:24), having the fear of God (Eph. 5:21), a joy that is from the spring of heaven (Psa. 16:11), and the Lord adding to the church daily such as should be saved (Acts 2:47). Reading the Bible, praying, being active in the ministry, doing specials, etc., can all be done, and the person still not make any progress in their spiritual life. I did that for many years in my own life. Have they moved towards holiness (1 Thess. 4:7)? Have they plowed through prayer and experienced God in a way that refined them spiritually, where the world loses its luster (1 John 2:15)? Have they come to the place where nothing offends them (Psa. 119:165)? You can ask a group of people if they are Christians or love God, and you can ask the same group about their progression, as mentioned earlier, and you will hardly see anyone care about such things. We very much want to have one foot in the world and one foot in a form of Christianity, but that will never do.

The church should be a place where those who have lived in darkness are brought into the marvelous light of God and live transformed lives. A church where they stand and testify that they were drunkards, homosexuals, transgenders, drag queens, drug addicts, prostitutes, wife beaters, atheists, followers of religion, and so forth; but now they testify that they have been brought to the place of repentance and have forsaken their former ways of sin, and they are followers of God to the glory of God. Jesus said, "I will build my church; and the gates of hell shall not prevail against it." – Matt. 16:18. It was expected for those who were saved to be different, but I didn't hear that preached anymore; why was that? Was it because we preach another gospel that does not bring about that kind of radical change?

I realized that what one may think as something that builds faith may, in reality, tear it down, even in "Christian" circles. It could be apologetics, blogs, articles, science, archeology, etc. For those proclaiming truth, unless life flows from within, there is nothing to give from an empty well; it may sound good but will show its fruit in creating doubt rather than the building up of faith. Science doesn't "prove" God, for science is subject to God, who created it and follows the laws He ordained for it. You divorce your externals such as apologetics, archeology, logic in competing with the world, etc., and unconditionally embrace the Person for all that He is (Heb. 11:6) and the bare word of God as illuminated by the Spirit of God (1 Tim. 6:20, 2 Tim. 3:1-7, 16-17, Eph. 4:14). Christ's deity is not proved because of man's ability, it is already a proven fact, but rather it is made effectual to man by God's revelation. These were some of the things I had to reconsider to ensure the proper view of them. Having heard that God loves you but hates your sin, I was confronted by the truth that the sinner is condemned to hell and not just his sin on that great and terrible day. The realignment was that God loves to show mercy to the penitent heart, though we have rebelled against God and sinned against Him. "But God commendeth his love toward us, in that, while we were yet sinners, Christ died for us" (Rom. 5:8) should bring us to the place of humility on the greatness of God's love rather than elevate the importance of man from a humanistic perspective. It is God who sentences them to hell, for they loved their sin and continued in it (Matt. 10:28, 25:41). Paul was concerned about the gospel being withstood by Elymas more than "loving the sinner and hating his sin" (Acts 13:8-11). Do we love sinners? A resounding "yes," but not at the expense of compromising truth. Preaching on hell, though done with brokenness and tears in realizing the final condition of fallen man, should be done from the standpoint that it brings us to the proper view that we rightly deserve it, and if God sent us there, He would be justified in doing so. Psa. 101:3-5 gives us a glimpse of David's desire to align himself with God in loving what God loves and hating what God hates, to the point of stating, "Whoso privily slandereth his neighbour, him will I cut off: him that hath an high look and a proud heart will not I suffer" (v5). I realized that the shallow roots of asking people to "just-believe" thinking to make the gospel more accessible to be embraced are, in reality, detrimental to the truth, for Jesus came to save us from our sins, not to let us continue in it, but to "go, and sin no more." – John 8:11, "lest a worse thing come unto thee." – John 5:14. God gave Himself for us, "that he might **redeem us from all iniquity**, and purify unto himself a peculiar people, zealous of good works." - Titus 2:14 *(emphasis mine)*.

I heard teachings that conveyed that there are no degrees of love in the sight of God when speaking about His children, irrespective of what they do. While it is true that we cannot earn God's love and His love is perfect toward us, there is a principle of essential love where He loves us with an everlasting love, but we also have the paradox of reciprocal love. In essential love, God's love remains the same in saving us, drawing us in mercy to shew forth His unchanging love upon us now and all of eternity. But reciprocal love is something altogether different. It is based on man's response in faith or unbelief. We are given many exhortations to pay careful attention to, such as, "God resisteth the proud, but giveth grace unto the humble." – James 4:6, "to this man will I look, even to him that is poor and of a contrite spirit, and trembleth at my word." – Isa. 66:2, regarding David "the Lord hath sought him a man after his own heart" – 1 Sam. 13:14, "For thus saith the high and lofty One that inhabiteth eternity, whose name is Holy; I dwell in the high and holy place, with him also that is of a contrite and humble spirit, to revive the spirit of the humble, and to revive the heart of the contrite ones." – Isa. 57:15, "Now the just shall live by faith: but if any man draw back, my soul shall have no pleasure in him." – Heb. 10:38.

As I saw missionaries come and go, I started realizing that this skewed view of salvation and straying away from Biblical Christianity has not only affected American circles with the plague of shallowness but has been propagated in the thousands by the missionaries who have carried the Americanized gospel to the world. It was not that they intended to but were taught in their colleges and churches, embraced it, and became vehement defenders of it. While the results that they may claim may not be as promised in the Scriptures (John 15:16, Acts 2:44-47, 4:31-33), when they see any result at all, they see it as justifying the entirety of their message and not being concerned about the majority who don't stay in the church or come to church or fall away. They are not concerned about the reproach that falls on the name of Christ because of the lifestyle of those supposed "Christians."

The statement that allows man's self-sufficiency states that God will not give you more than you cannot do. In Mark 11:13-14, we see Jesus coming to the fig tree and looking for fruit but finding none thereon proceeds to curse it. The tree did not bear fruit because "the time of figs was not yet" (v13). To call into account what was impossible for the tree to do and then curse it for not having the fruit should bring us to an important lesson. While it is impossible with man, it is possible with God when we live a life of faith. When we see the impossible done and are forced to acknowledge God, God is in that. Such is the nature of true outpourings of the Spirit in historical revivals.

3. Standing outside the camp to seek Him

God brought me to the crossroad where I needed to realize why I was here. It was not for my own personal betterment or gratification but to bring Him pleasure. That radically changed my perspective of God and life and all. When we think of the life of Abraham, it was not in the interest of God that Abraham should follow Him; instead, it was in the interest of Abraham that he followed after God. To Abraham, God was the center of his universe. And for his obedience, he was richly rewarded. "Thou art worthy, O Lord, to receive glory and honour and power: for thou hast created all things, and for thy pleasure they are and were created." – Rev. 4:11. I was brought to paths of loneliness to ensure my dealings were with God alone and to guard against anything that could corrupt His dealings with me in either stifling God's truth or thwarting the depth of His dealing. I came to certain truth revelations from standing outside the camp, as it were, and desiring His way in reproach and tears. "Let us go forth therefore unto him without the camp, bearing his reproach." – Heb. 13:13.

Below is a compilation of those conclusions. It brought me to being God-centered in everything we are and do as unprofitable servants (Luke 17:10), realizing the humbling and undeserving privilege that is ours when God calls us His friends (John 15:15).

- In true Christianity, I cater to God's needs instead of God catering to my needs. There is a difference between God as your Great Shepherd, where you follow Him in absolute submission and dependence upon Him, compared to a utility God who is there to meet your needs.
- I realize my life is about the glory of God instead of seeing God's purpose as to take me to heaven.
- I see God molding me as the chief end rather than wanting God to remove the problem or sickness.

- The proper focus on what He needs, and from that purpose flows everything as opposed to what others need and how I can meet that need by using God as a means to an end.
- In a church, preaching for God's needs to be met rather than for the congregation's needs by giving them truths that are live coals from the altar, from God's word.
- He never changes and is the same in His majesty as opposed to seeking Him for the sole purpose of meeting my life ambitions in sentimental Christianity.
- Humbling view of God's love for me (in all aspects of my life) while being grateful to Him for meeting my daily need, being made in the image of God, though I am here only to align with God's way vs. the elevation of man that God is there to fulfill my wants and the exaltation of man.
- The absolute pleasure and joy of fulfilling the role God created me to be.
- Needing to focus on God instead of looking at others on what they are or are not doing or desiring the approval of man.
- Praying for God's will to be done as mentioned in the Lord's prayer vs. man's will when they contradict one another.
- We submit to His Lordship rather than God needing to fit into our schedule and programs.
- Being created for His pleasure can only be fulfilled as per His way of salvation to restore us to holiness found in Him vs. trying to please Him with my flesh using carnal means, which is an abomination in His sight.

In looking at this, I see many parallel passages that reflect these truths. The Lord's Prayer focused on "Thy kingdom come, Thy will be done in earth, as it is in heaven." – Matt. 6:10, Solomon's conclusion after trying everything the world had to offer in wine, women, wealth, wisdom, and anything his heart desired or lusted after, "Let us hear the conclusion of the whole matter: Fear God, and keep his commandments: for this is the whole duty of man. For God shall bring every work into judgment, with every secret thing, whether it be good, or whether it be evil." – Eccl. 12:13-14, the exhortation to the church at Corinth, "Whether therefore ye eat, or drink, or whatsoever ye do, do all to the glory of God." – 1 Cor. 10:31, and that which is good for us, "He hath shewed thee, O man, what is good; and what doth the Lord require of thee, but to do justly, and to love mercy, and to walk humbly with thy God?" – Micah 6:8.

4. What is my Standing before God?

On many occasions during my time of removing the hindrances that could hide His face from me, the question kept coming to me regarding, "what does God think of me?" The Christian life, in essence, is a life that is lived before God's all-knowing and all-seeing eye. The Psalmist, regarding this truth, states, "O Lord, thou hast searched me, and known me. Thou knowest my downsitting and mine uprising, thou understandest my thought afar off" (v1-2). And he goes on in that Psalm 139 to speak of the impossibility of hiding from God where even darkness becomes as light and the deepest corners of the earth cannot hide His essential presence from us. I was brought to realize the madness of living for what man thinks of me and ignoring God's estimation of my life. Though this may be something that I know, of the nature of God and my daily awareness that He is there, there is a sense in which I had taken my eyes off Christ to look at the spirit of Americanized Christianity. It was as if I had stopped to look at a shop window from the street and was enthralled by the glitter and glamour of what was being displayed, and during this time, having left my Father's hand.

The hymn states it well "Turn your eyes upon Jesus, Look full in His wonderful face, And the things of earth will grow strangely dim, In the light of His glory and grace." – Helen Lemmel. The fanfare and display that I had gotten accustomed to did not help in my spiritual growth. Instead, it had stifled it while giving a form of pride that this was America, and those who propagate it around the world with this Americanized version are spreading the faith which was once delivered unto the saints. But where was the fruit? If there was one profession made, where are the ninety-nine who went thinking they were saved, finally to hear on that great and terrible day, "I never knew you: depart from me, ye that work iniquity" – Matt. 7:23? We need to consider seriously what Christ said, "Every plant, which my heavenly Father hath not planted, shall be rooted up." – Matt. 15:13. The Source matters. We must be cautious not to let the superficial "results" drive our theology. We must go to the foundation of doctrine and the application of revealed truth and its validity in light of the Scriptures. What does the Scripture promise in regeneration? A new heart, the outflow of a changed life that is visible, the inward witness of the Spirit, the desire of the newborn for prayer and the word, fruit that remains, deep enduring work of the Spirit, ongoing love for the lost, and so forth. There will be evidence in varying degrees. We see the command of the Scriptures to try the spirits, whether they are of God. We have people from other cults claiming supernatural healing, and they have genuine results. Does that mean we approve of the cult? The magicians of Egypt were also able to produce the same miracles with their enchantments that Moses did at the beginning, but we know that it was from the kingdom of darkness. "And no marvel; for Satan himself is transformed into an angel of light." - 2 Cor. 11:14, and it goes on to state that "it is no great thing if his ministers also be transformed as the ministers of righteousness" (v15). And this is not just speaking of open apostasy, but those who speak from the Bible. Jesus said, "This people draweth nigh unto me with their mouth, and honoureth me with their lips; but their heart is far from me. But in vain they do worship me, teaching for doctrines the commandments of men." – Matt. 15:8-9.

Americanized Christianity has not seen persecution, famine, perils, or death; she is happily waiting for the rapture to come so she can escape the pain. Such shallow views of "suffering" for Christ cannot be taken into a country like North Korea, where mentioning the word "God" could get you killed, a Christianity that needs to stand the test of persecution, a Christianity that needs to count the cost of following Christ, a Christianity that must take up its cross daily and follow the Lord, that must know that it is not about dying or even the promise of heaven that is attractive, but Christ who is all lovely, and walking by faith bearing His reproach is better than all the treasures of Egypt. Christ's charge to the church at Smyrna, which had already gone through tribulation, poverty, and other trials, His charge was not to take away the pain or the source of sorrow; instead, "Fear none of those things which thou shalt suffer: behold, the devil shall cast some of you into prison, that ye may be tried; and ye shall have tribulation ten days: be thou faithful unto death, and I will give thee a crown of life." – Rev. 2:10. They were called to be faithful unto death. God uses persecution to purify and purge His true church. And the lack of persecution can become detrimental to us when we rely on the arm of flesh rather than the power of God to keep us. We think we deserve better and may even question God when faced with trials like what God brought that church at Smyrna through.

Sidenote: Persecution has always been something that the followers of Christ are to expect. This certainty is stated in Christ's saying, "In the world ye shall have tribulation" - John 16:33, "And ye shall be hated of all men for my name's sake" – Matt. 10:22, and others. As mentioned earlier persecution refines us (1 Pet. 1:3-8), but it also shows the fleeting nature of this life (Prov 23:5, Matt. 16:19-21, Luke 12:15), reveals our true priorities (Heb. 10:34-36), reminds us of the nature of this conflict (Matt. 5:10-12, Eph. 6:12, Rev. 2:10), and restores our focus (Col. 3:1-5).

Coming to grips with my standing before God was crucial in ensuring that what truly mattered in life was Christ and, for His sake, to gladly put away everything this world affords; entertainment, sports, wealth, and even health. Americanized Christianity is popular and accepted because one can claim to be a Christian and can love the world and all the pleasures it offers, though we have sanctified it and called it "clean fun." We have "Christian" filters to watch R-rated movies and not miss out on the next big show, game, or movie. Yes, the filter blocked it, but your brain finished it, and you fantasized about it. Those acting in Hollywood (both men and women) that allow themselves to be displayed in sensual displays of lust, exposing themselves for the world to see, and getting top dollar for doing it are nothing more than glorified street prostitutes who do the same for money. We are "really" suffering for Jesus because it was cold, and we still came to church Sunday morning in our temperature-controlled cars, and someone cut us off, and we feel spiritual because we suffered silently. Jesus said that there is a cross to bear, a life of self-denial, a life that must endure hardness, that must be willing to lay down its life, "And ye shall be betrayed both by parents, and brethren, and kinsfolks, and friends; and some of you shall they cause to be put to death. And ye shall be hated of all men for my name's sake." – Luke 21:16-17. "If ye were of the world, the world would love his own: but because ye are not of the world, but I have chosen you out of the world, therefore the world hateth you." – John 15:19. Furthermore, we read, "Love not the world, neither the things that are in the world. If any man love the world, the love of the Father is not in him." – 1 John 2:15. There is no middle ground. Yes, Jesus is the prince of peace, but He is coming against the prince of darkness, and there is a conflict of kingdoms, and thus He said, "Think not that I am come to send peace on earth: I came not to send peace, but a sword. For I am come to set a man at variance against his father, and the daughter against her mother, and the daughter in law against her mother in law. And a man's foes shall be they of his own household." – Matt. 10:34-36. Instead, here I was, concerned about my standing before men, and allowed myself to be swallowed up by what my fellow believers were doing, what shoes they were wearing, what games they were playing, what cool toys they were flashing, and let the devil walk right through the door. God brought me to a season of reckoning, stripping me from what the world had to offer before He would reveal more openly about who He was and what He was like.

Biblical Christianity

My journey of this rediscovering the God of the Bible has been one of the most heart-searching and rewarding experiences. We worship the same God of the Old Testament and the New Testament, for if He changed for the better, it implies that something was lacking, and by the nature of needing to change, He ceases to be God. Christ, the uncreated and eternal *(past, present, and future)* Being, has that exclusive claim that there is no other way to have peace with God except through Him (John 14:6, Acts 4:12). The one true living God, co-equal in Trinity, undivided in substance, gave us one Book. It is ONE message given by God, the Author, written by 40 human penmen spanning 1600 years across three continents and three different languages. It speaks plainly of where we came from (Gen. 1:1, 26-27), why we are here (Rev. 4:11), why we have the problems that we see in every generation since the beginning (Rom. 5:12), and where we are going after we die (Rev. 20:11-15). We are faced today with an epidemic of spiritual blindness. What was once considered sin is now embraced and propagated from the halls and pulpits that are supposed to be the pillar and ground of the truth (1 Tim. 3:15). We are confronted with the question of why there is no discernment in the church. We read of the consequences of Israel who were in continual disobedience to God, where God said, "But my people **would not hearken to my voice**; and Israel would none of me. **So I gave them up unto their own hearts' lust**: and they walked in their own counsels." – Psa. 81:11-12 *(emphasis mine)*.

In a day when Biblical Authority is undermined on every side, the need is there to deviate a little to address this crucial topic. The Scriptures speak of themselves as given by God. We see in 2 Timothy 3:16-17 that, "All scripture is given by inspiration of God, and is profitable for doctrine, for reproof, for correction, for instruction in righteousness: That the man of God may be perfect, thoroughly furnished unto all good works." The term inspiration is different from what is commonly used today such as being inspired

61

to do something. This is far deeper, that it was God-initiated and God-breathed. God chose the penmen through whom it would be codified. "For the prophecy came not in old time by the will of man: but holy men of God spake as they were moved by the Holy Ghost." – 2 Pet. 1:21. We believe in supernatural inspiration (God-breathed), infallibility (reliable and trustworthy), inerrancy (without error or contradiction), accurate transmission, and providential preservation for all generations. The Bible does not "contain" the word of God, it "is" the word of God. It was once given (Jude 1:3) and forever settled (Psa. 119:89, Rev. 22:18-19) in its sixty-six books. Jesus spoke many times saying "It is written" or "Have ye not read?" quoting the Scriptures with the assurance of its content thousands of years after it was given and read in the synagogues and studied by the religious leaders of His day. This is not just in the original autographs, but also in how God preserved the copies, apographs, through the centuries. Jesus said, "Heaven and earth shall pass away, but my words shall not pass away." – Matt. 24:35. And He is the same yesterday, today, and forever (Mal. 3:6, Heb. 13:8). We go to the Scriptures to receive truth to change our lives and not to see if it agrees with what we have to say. Since God knows mankind from the beginning to the end the Bible is authoritative in its message given to all generations irrespective of culture, time, or technological advancements.

The same God who condemned the sin of Sodom in homosexual relationships (Lev. 18:22, 20:13) is the same God who said, "For this cause God gave them up unto vile affections: for even their women did change the natural use into that which is against nature: And likewise also the men, leaving the natural use of the woman, burned in their lust one toward another; men with men working that which is unseemly, and receiving in themselves that recompence of their error which was meet." – Rom. 1:26-27. The same God who instituted the home and gave the definition of marriage as only between one man and one woman for life (Gen. 2:22-24) is the same God who said, "And said, For this cause shall a man leave father and mother, and shall cleave to his wife: and they twain shall be one flesh? Wherefore they are no more twain, but one flesh. What therefore God hath joined together, let not man put asunder." – Matt. 19:5-6. The same God who said that He created humans immutable as male and female (Gen. 1:27) with no other gender to be added or changed to is the same God who said, "And he answered and said unto them, Have ye not read, that he which made them at the beginning made them male and female" – Matt. 19:4. The same God who pronounced pre-marital sex or adultery as an abomination (Exo. 20:14, Lev. 20:10-11) is the same God who said, "Marriage is honourable in all, and the bed undefiled: but whoremongers and adulterers God will judge." – Heb. 13:4. The same God who began His judgment from the sanctuary (Eze. 9:6-7) is the same God who said "For the time is come that judgment must begin at the house of God" - 1 Peter 4:17. The same God who calls cross-dressing as an abomination (Deut. 22:5) is the same God who said, "Doth not even nature itself teach you, that, if a man have long hair, it is a shame unto him?" – 1 Cor. 11:14 and further condemns such works of the flesh in 1 Cor. 6:9-10. He does not change, and His holiness nor His response to sin has or will ever change. Thus, the judgment for those who die in their sin and are cast into the lake of fire will be forever (Rev. 20).

I drove by a "church" with a rainbow flag and a saying that "God loves everyone unconditionally." While "God so loved" with a love that is full of pity and compassion, this same love is not willing that any should perish, but that all should come to repentance; it is a love that sent His only begotten Son to come to save us from our sins and bring us to God. What is the goodness of God? It is the kindness God shows to unworthy creatures, us. God does not condone sin, for the nature of God is that "Thou art of purer eyes than to behold evil, and canst not look on iniquity" – Hab. 1:13. "The Lord is slow to anger, and great in power, and will not at all acquit the wicked" – Nah. 1:3. I realized that Americanized Christianity and Biblical Christianity are diametrically opposed to each other. I also see the stark warning that God gave "Know ye not that the unrighteous shall not inherit the kingdom of God? Be not deceived: neither fornicators, nor idolaters, nor adulterers, nor effeminate, nor abusers of themselves with mankind, Nor thieves, nor covetous, nor drunkards, nor revilers, nor extortioners, shall inherit the kingdom of God." – 1 Cor. 6:9-10. This was addressed to those who were homosexuals, transgenders, queers, idolaters, etc., but whom God had redeemed "And such were some of you: but ye are washed, but ye are sanctified, but ye are justified in the name of the Lord Jesus, and by the Spirit of our God" (v11). There is hope for those who will seek repentance and turn to Christ from their sin. Jesus said to a woman caught in the act of adultery, in forgiving her sin, to "go, and sin no more." – John 8:11. To the man who was healed at the pool of Bethesda Jesus said, "Behold, thou art made whole: sin no more, lest a worse thing come unto thee." – John 5:14. The standard for living-out the truth in holiness is much higher for a true Christian. "That ye would walk worthy of God, who hath called you unto his kingdom and glory." - 1 Thess. 2:12. Personal holiness is that which reflects God's heart.

There is another "jesus" running around in America who, in the name of Christ, not only condones sin but allows his followers to continue in it, "turning the grace of our God into lasciviousness, and denying the only Lord God, and our Lord Jesus Christ" - Jude 1:4. Thus, this "jesus" has zealous believers who actively practice and continue in their sin of homosexuality, drunkenness, and such, while calling themselves "Christians," not knowing that "the grace of God that bringeth salvation hath appeared to all men, Teaching us that, denying ungodliness and worldly lusts, we should live soberly, righteously, and godly, in this present world" - Titus 2:11-12. "Christian" in name but lost.

That is an argument that is out there which states that passages which are given such as, to put off the old man (Eph. 4:22-32), let not sin reign in your mortal bodies (Rom. 6:12), come out from among them, and be ye separate (2 Cor. 6:17), and all such truths justify an acceptance of sin (with the possibility of continuing) in the life of a believer. But to be truthful to the Scriptures, we must realize that there are parallel passages that speak of a line that has been drawn, such as, shall not inherit the kingdom of heaven (1 Cor. 6:9-10), not every one that saith Lord, Lord, shall enter into the kingdom of heaven (Matt. 7:21), strive to enter in, for many will seek but not be able to (Luke 13:24), the unpardonable sin (Matt. 12:31-33), which in turn signifies that those who cross the line, having made a profession of faith, and continue in unrighteousness, are showing by their lifestyle that they had never passed from death unto life. And the passages that exhort to put off the old man and to put on the new man and such are for those like David when he was confronted by Nathan, to repent and find restoration in Christ, with the warning to examine oneself if they have truly believed (2 Cor. 13:5, Heb. 6:4-9). In regeneration, you receive a new nature and are made a partaker of the nature of God, where once we had displayed the nature of Satan. And to declare that nothing has changed is an absurdity of the devilish kind.

Mocking God: We received a thank you card from a church member, read from the pulpit, thanking the church for praying for her recent cancer treatments and saying that God answers prayers from the church. But this same person has not attended a single church service for many years and is not even interested in watching the Livestream, in blatant disobedience to God. This is a mockery. **We are mocking God when:** we know what to do but pray so we can ask God's help; we preach salvation, but we accept decisions not caring if they were born of God; we speak of the purity of the Bride but don't care about the glory of God or the name of Christ being polluted in our converts; we pray for God to work or desire the moving of the Holy Spirit, but we don't pay the sacrifice needed actually to see it happen; we say that only God can save, but we have all the trimmings of roman's road, sinners' prayer, give human assurance, and such; we say God answered prayer but justify any outcome to save our face; we don't expect any change in our coverts but justify willful sinning as expected in the life of a Christian; we speak of pleasing the Lord but lack taking action on known sin in His church; we speak about God but do not give the people GOD;

we boast of numbers to prove our worth; we speak of God's purpose but focus on heaven and detest repentance and submission to Christ. And we are reaping what we are sowing (Gal. 6:7). And God says, "when ye spread forth your hands, I will hide mine eyes from you: yea, when ye make many prayers, I will not hear: your hands are full of blood." – Isa. 1:15.

We see the judgments of God, which was unto death, that we are familiar with from the Old Testament, such as during the time of Korah (Num. 16:1-35) repeated in the New Testament with Ananias and Sapphira (Acts 5:1-11), a fornicator given over to Satan for the destruction of the flesh (1 Cor. 5:5), Hymenaeus and Alexander delivered unto Satan, that they may learn not to blaspheme (1 Tim. 1:20), those who partook of the Lord's supper unworthily had died (1 Cor. 11:29-30), the Lord's warning of the unpardonable sin (Matt. 12:31-32) and further stated in 1 John 5:16. We tremble when reading passages like Ezekiel 5 where God with no uncertain term declared, "Behold, I, even I, am against thee" (v8). We see the terror of the Lord when five men with a destroying weapon in their hands were told to follow the man who had marked those who were the Lord's and to "Go ye after him through the city, and smite: let not your eye spare, neither have ye pity: Slay utterly old and young, both maids, and little children, and women: but come not near any man upon whom is the mark; and begin at my sanctuary. Then they began at the ancient men which were before the house. And he said unto them, Defile the house, and fill the courts with the slain: go ye forth. And they went forth, and slew in the city." – Eze. 9:5-7.

We see the final judgment of the lost cast into the lake of fire by the Lord Jesus Christ, "For the Father judgeth no man, but hath committed all judgment unto the Son:" – John 5:22. "And whosoever was not found written in the book of life was cast into the lake of fire." – Rev. 20:15. As much as the American church has shared about the love of God, and He is merciful, and a God of love (agape) who is self-giving and sacrificial, the church has failed to embrace the Biblical God who is also holy and rules with absolute sovereignty and unfathomable power. The God who declares, "Nay but, O man, who art thou that repliest against God? Shall the thing formed say to him that formed it, Why hast thou made me thus?" – Rom. 9:20. And to the wicked, "What hast thou to do to declare my statutes, or that thou shouldest take my covenant in thy mouth? Seeing thou hatest instruction, and casteth my words behind thee. … These things hast thou done, and I kept silence; thou thoughtest that I was altogether such an one as thyself: but I will reprove thee, and set them in order before thine eyes. Now **consider this, ye that forget God, lest I tear you in pieces, and there be none to deliver**." – Psa. 50:16-17, 21-22 *(emphasis mine)*.

In Biblical Christianity, we see the entire Bible and God's dealing with Israel as a pattern for how He deals with His church, that is us, for He changes not (Mal. 3:6, Heb. 13:8, Rev. 1:8). The below gives a glimpse of how God dealt in the Old Testament compared with how He dealt with Jews and Gentiles in the New Testament.

- Reflections of grace in the Old Testament in the lives of Rahab the harlot, Ruth the Moabitess, mercy shown to Nineveh who were the enemies of God and His people compared to "the grace of God that bringeth salvation hath appeared to all men" in Titus 2:11.
- Jeremiah, Ezekiel, Hosea, and others, prophesy against Israel that sinned against God compared to the sin of pride. Isa. 57:15, Amos 4 vs. James 4:6, 1 Peter 5:5.
- Blessings and warnings in the book of Hebrews with the word "lest." 2 Cor. 5:10-11 compared to Deut. 28.
- The greater the love of God shown at Calvary, the greater the accountability to obey Him under His Lordship. Gal. 5:13.
- Warnings in Revelation to the seven churches (Rev. 2 and 3) and the Corinthian church to repent (1 Cor. 3:16-17, 5:5)

- compared to the judgment of God upon Samson (with his eyes put out) and Israel given over to sin. Psa. 106:14-15.
- Samson wist not that the Lord was departed from him (he didn't even know it), ICHABOD where the glory of God had departed (1 Sam. 4:21-22), compared to the church given over in removal of the manifest presence of Christ, and the loss of the fear of God. Exo. 33:7, 15-16, Hos. 5:6, 15, Hab. 3:2 vs. Eph. 4:30, 1 Peter 1:17, Heb. 10:31, Rev. 2:5.
- The conditional promise of "I will never leave thee, nor forsake thee" vs. God fighting against Israel. Deut. 31:6, 8, Isa. 63:10 vs. I Cor. 5:1-5, 1 John 5:16
- God gives us over to our lusts if we fail to heed His call. If we only like to hear what we already want to do, He will send prophets and teachers of itching ears who will send us to our destruction. Prov. 1:28-29, Eze. 14:3-4, 18:30, 1 Kings 22:19-23 vs. 1 Tim. 4:1-2, 2 Tim. 4:3-4, 2 Peter 3:16-17.
- Dealing with sin in the camp and the times of God's warning for maintaining the purity of the Bride in the New Testament. Josh. 7:11-12, Num. 25:6-8 vs. Matt. 18:15-17, 25:41, 1 Cor. 11:27-31, 1 Peter 4:17, Rev. 2 and 3.
- Though we don't serve the shadows of the law, which have been fulfilled in Christ, much more is required under grace to walk in fear of the Lord and all His ways. Gen. 17:1 vs. Matt. 5:48, Rom. 1:28-32, 13:14, Titus 2:11-12, 1 Cor. 6:9-10, Gal. 5:13, 6:7-8, 1 Peter 1:17.

There are so many voices that seem to drown out the truth, the unadulterated truth. But when confronted by those voices, many who seem genuine, we must not be pulled into every wind of doctrine (Eph. 4:14) but lay our deep anchor into the word of God of what God has revealed. While others may declare "success" by the display of their ways of serving Christ, we must stay the course of letting the word be our guide and anchored upon Christ Himself. On that last day, it shall be revealed what sort it is (1 Cor. 3:13). If we truly grasped the gravity of what it means to walk in fear of the Lord in light of this great God of the Bible, we would realize the greatness of Christ's sacrifice, worship Him in adoration and with love that has been shed abroad in our hearts (Rom. 5:5), and the need to sojourn here in fear (1 Peter 1:17), knowing that our God is a consuming fire (Heb. 12:29).

The Trustworthiness of God

In a world that has gotten used to broken promises, fathers who divorce their wives over trivial matters, and ministers who abandon the faith or are caught in gross sin, the topic of trustworthiness is hard to wrap our minds in. When I was going through this season of God removing the chaff from the wheat and clearing my doubts about what I believed in, from the time I was saved and struggling to find sanity at times, God brought me to where He stripped me away from everything around me that I had confidence in, false notions that I had come to agree with. Instead, God, in His love, turned me back to Himself and walked with me through the valley, bringing me to the place of casting myself upon the trustworthiness of God. This trustworthiness had to be painfully divorced from the confidence one could place in a fallen man (Psa. 118:8). This time of God turning me back was not an intellectual agreement of historical truths that I had been brought up in; instead, it was a fresh revelation from the most high God in dealing with me through this time of restoration.

In not going to great lengths regarding these truths, I will touch on a few ways that God showed His trustworthiness in bringing me back through many seasons of prayer, questions, and uncertainty.

- I came to see the trustworthiness of God in Creation when God created this world in six literal 24-hour days and the apparent proof that is all around us. "The heavens declare the glory of God; and the firmament sheweth his handywork." – Psa. 19:1.

69

- I realized the trustworthiness of God in seeing His hand upon my recollection of the past and present with a glorious promise of the future. His supernatural revelation regarding the name to be given and gender before birth when it was not permitted by Indian law to determine the sex until birth. His prevenient grace in my school years, times when I should have perished, if not for His supernatural protection and faithfulness. "It is of the Lord's mercies that we are not consumed, because his compassions fail not. They are new every morning: great is thy faithfulness." – Lam. 3:22-23.

- I was reminded of the trustworthiness of God when He met me on that glorious day in April 1996. I was not seeking God, but He found me. Not a religion, not a tradition, but a daily reality and an enduring relationship with the living God, the One who created us and loved us for Himself. "Therefore if any man be in Christ, he is a new creature: old things are passed away; behold, all things are become new." – 2 Cor. 5:17.

- I was brought to see the trustworthiness of God in His providence. His faithfulness in bringing me to America from India and sustaining me, allowing me to meet my wife from the Philippines in California, and the miraculous way that a vision was given to my dad from Matthew 7:11, who was determined on a traditional arranged marriage, but the assurance from God that was given that this was His doing. "This is the Lord's doing; it is marvellous in our eyes." – Psa. 118:23.

- I was overwhelmed with the trustworthiness of God at work. The way that He made way for bringing me to the US, His hand of protection during multiple layoffs and the 2000-2002 dot-com crash. His hand in leading me when everyone discouraged me from joining a particular tech company where God not only blessed but prospered His child in a way that I never imagined. "He that dwelleth in the secret place of the most High shall abide under the shadow of the

Almighty. I will say of the Lord, He is my refuge and my fortress: my God; in him will I trust." – Psa. 91:1-2.

- The trustworthiness of God in the history of revivals where, when dire circumstances were seen, God rained down His glorious outpouring of His Spirit; like the Moravian Revival of 1727, where a twenty-four-hour prayer meeting was started and continued unbroken for a hundred years. A historian writing on that event said, "In 20 short years, that bunch of Moravians did more for missions than all the church put together in 200 years." "The Lord hath made bare his holy arm in the eyes of all the nations; and all the ends of the earth shall see the salvation of our God." – Isa. 52:10.

- I witnessed the absolute sovereignty of His power to perfectly fulfill hundreds of prophecies regarding world events, the life and mediatorial work of Christ, future foretold events that have been fulfilled, scientific and archeological revelations, etc., many of which were written thousands of years prior. And He was able to preserve the lineage of Christ through the seed of David despite Israel's rebellion and exile. His ability and faithfulness to preserve and keep His word for all generations and to have a faithful remnant in all generations. "God is not a man, that he should lie; neither the son of man, that he should repent: hath he said, and shall he not do it? or hath he spoken, and shall he not make it good?" – Num. 23:19.

- I remember the trustworthiness of God in times of my life when being spared from accidents and in His sustenance during the death of loved ones, including my dad. His tender care when someone you love and trust has responded to you with evil against those you love. "But it is good for me to draw near to God: I have put my trust in the Lord God, that I may declare all thy works." – Psa. 73:28.

- His trustworthiness in the many ways God showed mercy in protecting and restoring me when I went a whoring after this world as a prodigal; He had compassion on me to bring me unto Himself as He did to the lost sheep. "I will mention the lovingkindnesses of the Lord, and the praises of the Lord, according to all that the Lord hath bestowed… which he hath bestowed on them according to his mercies, and according to the multitude of his lovingkindnesses." – Isa. 63:7. "But when he was yet a great way off, his father saw him, and had compassion, and ran, and fell on his neck, and kissed him… For this my son was dead, and is alive again; he was lost, and is found" – Luke 15:20, 24.

- I was confronted with the trustworthiness of God in His unchanging word, meeting the needs of the ministries that He has placed me in, opening my eyes and understanding, and His impressions by His Holy Spirit and leading me into the place of prayer. "And I will bring the blind by a way that they knew not; I will lead them in paths that they have not known: I will make darkness light before them, and crooked things straight. These things will I do unto them, and not forsake them." – Isa. 42:16.

- I came to fully desire and embrace the trustworthiness of God for my future and the world to come. Though we walk by faith and not by sight, God brought me to a faith that produced sight. "But as it is written, Eye hath not seen, nor ear heard, neither have entered into the heart of man, the things which God hath prepared for them that love him. But God hath revealed them unto us by his Spirit: for the Spirit searcheth all things, yea, the deep things of God." – 1 Cor. 2:9-10.

I think of the kindness and tenderness of Christ where in His patience and care, He guides me, and at times of falter, His love upholds me. He has proven again and again that "a bruised reed shall he not break, and smoking flax shall he not quench" – Matt. 12:20. What love, what grace, what patience. I love thee, oh Lord. I am weak, but thou art strong (2 Cor. 22:10). Though much more can be said, one truth that stands alone in my long and lonely road to recovery is that **God is trustworthy**. This was much needed in my time to not only seek Him but to find Him. It brought me to new heights of His love, new depths of His grace, and new experiences of His attributes. I can say with speechless adoration, "O give thanks unto the Lord; for he is good; for his mercy endureth for ever." – 1 Chr. 16:34. "O taste and see that the Lord is good: blessed is the man that trusteth in him." – Psa. 34:8.

Found Wanting

When one endeavors by the grace of God to seek the old paths, the greater realization comes that God, in His infinite mercy and love, has given us precious promises, "Draw nigh to God, and he will draw nigh to you." – James 4:8, "Being confident of this very thing, that he which hath begun a good work in you will perform it until the day of Jesus Christ:" – Phili. 1:6, "Faithful is he that calleth you, who also will do it." – 1 Thess. 5:24. When Belshazzar summoned Daniel to the court in fear of that writing on the wall, we see a reckoning where he had to face the reality of God and what he ignored in not taking into account how his father Nebuchadnezzar was humbled. Thus, when the judgment was pronounced, "Mene; God hath numbered thy kingdom, and finished it. Tekel; Thou art weighed in the balances, and art found wanting. Peres; Thy kingdom is divided, and given to the Medes and Persians." – Dan. 5:26-28; it was God's final judgment with no place for repentance. In the life of Peter, after he betrayed Christ with a curse, though he was found wanting, he found restoration in the place of bitter weeping and submission to Christ (Matt. 26:75). There are some critical areas that God started dealing with me about where I had to come to the proper diagnosis of the situation to have the correct remedy. These truths were not formed in a short period of time but have been continually seeded and matured since their initial inception in 2005. It continues to affirm the lack thereof and our great need in America. We have already seen some of these truths in earlier sections on GOD and Biblical Christianity. Below were other areas that I had to relearn, which were found wanting in Americanized Christianity; these were found wanting from

73

churches that believed in the Bible and were sincerely propagating the "gospel."

God in the Midst

What distinguishes a church meeting from all other gatherings of religions or cults? It is God in the midst of His people. Think of the times when the pillar of cloud by day and the pillar of fire by night dwelt among the camp. It was for all the world to know that the only true God dwelt in the midst of His people. "And they will tell it to the inhabitants of this land: for they have heard that thou Lord art among this people, that thou Lord art seen face to face, and that thy cloud standeth over them, and that thou goest before them, by day time in a pillar of a cloud, and in a pillar of fire by night." – Num. 14:14. The implication of what that meant, "Defile not therefore the land which ye shall inhabit, wherein I dwell: for I the Lord dwell among the children of Israel." – Num. 35:34. "(For the Lord thy God is a jealous God among you) lest the anger of the Lord thy God be kindled against thee, and destroy thee from off the face of the earth." – Deut. 6:15. We see God's promise in Joel 2:27, "And ye shall know that I am in the midst of Israel, and that I am the Lord your God, and none else: and my people shall never be ashamed." We see the absence of God in the midst of His people in times such as ICHABOD, in Ezekiel, and the New Testament, when Jesus said of the temple, "Behold, your house is left unto you desolate: and verily I say unto you, Ye shall not see me, until the time come when ye shall say, Blessed is he that cometh in the name of the Lord." – Luke 13:35. It was not God's house anymore but a place of rituals and empty sacrifices. And God was not going to come into His temple until after His return in Rev. 1:7.

We have already seen that just claiming Matt. 18:20 is not enough. W. B. Hinson, a preacher of bygone years, said, "There is something worse than an empty church. It is an offended God." We see the pattern in the Old Testament of the Tabernacle that was in the midst of the people, and all the 12 tribes were to be pitched around about the Tabernacle. And when the pillar of cloud moved, they were to go where God went, led by God. And **what is the manifest presence of Christ** in the midst of His people? It is the evidence of deep conviction of sin and the worship of saints in the beauty of holiness, the free course of the word of God as a flood into the community with lasting effects, the arrest of sin by the Spirit and His transformative power among God's people, the revelation of the nature of Christ among His children to be Christ-bearers, the glory of God coming down that brings awe and wonder into the audience, being made partakers of the joy of the Lord, at times bowed down into stillness as they are brought to the reality of this sacred Person in their midst, fear of the Divine that causes one to restrain themselves lest they say or do anything that will grieve Him. Those who attend worship are so transformed in meeting Christ that they forget the preacher and leave in enraptured love having experienced their Savior. Instead of talking about the Super Bowl or lunch plans and enjoying the services in jollity and fun, people are ushered into meeting the eternal God where He meets with them, and they are filled with the God of the word. We hear of certain expressions in times past by those who have been in His manifest presence that is unknown to us; statements such as, the people began to groan under the weight of His presence, they pressed into God, prevailing with God in prayer, etc.

It was the custom when there were mighty preachers in London for people to go "sermon-tasting." A man and his wife once heard two great preachers, one on Sunday morning and the other on Sunday evening. The whole day long the man kept saying of the morning preacher, "What a wonderful preacher, what a wonderful preacher!" In the evening, he and his wife went to hear Charles Haddon Spurgeon. Down the steps of the Metropolitan Tabernacle they came, the tears rolling down their cheeks, and saying, "Oh, what a wonderful Saviour! Oh, what a wonderful Saviour I have!" Do we go home enraptured with Christ or do we continue our worldly conversation from where we left off when we were on our way to Church?

75

There were only four outcomes of that early church in the book of Acts: either the rejection of the message, repentance, riot, or communities transformed by the power of God. Christ was never popular with the world in His day nor during that early church because it was a battle between two kingdoms. The kingdom of God against the kingdom of Satan. Jesus said regarding the enemies of Christ whom the world loves. "Woe unto you, when all men shall speak well of you! for so did their fathers to the false prophets." - Luke 6:26. Today, we are preaching a popular Christ that the world loves. I believe in the joy of the Lord, but not the cheap fun that is worked up; instead, the joy produced by the fruit of the Spirit, which flows from a heart full of love. Americanized Christianity has lost its sense of the magnitude of what it means to meet God.

What is the high view of God? Having a high view of God is not about us lifting God up. He is already high and lifted up, and there is no change in Him. Just as the Sun shines in all its glory all the time and just our perception of it changes when we see a cloudy day, we need to acquaint ourselves with God, who always is. It would be foolish to the extreme to say that the Sun revolves around me, but it is insanity to say that God revolves around me. To come to the conviction of the greatness of God and the smallness of man is crucial to have the proper view of God. Read Isaiah 40 sometimes and see statements such as "Who hath measured the waters in the hollow of his hand, and meted out heaven with the span, and comprehended the dust of the earth in a measure, and weighed the mountains in scales, and the hills in a balance? Behold, the nations are as a drop of a bucket, and are counted as the small dust of the balance: behold, he taketh up the isles as a very little thing" (v12, 15). The vastness and intricacies of space that man is astounded by, with some galaxies over a million light-years in diameter, with our Milky Way having over 100 billion suns. While numbers lose their meaning on the vastness, Scriptures convey it by saying, "he made the stars also." – Gen. 1:16. This is the God who "telleth the number of the stars; he calleth them all by their names." – Psa. 147:4. Isaiah captures the essence of it that moves us to awe and wonder, "Lift up your eyes on high, and **behold** who hath created these things, that bringeth out their host by number: he calleth them all by names by the greatness of his might, for that he is strong in power; not one faileth." – Isa. 40:26 *(emphasis mine)*. This beholding must be one that causes us to bow ourselves to the ground in light of this great God. Nebuchadnezzar, the king of Babylon who ruled the world, acknowledged this when he said, "I blessed the most High, and I praised and honoured him that liveth for ever, whose dominion is an everlasting dominion, and his kingdom is from generation to generation: And all the inhabitants of the earth are reputed as nothing: and he doeth according to his will in the army of heaven, and among the inhabitants of the earth: and none can stay his hand, or say unto him, What doest thou? ...Now I Nebuchadnezzar praise and extol and honour the King of heaven, all whose works are truth, and his ways judgment: and those that walk in pride he is able to abase." – Dan. 4:34-35, 37. Can you imagine the greatness of Christ, "from whose face the earth and the heaven fled away; and there was found no place for them." - Rev. 20:11? We think of the unknownness of God, where there is only darkness after a certain point when we peer into God. We meditate on His nature, such as ineffable (indescribable) and inscrutable (unsearchable and impossible to comprehend). God is not limited by Time, Matter, or Space. He declared of Himself "I AM THAT I AM" (Exo. 3:14) stating that He always was, is, and will be, in eternity to come (Rev. 1:8). God is above Time and thus created Time, His omniscient; He is above Matter and thus created the worlds and the heavenly bodies, His omnipotence; He is above Space and thus created and upholds all Space in the Universe, His omnipresence. We have lost sight of the greatness of God. We struggle to grasp the thought that this God comes and lives inside vessels of clay, in hearts that have been regenerated to show a lost and dying world of His greatness.

Some may contest that the desire to see God work through the Holy Spirit is there, but what are the fruits of such desire? Does it permeate everything we do, or is it an afterthought or something we remind ourselves of at the beginning of a service? Is our foundational understanding when approaching the pulpit one of bearing in mind the Lordship of Christ, His holiness, His call to take up our cross and follow Him, the fear of God, and so forth, that weighs heavily in our hearts when sharing the eternal truths of God? If we can switch from joking around to spiritual things and jump back to trivial matters and back to spiritual, this roller coaster shows us the reality that we fundamentally don't understand the nature of the two kingdoms and what it means to have God in the midst of His people. If the devil is not playing and he "as a roaring lion, walketh about, seeking whom he may devour:" (1 Peter 5:8), where we see his handiwork in the death and destruction brought about in this world, if that is the enemy we are facing and it is spiritual warfare, then it is warfare until the end. I am not here to entertain people but to prepare them for war and to fight the good fight of faith (1 Tim. 6:12). The Roman soldier sailed through rivers of blood to win the prize of victory, and we want to be entertained into heaven. I don't care if a sermon I preached was a blessing or changed someone's life for the better; my only concern is, was the Person of Christ revealed? Not the archeological Christ, or the historical, or theological, or the sentimental, but the living Christ making Himself known in the midst with manifest evidence. Did it produce faith where doubts were forced to flee? Was the Spirit honored, and did the word of God have free course? Did they go out having met the living God and not by being impressed with the eloquence of a man? Did they go out in new vigor to serve their Master in blood, sweat, and tears? When delivering a message, do I see what God sees? do I feel what God feels? do I hear what God hears? I don't want them to thank me; I want them to leave saying, "what a glorious Christ." A man who realizes the eternal implication of the word being preached trembles. The implication is twofold. One is his accountability to God on what is being said while handling the word of God, and the second is the implication of the living Word of God to use the written word of God by His Spirit where we tremble at the thought of the response of the man who hears it. To such a man will God look upon (Isa. 66:2).

When Christians spoke, the world stopped and took notice when the burning presence of God was in their midst. During times of God's power manifested in this particular denomination many decades prior, sinners would cross the street when passing the church lest they come under conviction and get saved. We see this in the early church where "And of the rest durst no man join himself to them" – Acts 5:13. Several years ago, I spoke to an old missionary who ministered among the fairgrounds of America. While stationed in London in his younger years, he went to the Westminster Chapel in London, where Dr. Martyn Lloyd-Jones was pastoring. He mentioned that when He went into the auditorium, he could suddenly sense an unmistakable presence of God. Immediately I asked him a question since he had been to churches all over America when working at the fairgrounds, if he could say the same in America in any of the churches he attended over the years, he could not.

Consider this. You can have a young person who professes to be a Christian, go for youth camp from their childhood to their teen years, with no technology during their camp week, maybe over seven years, attend church all their lives, and leave home for college and have no interest in Christ, or be revealed of their need, whatever it may be. How is that possible? If they have nothing on the inside that moves them to conform to what's preached on the outside by the Spirit through the word, there is no reason for me to believe that they have the Spirit of God in them, but it speaks to the reality that they are but lost. They come home with more information but not with the new life that has entered and changed them from the inside for the rest of their lives. And if those who are saved jump straight back into the world without a second thought and are not moved to consider what they have learned during the week, something is seriously wrong. In looking at the reality around me, I cannot but come to the conclusion that we are under Divine judgment. Sin has been left unrestrained in the church and the nation, conviction of sin in producing godly sorrow and brokenness in the heart of the hearers unknown, prayer that is just a ritual, spiritual drunkenness that lacks discernment of our condition, coldness of heart in the church, and many other symptoms speak of the state of God's displeasure that is upon us. The greatest tragedy is that we don't know God in this post-Christian era in America.

The Fear of God

The natural response when encountering the greatness of God is fear, and "fear not" is the general outcome that is first uttered when a man meets God or an angel. Fear, in the sense of a natural response, has the thought of intimidation, torment, and self-preservation. But the fear of God has the response of meeting with someone who is infinitely powerful with awe and wonder. Like Mary, it almost has a thought of uneasiness when facing a God who knows everything. It is not just a sense of reverence that signifies deep respect but also the solemnness that we are dealing with holy things and sacred things, which has intense consequences, and sin in the presence of a holy God is an abomination. This sense of man's unworthiness compared to God's perfection will bring us to submit to the all-knowing, sovereign God in love. A proper fear of God built on God's holiness can help us forsake sin and create a desire for us to live in His presence. While we can come boldly to the throne of grace, the right approach to it would be with fear and trembling. We read again and again in the Scriptures of this matter where "The fear of the Lord is the beginning of wisdom: and the knowledge of the holy is understanding." – Prov. 9:10. This truth can bring us to that proper understanding of who God is. Jesus said, "And fear not them which kill the body, but are not able to kill the soul: but rather fear him which is able to destroy both soul and body in hell." – Matt. 10:28. The God of the Bible not only proved His love on the Cross and places great value upon the soul of man, but He also proves His sovereignty that He gives life and, when necessary, brings about death and destruction. God states the man to whom He will look will be the one "that is poor and of a contrite spirit, and trembleth at my word." – Isa. 66:2.

In the natural world, you realize the danger of facing an approaching train and the need to get off the track knowing the impossibility of the outcome that would be in your favor. Though it is impossible to equate it with this, the greatness of God, His omnipotent power, and the nature of who He is should cause us in awe to fear Him and cause us to eschew evil. "The fear of the Lord is to hate evil: pride, and arrogancy, and the evil way, and the froward mouth, do I hate." – Prov. 8:13. To the question, "which is the great commandment in the law?" that Jesus responded to (Matt. 22:36-38) is given in Deuteronomy 10:12, which says, "And now, Israel, what doth the Lord thy God require of thee, but to fear the Lord thy God, to walk in all his ways, and to love him, and to serve the Lord thy God with all thy heart and with all thy soul." The commendation of that early church was, "Then had the churches rest throughout all Judaea and Galilee and Samaria, and were edified; and walking in the fear of the Lord, and in the comfort of the Holy Ghost, were multiplied." – Acts 9:31. In the midst of the worship that is taking place in heaven at this very moment, we hear, "And a voice came out of the throne, saying, Praise our God, all ye his servants, and ye that fear him, both small and great." – Rev. 19:5. Peter's exhortation after reminding them to be holy (1 Peter 1:15-16) was to reflect on that and "pass the time of your sojourning here in fear" for there is a God who sees all things and "judgeth according to every man's work" – 1 Peter 1:17. It by the fear of the Lord that men depart from evil (Prov. 3:7, 16:6).

Americanized Christianity has no sense of the fear of God. You read again and again of that early church and how that "great fear came upon all" inside and outside the church. They had such power that the world feared them and was afraid to blaspheme the name of Christ. Today there is no fear of God in the churches, let alone in the world. There is a shallow play of words with no outcome of their reality. And blaspheming the name of Christ is all around us, in lyrics, stage plays, movies, and such. There is no sense of the awe of meeting a holy God and the implication of what that means. We don't see Moses strolling into the holy of holies; or the priest who had ropes tied to his ankles entering into that place of the Shekinah glory, having covered himself with the tokens of the covenant lest he is killed, and they will have to pull him out by the feet; we don't see John when he saw the glorified Christ having a chat with Him, instead "And when I saw him, I fell at his feet as dead." – Rev. 1:17, and God had to raise him up. I hear during preaching time which generally has a "joke time" at the beginning so the people can be put at ease and then go to a more "serious time," you hear preachers explain their personal love life and try to wow the audience. There is no sense of the reality that the audience is there to meet God and not hear some thoughts or clichés about Him or be entertained by the man in the pulpit. Bringing the word from the Lord must have a sense of what is taking place in standing before men on behalf of God. Americanized Christianity is popular because it tries to attract fallen men by lessening the reality of the awful presence of the God of the Bible. "For the Lord your God is God of gods, and Lord of lords, a great God, a mighty, and a terrible, which regardeth not persons, nor taketh reward" – Deut. 10:17. The response of Jacob encountering God, "And he was afraid, and said, How dreadful is this place! this is none other but the house of God, and this is the gate of heaven" – Gen. 28:17.

Do we approach holy things with a sense of apprehension about their consequences? King Uzziah tried to handle what he was not supposed to and was struck with leprosy as they beheld him (2 Chr. 26:16-20). Do we carefully apply what God said, "to this man will I look, even to him that is poor and of a contrite spirit, and trembleth at my word." – Isa. 66:2. The proper fear of God for His children is without torment since he can love his heavenly Father with a love that is without condemnation but reverence. And the genuine love for God should motivate us to have that proper fear of God without torment. "There is no fear in love; but perfect love casteth out fear: because fear hath torment. He that feareth is not made perfect in love." - 1 John 4:18. Yes, there is great joy in the presence of Christ but not the frivolous fun in cracking jokes and being in step with the world. The joy of Christ is a wellspring that flows from the heart, sanctified and desirous of her Beloved. We see the glorious exchange of love, joy, and longing in that beautiful book of the Song of Solomon. I see the Song of Solomon as this; God initiated redemptive love, and my response in reciprocal love to Him seeing the enjoyment of each other in a sacred context through natural and human imagery. What love could be more overwhelming than realizing, "I am my beloved's, and my beloved is mine" – Song. 6:3.

The Holiness of God

The fundamental nature of God is that He is holy. The call for every Christian is, "Because it is written, Be ye holy; for I am holy." – 1 Peter 1:16. This is utterly lacking in our perspective of God because of our low view of God. Once our view of God is lowered, everything else gets affected by that, and one of the first areas it impacts is the area of God's nature regarding His holiness. The lack of this truth bleeds into other areas, such as the lack of the proper fear of God and having no concept of what it means to tremble at God's word because of the nature of how wicked sin is in light of the holiness of God. This is seen in the lack of preaching on the reality of the horrors of hell. We see that hell is a literal place (the unquenchable fire that burns – Matt. 5:22, 25:41, Mark 9:42-48, Luke 16:28, Jude 1:7; outer darkness – Matt. 8:12, 22:13, 25:30, Jude 1:13; bottomless pit – Isa. 14:15, Rev. 9:1-2); it is a place of torment of the body (Matt. 5:29-30, Luke 16:23-24); the torment of the mind (Luke 16:25); where there is no hope (Rev. 14:9-11); it continues (after the Great white throne Judgment in Rev. 20:11-13) into the lake of fire (Rev. 20:14-15) as an everlasting fire; it is forever (Matt. 25:41, Rev. 20:10); it was created where the wrath of Almighty God will be poured out on supernatural beings (Matt. 25:41, 2 Peter 2:4); it makes it indescribable on its torment for mortal humans (Psa. 9:17). I believe that every beauty of nature that someone enjoyed in this life, maybe a bird singing, the grass they walked on, an animal that they loved, a beautiful scenery, vastness of space, the spectacular beauty of the eye, every memory of them will be a torment for the dammed in hell, for the heavens declare the glory of God (Psa. 19:1-3), and creation's cry will declare the judgment of God to those who saw that glory and rejected the God who made them. The greatness of the immense suffering and pain of hell is even more compounded when we realize that hell is a place where there is no hope because it is forsaken by God, from whom all goodness flows. Furthermore, to realize that it is "forever" speaks of the unimaginable pain and eternal torment. Jesus was graphic in telling the truth of it when He gave warnings like, "And if thine eye offend thee, pluck it out, and cast it from thee: it is better for thee to enter into life with one eye, rather than having two eyes to be cast into hell fire." – Matt. 18:9. His description in Luke 16 of the rich man in hell with the reality such as, "And in hell he lift up his eyes, being in torments" (v23), "Father Abraham, have mercy on me, and send Lazarus, that he may dip the tip of his finger in water, and cool my tongue; for I am tormented in this flame" (v24). The more you meditate on the burning holiness of God, the more you are confronted with the horror of the justness of someone being sent to hell because of their sin and trampling the blood of Christ under them, who is the ONLY way of escape. "It is a fearful thing to fall into the hands of the living God." – Heb. 10:31.

The seraphims could not look upon God, nor could they show any signs of immodesty, "And one cried unto another, and said, Holy, holy, holy, is the Lord of hosts: the whole earth is full of his glory." – Isa. 6:3. We see the fearful question asked in Isa. 33:14, "Who among us shall dwell with the devouring fire? who among us shall dwell with everlasting burnings?" It states the conditions that must be met for approaching such a Holy One, similar to Psa. 24:3-4. Think of the utter depravity of man thinking he can bring something to such a God who is a consuming fire, One who poured His wrath upon His own dear Son to the point where Christ cried out, "My God, my God, why hast thou forsaken me?" – Matt. 27:46. He was forsaken so we can be accepted, and for the man who is a worm standing in arrogance and saying he is going to make a "decision" that suits him and is presented with a God who is begging for him to make the right choice, while silently waiting in impotence, such low representation of God is beyond abomination. It is reducing God's nature and bringing it under the harsh scrutiny of fallen man to equate it with the imperfections that we are used to.

The question begs to be asked if "decision" was so pivotal to the matter of salvation, why is it not once mentioned in the entire New Testament when calling sinners to repent? **It was expected as more of a response of an awakened heart than a decision with intellectual importance.** If one disobedience in the garden of perfection hardened Adam and Eve's hearts where they hid from God, think about the multitude of sins that we commit from the abundance of our hearts and for someone to believe that we have the ability of ourselves to make a decision for righteousness is to be ignorant of the awful nature of sin. Jesus did not just provide the way of salvation; He is the executor of it also in human hearts. Titus 2:11 says that the "grace of God that bringeth salvation." It brings salvation all the way until the work is complete. He not only came to seek but is mighty to save that which was lost (Luke 19:10). The word "to save" speaks of active participation on the part of God. How depressing it is to say that God had provided a way; now it's up to you to understand it and decide for yourself based on how well the preacher can convince you. Man is lost, calls evil good and good evil, and sin not only blinds but also binds us, where we need Divine intervention.

Sadly, we see this presented as the norm in Americanized Christianity because of our low view of God. In the imagination of man's fallen heart, he has devised mythology and "gods" that represent his fallen nature and are bound by the lust of the eyes, the lust of the flesh, and the pride of life (1 John 2:16). As much as we reject them, we have been guilty of falling into the same snare where we have devised a god of our own making who has a skewed representation of holiness that we can manage, living our lives unaffected by the true nature of God. The more we are confronted with the holiness of God and His perfection, the more we will desire to put away shallow representations of God and worship Him in spirit (by the Spirit in the regenerated man) and in truth (of who God is). "God is a Spirit: and they that worship him must worship him in spirit and in truth" - John 4:24. Holiness of God and the sinfulness of sin cannot coexist, and if the Holy Spirit indwells the temple of the believer, then the other has to go, we cannot serve God and mammon.

Think of this scene in Revelation of the beasts and the elders who worship God, "And when those beasts give glory and honour and thanks to him that sat on the throne, who liveth for ever and ever, The four and twenty elders fall down before him that sat on the throne, and worship him that liveth for ever and ever, and cast their crowns before the throne, saying, Thou art worthy, O Lord, to receive glory and honour and power: for thou hast created all things, and for thy pleasure they are and were created." – Rev. 4:9-11, or the holiness of God in judgement of those cast into the lake of fire where, "The same shall drink of the wine of the wrath of God, which is poured out without mixture into the cup of his indignation; and he shall be tormented with fire and brimstone in the presence of the holy angels, and in the presence of the Lamb: And the smoke of their torment ascendeth up for ever and ever: and they have no rest day nor night, who worship the beast and his image, and whosoever receiveth the mark of his name." – Rev. 14:10-11, **is that the God you meet during your worship service?** If one goes to a worship service and has an experiential roller coaster of "worship" that moved their emotions to a sentimental Christ or in an orthodox church in singing hymns, but goes home unchanged, unrepentant of sin in their lives that needs to be put away, never having a sense of the holiness of God because of their time in church, or having no impact on their life when beholding His holiness, if this is true then all you have experienced is Americanized Christianity that serves an UNKNOWN GOD, a god of our imagination, and not the God of the Bible. No matter how good it made you feel, you fed your flesh and went home thinking all was well between you and God. In true worship, there

THE REMAKING

is awe and speechless adoration of this great God where we experience His majesty, which humbles us to not only worship Him in the beauty of holiness (Psa. 96:9) but will move us to obedience while we rejoice in Him. "Serve the Lord with fear, and rejoice with trembling" – Psa. 2:11. It will cause us to "work out your own salvation with fear and trembling." – Phili. 2:12, for "It is a fearful thing to fall into the hands of the living God." – Heb. 10:31. In Habakkuk 2:20, it states, "But the Lord is in his holy temple: let all the earth keep silence before him." And worship at times is this stillness in the presence of God who met Elijah and spoke with that still small voice (1 Kings 19:12, Psa. 46:10). We think of the revival in China with Jonathan Goforth, where there were times of stillness, where the congregation sat in absolute silence as they were confronted with the living God.

From such an understanding of the nature of God, we realize the need to come out from among them and be ye separate, to live separated lives unto the Lord, worthy of the name we bear. There must be a distinction between the profane against what is godly, for we war against the kingdom of darkness and are of the kingdom of Light (2 Cor. 6:14-18).

The Sinfulness of Sin

Americanized Christianity has forgotten the holiness of God and thus has destroyed the true magnitude of the sinfulness of sin. So, one could make sin as just breaking God's law, or something we all do and mention it as a passing statement of, "For all have sinned, and come short of the glory of God" – Rom. 3:23. While sin is a transgression of the law, it is more than that; it is who we are, both are inseparable. What we do is the fruit of who we are within. This is a matter of the heart. **Thus, even a child, though he may not have committed heinous crimes, can still be convicted before a holy God because of who he is**. Jeremiah stated, "The heart is deceitful above all things, and desperately wicked: who can know it?" – Jer. 17:9. Though the law applied to the conscience can expose the failings of man, only the Spirit can effectually affect the depravity of man of who he is and not just what he has done. There is a term in Romans 7:13 called "exceeding sinful." It is to bring us in contact with the perfection of God that reflects on the corruption of man who is dead in trespasses and sins (Eph. 2:1). The same heart that Hitler had when he butchered millions of lives is the same heart we possess; the same heart that you hear of in the torture cells of the dark ages when they used instruments of torture to tear men, women, and children into pieces or pulled their tongues using tongs, is the same heart we possess; the same heart that lives a moral life but denies the God who created them and gives them their very breath is the same heart we possess. This is not just a statement of formality but the reality of me and you of what is on the inside. And the finality of sin is death and after which the judgment (Rom. 6:23, James 1:15). "And as it is appointed unto men once to die, but after this the judgment:" – Heb. 9:27.

Sin is indeed the transgression of the law (1 John 3:4), but it is also an attack on the character of God in enthroning themselves as a god. Thus, sin equates the "divinity of self" in elevating their heart to what Lucifer said in his heart, "I will ascend into heaven, I will exalt my throne above the stars of God: I will sit also upon the mount of the congregation, in the sides of the north: I will ascend above the heights of the clouds; I will be like the most High." – Isa. 14:13-14. And in our fallen state, when we sin, we take the image of Satan against God in joint rebellion to dethrone God. Jesus said, "Ye are of your father the devil" - John 8:44. We bear the image of our father and take on his nature of evil. This is the state of all who are born into this world. They may bring about great evil, be moral in the eyes of men, give to charity, etc., but the nature of their hearts remains the same. Thus, Jesus said, "the wrath of God abideth on him" - John 3:36, not based on what he does but who he is. For the Christian, sin should be something he abhors and hates, for it does the same within the ranks of the family to spite his heavenly Father. Thus, the heinousness of sin is echoed in the passages such as Isaiah

53 on the reflections of the spotless Lamb to be offered in our place. We see darkness in passages such as, "He is despised and rejected of men; a man of sorrows, and acquainted with grief: and we hid as it were our faces from him; he was despised, and we esteemed him not. …Yet it pleased the Lord to bruise him; he hath put him to grief: when thou shalt make his soul an offering for sin" (v3, 10). The corruption that was to be placed upon Jesus, who became sin for us, caused Him to cry out from his pure sinless heart, "O my Father, if it be possible, let this cup pass from me: nevertheless not as I will, but as thou wilt." – Matt. 26:39. In the unbroken union where Jesus entered into the abyss too deep to ponder when He cried with a loud voice, "Eli, Eli, lama sabachthani? that is to say, My God, my God, why hast thou forsaken me?" – Matt. 27:46. Maybe in Gethsemane, the thought of being separated from His Father was too much. But still, He went in obedience displaying His love to God, who loved this world. Can we fathom such love? We are unable to do so. The God who dwells in thick darkness entered into the blackness of sin and took the full brunt of God's wrath in His own body (1 Peter 2:24) on our behalf.

And we tremble to remember the event when He took His own blood to the holy of holies and offered it as the once-for-all perfect, never to be repeated sacrifice to turn the wrath of God that is upon us. "Neither by the blood of goats and calves, but by his own blood he entered in once into the holy place, having obtained eternal redemption for us." – Heb. 9:12. To reckon the sinfulness of sin, look upon the justice of God that fell upon the Person of God (Jesus Christ) who as God died in our place that the perfection of God's judgment can be satisfied by the unblemished Lamb who is the only one who can atone for our sin. All the rivers of blood that flowed through the ages from Adam to Christ were satisfied with that one sacrifice which was the fulfillment of the shadows that we were given before that event as heaven stood still, and sinful man was reconciled to God. Man, vile and depraved, could never be reconciled, for he was hopelessly sinful. "Who can bring a clean thing out of an unclean? not one." – Job 14:4. And God could never justify the ungodly. Then we hush as we read, "But God, who is rich in mercy, for his great love wherewith he loved us, Even when we were dead in sins, hath quickened us together with Christ, (by grace ye are saved;)" – Eph. 2:4-5. And God declares, "For mine own sake, even for mine own sake, will I do it" – Isa. 48:11. All of grace, Hallelujah, what a Savior! (Eph. 2:8-9). Thus, the Psalmist cries out ecstatically, "Blessed is he whose transgression is forgiven, whose sin is covered. Blessed is the man unto whom the Lord imputeth not iniquity, and in whose spirit there is no guile." – Psa. 32:1-2.

Americanized Christianity has been found wanting to take such sacred topics and attract fallen men with the carnal desire of going to heaven while making sin nothing more than a hindrance to getting there. People want to get saved from hell but don't want to be saved from sin. In the Scriptures, we see these truths interconnected, such as repentance, Lordship, and so forth, as part of this great invitation by God to man; for if a man is not willing to turn from who he is and submit to the One who can deliver him, how can he have any hope of ever being able to enter into the finished work of Christ that was done on his behalf; it is preposterous to consider someone being told to embrace Christ for heaven while having no thought of turning from sin or laying down his weapons of rebellion. "He that covereth his sins shall not prosper: but whoso confesseth and forsaketh them shall have mercy." – Prov. 28:13. And Jesus came to save us from our sins, not just for the future but from the dominion, corruption, and power of sin while living here on earth (Matt. 1:21).

The Wrath of God

When we think of the holiness of God and the punishment of sin that was laid upon His dear Son in our place, we must face the reality of what it means to further ponder on the topic of the wrath of God. Good is because of the absence of evil; Truth is because of the absence of lie; Light is because of the absence of darkness. God's rightness in His judgments is because of His nature of not tolerating sin, for there would be no heaven if sin were allowed into it. In the sacrifice of Christ (1 John 4:10), we see that God's wrath was not only appeased but also His sacrifice satisfied the justice of God where Christ took the wrath of God upon Himself that was meant for us because of our sin. Wrath, in human terms, has the meaning of anger without control, something like a shotgun where it explodes and destroys everything in its direct path and causes collateral damage. But God, who is all-knowing, is also in perfect control over all things, including pouring judgment upon sinners that are precisely on time and to the exact extent that it is deserved. Abraham rightly said, "Shall not the Judge of all the earth do right?" – Gen. 18:25. Here is a fearful picture of God declaring His righteous judgment in Zephaniah 3:8. This is not someone's perspective, but God Himself who declares "to pour upon them mine indignation, even all my fierce anger: for all the earth shall be devoured with the fire of my jealousy." We serve a jealous God who declared, "For thou shalt worship no other god: for the Lord, whose name is Jealous, is a jealous God:" – Exo. 34:14. A jealousy that is synonymous with His holiness where He rightfully deserves the adoration and worship of His creation. "Behold therefore the goodness and severity of God" – Rom. 11:22. "Knowing therefore the terror of the Lord, we persuade men" - 2 Cor. 5:11. "Kiss the Son, lest he be angry, and ye perish from the way, when his wrath is kindled but a little. Blessed are all they that put their trust in him." – Psa. 2:12. It is God who is to be feared who "is able to destroy both soul and body in hell." – Matt. 10:28.

God told His people, "thou refusedst to be ashamed." – Jer. 3:3. There is a point we know not when where God stops drawing a lost man who has spurned the grace of God enough that the Spirit of God takes flight, never to convict again, never to produce tears of brokenness, forever lost. He may live a hundred years after that but is sure of hell, just as when he rejected the call of God for the last time. There is a frightful phrase, "prepare to meet thy God, O Israel" in Amos 4. God sent pestilence, famine, and wars and kept trying to bring Israel back to Him, where God declares, "yet have ye not returned unto me, saith the Lord" five times. When they rejected the call of God, He finally said they would be destroyed without remedy. "He, that being often reproved hardeneth his neck, shall suddenly be destroyed, and that without remedy." – Prov. 29:1. What a fearful thought of being given over with no hope of restoration. "Ephraim is joined to idols: let him alone." – Hos. 4:17. "God gave them over to a reprobate mind, to do those things which are not convenient" – Rom. 1:28. Esau seeking repentance with tears (Heb. 12:16-17), Judas repented himself and committed suicide (Matt. 27:3). They could not find the place of true repentance which comes from God. "Because I have called, and ye refused; I have stretched out my hand, and no man regarded… Then shall they call upon me, but I will not answer; they shall seek me early, but they shall not find me" – Prov. 1:24, 28. To such a one, the wrath of God is assured where there is no hope of mercy.

Some consider the wrath of God in an eternal hell as something not acceptable in their sight. Their justice of God is skewed, and they have become their own god instead of submitting to the righteousness of Christ. They base their acceptance of judgment on their skewed standard of morality. The word of God is not a book under evaluation, but it is the command of God given for mankind to obey. It is we who need to correct ourselves when approaching the Bible, the infallible truth. And the man who questions the validity of hell or the wrath of Almighty God under the guise of rational grounds has an ulterior motive; he loves his sin and wants to continue in it and thus is concerned about the judgment of God that he sees around him and the eternal judgment to come. "And this is the condemnation, that light is come into the world, and men loved darkness rather than light, because their deeds were evil." - John 3:19. God is holy, and sin challenges the holiness of God. God, in His love to preserve what is pure, in perfect wrath, purges that which is evil. A gospel that makes provision for someone to continue in their sin is a false gospel.

The depravity of sin is far greater than we can ever imagine, and a man who has spurned the blood of Christ and questioned the validity of an eternal hell is playing with fire. What is man in the eyes of God? He is fallen, deplorable, unholy, wicked, and depraved. God owes him nothing. For such a one to turn his polluted mind and bring a holy God under his fallen morality is the height of madness. "The fool hath said in his heart, There is no God. They are corrupt, they have done abominable works, there is none that doeth good." – Psa. 14:1. If the heavens are not clean in His sight and He putteth no trust in His saints, "How much more abominable and filthy is man, which drinketh iniquity like water?" – Job 15:16. While it is true that God does not take pleasure in the death of the wicked but that the wicked would repent (Eze. 33:11); such desire of God for man is always shown before the separation of physical death and not after. "For what shall it profit a man, if he shall gain the whole world, and lose his own soul?" – Mark 8:36. Will the eternal God look upon a man in hell and desire to pardon him of the very reason that he is judged for? by doing such to the one who has rejected His Son would be to consider the blood of His own Son an unholy thing. What abomination is this? He is a God who cannot change and will not change his judgment against sin. The wrath of God is eternal, for when a sinner enters into hell, the sinner is not paying to atone for his sin, or as the Roman Catholic church falsely teaches regarding "Purgatory," as the place for expiating their sins before going to heaven; no, he is in final judgment. The wages of sin is death, but hell and the lake of fire (the final place of the damned) is the execution of that judgment, and sin can never be paid for after death, for it is too late. The rich man who went to hell in Luke 16 did not ask for forgiveness, for he knew that mercy had ended; he did not ask to be let out, for he knew he had no hope of being freed.

When we read the finality of those who reject Christ, "And death and hell were cast into the lake of fire. This is the second death" – Rev. 20:14; it carries the weight that the second death is worse than the first death, where you find yourself in hell; the second death is where death and hell are cast into something more terrible called the lake of fire. "But the fearful, and unbelieving, and the abominable, and murderers, and whoremongers, and sorcerers, and idolaters, and all liars, shall have their part in the lake which burneth with fire and brimstone: which is the second death." – Rev. 21:8. There is a quote from Jonathan Edwards that haunts me, "Wicked people will on the day of judgment see all there is to see of Jesus Christ, except His beauty and loveliness."

Sometimes one can consider the topic of the wrath of God as an Old Testament subject (Exo. 32:10, 12, Num. 16:46, 2 Kings 22:13, etc.). Still, we see that Jesus warned us about the wrath of God in that literal place of torment, the place called hell (Matt. 5:29-30, Luke 16:19-31). We see similar warnings from John the Baptist (Luke 3:7) and the apostle Paul (Rom. 1 and 2), human penmen for the Divine author. It is consistent with the Old Testament, for we serve one God who will judge sin. We see the various portrayals of God's wrath as seen already, but also in Revelation 6:15-17 "And the kings of the earth, and the great men, and the rich men, and the chief captains, and the mighty men, and every bondman, and every free man, hid themselves in the dens and in the rocks of the mountains; And said to the mountains and rocks, Fall on us, and **hide us from the face of him that sitteth on the throne, and from the wrath of the Lamb**: For the great day of his wrath is come; and who shall be able to stand?" *(emphasis mine)*. Gentle Jesus, meek and mild, who identified Himself with the suffering of men, is the same Jesus who will pour out His wrath upon the wicked. "Of how much sorer punishment, suppose ye, shall he be thought worthy, who hath trodden under foot the Son of God, and hath counted the blood of the covenant, wherewith he was sanctified, an unholy thing, and hath done despite unto the Spirit of grace? For we know him that hath said, Vengeance belongeth unto me, I will recompense, saith the Lord. And again, The Lord shall judge his people." – Heb. 10:29-30. This is the same Jesus who warned the church in Ephesus that He hated the deeds of the Nicolaitanes (Rev. 2:6). To Thyatira, Jesus spoke regarding a so-called "prophetess" named Jezebel who brought great evil into that church, Jesus said of her, "Behold, I will cast her into a bed, and them that commit adultery with her into great tribulation, except they repent of their deeds. And I will kill her children with death; and all the churches shall know that I am he which searcheth the reins and hearts: and I will give unto every one of you according to your works." – Rev. 2:22-23. In Revelation 19:11-16, He is described as "His eyes were as a flame of fire ... And he was clothed with a vesture dipped in blood: and his name is called The Word of God." (v12-13), "And out of his mouth goeth a sharp sword, that with it he should smite the nations: and he shall rule them with a rod of iron: and he treadeth the winepress of the fierceness and wrath of Almighty God" (v15). In John, we see the state of everyone born into this world, where the wrath of God abideth on him, as in, at present, and not something that will happen in the future. "He that believeth on the Son hath everlasting life: and he that believeth not the Son shall not see life; but the wrath of God abideth on him." – John 3:36. It will be fully experienced upon the entrance of death.

Repentance

The sinner must be brought to the place by the Spirit, where he realizes that he rightfully deserves hell because he has offended a good God. The law and the conscience can aid in that, but the Spirit reveals it to the heart. Escaping hell or gaining heaven can unintentionally become a wrong motivator for coming to Christ purely for self-preservation rather than being made to feel that they are justly deserving of it. We see this declaration by the thief on the cross, "And we indeed justly; for we receive the due reward of our deeds: but this man hath done nothing amiss." – Luke 23:41. Finishing a sermon with a story can often move us to the emotional in sentimentalism, though it may help connect the truth; the concern is that where the truth must flow from the mind to the heart and ultimately affecting the will, that flow can be overlooked. While emotion can be part of this, the emotion of itself can be dangerous. Emotion can move us to the altar or make a decision and never be impacted by the truth to let it change us. Thus, emotions can fulfill the response to ease the nagging of the conscience to quieten it though the man remains in his fallen state. A good self-evaluation will be to consider whether they will still come being burdened for their soul if we don't give the altar call. If it is the Spirit, they will. But the Spirit takes the law of God and crushes man's righteousness to bring him as a little child to the Savior. **Repentance is not just a change of mind but a change of mind that affects the heart, which is proved by a change of course**. We see Christ's sharp rebuke of Chorazin and Bethsaida that if Tyre and Sidon had seen the works that Christ had done, they would have brought forth fruits meet for repentance in their outward response of sackcloth and ashes because of the inward work of the Spirit, and they would have been spared. "Then began he to upbraid the cities wherein most of his mighty works were done, because they repented not: Woe unto thee, Chorazin! woe unto thee, Bethsaida! for if the mighty works, which were done in you, had been done in Tyre and Sidon, they would have repented long ago in sackcloth and ashes." – Matt. 11:20-21. The Thessalonians were reminded of "how ye turned to God from idols to serve the living and true God" - 1 Thess. 1:9. Suppose someone walked into your church who was living in open sin and said, I love my sin, but I like to go to heaven; what would you tell them? Americanized Christianity will say, tell them to make a decision, and then God will deal with their sin. But that is being unfaithful to Christ who said, "except ye repent, ye shall all likewise perish." - Luke 13:3. By the very fact that they don't see sin as God sees it proves that the Spirit has not brought that needed conviction of sin into their lives, which is essential for regeneration and why Jesus came for (Matt. 1:21). Lester Roloff stated, "unless we preach repentance, if our church is filled and its membership rolls increased, they'll have to be increased with unregenerated people."

When Graceless, who later became Christian (in Pilgrim's Progress), saw the burden on his back, he was being crushed by the weight of it and was desirous of finding a way to get rid of it, and when he came to the foot of the cross, he was set free from the law of sin and death. Repentance is not just a turning from (unholiness) but a turning to the Savior (holiness). To bring a sinner to desire Christ for salvation from sin while not desirous of letting go of his sin is an absurdity of the devilish kind. Some say that repentance is to turn from unbelief to believing in Jesus. But that is a strange doctrine that speaks of someone who already believes in the truths of the Scriptures but has no desire to turn from their wicked ways (Isa. 55:7), neither to confess and forsake them (Prov. 28:13), but desires to seek forgiveness. If we are not telling them to confess and forsake their sin, we are, in essence, telling them that they can embrace their sin and be saved. **There are times when our silence speaks greater than our words.** It can be likened to a thief who desires pardon but has that which he has stolen hidden away. **How can his "believe" imply repentance when his heart has not been moved to hate his sin?** If a man has no desire to change his ways, he is not convicted of sin. Repentance is not about just changing one's mind regarding what they are trusting in to take them to heaven; it is the result of seeing who they are before a holy God, a sinner with self-righteous works that amount to filthy rags (Isa. 64:6). And only the Holy Spirit can produce that. Some falsely state that repentance is the same as believe, but in Matthew 21:32 Jesus explicitly states that "For John came unto you in the way of righteousness, and ye believed him not: but the publicans and the harlots believed him: and ye, when ye had seen it, **repented not afterward, that ye might believe him**" *(emphasis mine)*. Agreement to the word of God does not inherently mean conviction of sin by the Spirit. The devils believe to the point of trembling at the implications of what the word of God says (James 2:19); does that mean they hate their sin? Or that they have repented of their evil ways? When "Zacchaeus stood, and said unto the Lord: Behold, Lord, the half of my goods I give to the poor; and if I have taken any thing from any man by false accusation, I restore him fourfold" (Luke 19:8), it was after this outflow that, "Jesus said unto him, This day is salvation come to this house, forsomuch as he also is a son of Abraham" (v9).

While we recognize that repentance is a gift from God (to the Jew in Acts 5:30-31, to the gentiles in Acts 11:17-18, 14:27, in daily witness in 2 Tim. 2:24-26), one of the ways that repentance manifests itself is godly sorrow for sin, that not only has he offended God's law but that he has offended God Himself. It brings him to hate his sin, and he now abhors the transgression that he once loved. "For I will declare mine iniquity; I will be sorry for my sin." – Psa. 38:18. "For godly sorrow worketh repentance to salvation not to be repented of: but the sorrow of the world worketh death." – 2 Cor. 7:10. This sorrow of the world in 2 Corinthians 7:10 is not repentance; it is remorse because of getting caught. And godly sorrow that worketh repentance is not about doing "good works." True repentance shows the state of a penitent man when being awakened by the Spirit to the reality of his wicked heart before God, the fruit of what is happening in his heart. If sin is seen as nothing more than an inconvenience to get to heaven or that it hurts others, the sinner will try to make amends for the betterment of his life or others he loves. Instead, if the goodness of God, as in the prodigal in remembering God's blessings upon his father (Luke 15:17), brings him to repentance (Rom. 2:4), it will immediately reflect on his offense to this good God. Thus, the prodigal son's first statement of reconciliation was, "Father, I have sinned against heaven, and before thee, And am no more worthy to be called thy son" (v18-19). Such is the repentance that brings about salvation that is not to be repented of but ends with the finality of joy from the well of sorrow.

Psalm 116 has a beautiful picture of the sorrow of the night and the joy that cometh in the morning. Have those who desired Christ for salvation said, "The sorrows of death compassed me, and the pains of hell gat hold upon me: I found trouble and sorrow. Then called I upon the name of the Lord; O Lord, I beseech thee, deliver my soul." (v3-4)? Have they embraced the promise that "Gracious is the Lord, and righteous; yea, our God is merciful" (v5)? Were they brought low so that the Lord alone could be their help (v6)? Have they had the witness of the Spirit of a heart made clean, to cry out, "Return unto thy rest, O my soul; for the Lord hath dealt bountifully with thee. For thou hast delivered my soul from death, mine eyes from tears, and my feet from falling" (v7-8)? Have they, in obedience to Christ, said, "I will walk before the Lord in the land of the living" (v9)? We have cheapened grace and produced counterfeits. True grace always results in those redeemed moved with deep gratitude for so great salvation with lifelong submission to Christ.

As with anything true, we realize that there is a false kind of repentance as well. Judas repented, but it was the repentance unto dead works (Heb. 6:1), and he went and hung himself (Matt. 27:3-5). Repentance unto dead works is attempting to find merit for good works or doing penance, which leads to death; it springs from the self-righteous heart that is deceitful and desperately wicked (Jer. 17:9). Speaking of Esau in losing his birthright, "he was rejected: for he found no place of repentance, though he sought it carefully with tears." – Heb. 12:17. The **1828 Webster Dictionary** defines "Repentance" as below.

1828 Webster Dictionary

Repentance: 1. Sorrow for any thing done or said; the pain or grief which a person experiences in consequence of the injury or inconvenience produced by his own conduct.

2. In theology, the pain, regret or affliction which a person feels on account of his past conduct, because it exposes him to punishment. This sorrow proceeding merely from the fear of punishment, is called legal repentance as being excited by the terrors of legal penalties, and it may exist without an amendment of life.

3. Real penitence; sorrow or deep contrition for sin, as an offense and dishonor to God, a violation of his holy law, and the basest ingratitude towards a Being of infinite benevolence. This is called evangelical repentance and is accompanied and followed by amendment of life.

Repentance is a change of mind, or a conversion from sin to God.

Godly sorrow worketh repentance to salvation. 2 Corinthians 7:9. Matthew 3:8. Repentance is the relinquishment of any practice, from conviction that it has offended God.

In his book "Evangelism" James A. Stewart, speaking on repentance, states, "Three Greek words are used in the New Testament which represent different phases of repentance. First is *Metanoeo*, which means a change of mind (Matt. 3:2, Mark 1:15, etc.). The second is *Metamelomai*, which means a change of heart (Matt. 21:29, 32, Heb. 7:21, etc.). Third, *Metanoia*, which means a change of course or life (Matt. 3:8, 9:13, Acts 20:21). These three must go together for genuine repentance."

We see this emphasized in the repentance of David compared to the repentance of Saul; both were confronted by men sent from God. One was of the evangelical kind unto life, and the other was of the legal type unto death.

Evangelical Repentance	Legal Repentance
The sinner sees himself condemned before a holy God and does not seek to shift the blame. David said, "Against thee, thee only, have I sinned, and done this evil in thy sight" – Psa. 51:4. Bathsheba is not mentioned once in the entire confession of David in Psalm 51. True repentance is principally toward God before seeing their sin as against others	The sinner is willing to take the blame partly but will look for others who may have caused him to sin. Saul said, "I have sinned: for I have transgressed the commandment of the Lord, and thy words: because I feared the people, and obeyed their voice." - 1 Sam. 15:24

The sinner desires freedom from the source of sin, to have a pure heart, and to be rid of the crushing penalty of sin. David said, "Wash me throughly from mine iniquity, and cleanse me from my sin." – Psa. 51:2	The sinner desires freedom from the penalty of sin but not with sin itself. Saul said, "Now therefore, I pray thee, pardon my sin, and turn again with me, that I may worship the Lord." - 1 Sam. 15:25
Realizes the effect sin has on others in front of a holy God. David said, "Restore unto me the joy of thy salvation; and uphold me with thy free spirit. Then will I teach transgressors thy ways; and sinners shall be converted unto thee." – Psa. 51:12-13	Arises from the remorse of getting caught or wanting to make amends to please the people and is willing to justify it. "And Saul said, They have brought them from the Amalekites: for the people spared the best of the sheep and of the oxen, to sacrifice unto the Lord thy God; and the rest we have utterly destroyed." - 1 Sam. 15:15
Is willing to flee from sin and put it away. David said, "For I acknowledge my transgressions: and my sin is ever before me." – Psa. 51:3	Is desiring relief from the guilt with no intention of completely forsaking it but shifts the blame. Saul said, "But the people took of the spoil, sheep and oxen, the chief of the things which should have been utterly destroyed, to sacrifice unto the Lord thy God in Gilgal." - 1 Sam. 15:21
He desires complete cleansing to ensure he is completely purified and right before God. David said, "Purge me with hyssop, and I shall be clean:	May show remorse, but the fruits of this repentance will be temporary where his inner heart is not changed to desire consistently after holiness. Saul wanted to force the matter

wash me, and I shall be whiter than snow." – Psa. 51:7	when "And as Samuel turned about to go away, he laid hold upon the skirt of his mantle, and it rent." - 1 Sam. 15:27
Is willing to come clean no matter the cost or the consequences. David said, "Against thee, thee only, have I sinned, and done this evil in thy sight: that thou mightest be justified when thou speakest, and be clear when thou judgest." – Psa. 51:4	He is willing to come clean based on how much it will cost him. Saul said, "Then he said, I have sinned: yet honour me now, I pray thee, before the elders of my people, and before Israel, and turn again with me, that I may worship the Lord thy God." - 1 Sam. 15:30
Repentance comes from God by the conviction of the Holy Spirit. David said, "Create in me a clean heart, O God; and renew a right spirit within me." – Psa. 51:10	Repentance that man works up. Even after being confronted by Samuel (v18-19), Saul was blind to his disobedience. "And Saul said unto Samuel, Yea, I have obeyed the voice of the Lord, and have gone the way which the Lord sent me, and have brought Agag the king of Amalek, and have utterly destroyed the Amalekites." - 1 Sam. 15:20
He is concerned about his fellowship with God more than the friendship of man. David said, "Cast me not away from thy presence; and take not thy holy spirit from me." – Psa. 51:11	Is concerned about the fear of man and his position before them. Saul said, "Then he said, I have sinned: yet honour me now, I pray thee, before the elders of my people, and before Israel, and turn again with me, that I may worship the Lord thy God." - 1 Sam. 15:30. He

	has no true repentance which is toward God
He knows God desires a pure heart and cannot be fooled by our pretense. David said, "For thou desirest not sacrifice; else would I give it: thou delightest not in burnt offering. The sacrifices of God are a broken spirit: a broken and a contrite heart, O God, thou wilt not despise." – Psa. 51:16-17	Does not have the proper view of God and perspective of His impeccable holiness and the utter darkness of one's sin. Saul said, "But the people took of the spoil, sheep and oxen, the chief of the things which should have been utterly destroyed, to sacrifice unto the Lord thy God in Gilgal." - 1 Sam. 15:21
Seeks no self-justification for the action of why he did it but realizes that sin is bigger than what he can handle. David said, "Behold, I was shapen in iniquity; and in sin did my mother conceive me." – Psa. 51:5	He views sin lightly, asking Samuel and not God for pardon, and believes that the end justifies the means. Saul said, "Now therefore, I pray thee, pardon my sin, and turn again with me, that I may worship the Lord." - 1 Sam. 15:25
Receives an accurate perspective of God and how He views sin. David said, "For thou desirest not sacrifice; else would I give it: thou delightest not in burnt offering." – Psa. 51:16	Has a faulty view that God will be pleased in the grand scheme of things since we are doing it for the "right" reasons. "And Saul said unto Samuel, Yea, I have obeyed the voice of the Lord, and have gone the way which the Lord sent me, and have brought Agag the king of Amalek, and have utterly destroyed the Amalekites. But the people took of the spoil, sheep and oxen, the chief of the things which should have been utterly destroyed, to sacrifice

	unto the Lord thy God in Gilgal." - 1 Sam. 15:20-21
He falls on the mercy of God for pardon. It's all about God and our focus upon Him. David said, "Have mercy upon me, O God, according to thy lovingkindness: according unto the multitude of thy tender mercies blot out my transgressions." – Psa. 51:1	God becomes distant, one with whom we need to somehow get right with, so we can be cleared in our conscience. Has the view of "It's all about me." At the end of the discourse, Saul addressed God as "thy God." "Then he said, I have sinned: yet honour me now, I pray thee, before the elders of my people, and before Israel, and turn again with me, that I may worship the Lord thy God." - 1 Sam. 15:30
Desires protection for the future. David said, "Do good in thy good pleasure unto Zion: build thou the walls of Jerusalem." – Psa. 51:18	The desire is about dealing with the here and now with little concern about whether he will repeat it in the future. Saul never expressed his desire for God to protect him in the future against such transgressions.

Though many churches don't believe in preaching on repentance, there is a man in hell at this very moment who believes in it. "And he said, Nay, father Abraham: but if one went unto them from the dead, they will repent." – Luke 16:30. Though much more can be said here, I was brought to the place of conviction of the truths that were found wanting in Americanized Christianity which emphasizes "believe" but places little emphasis on the source of the reason why Christ came (Matt. 1:21) and the need to turn, in thought and proved by its action, for what He died for. We see the stark warning in Ezekiel 13:22, "Because with lies ye have made the heart of the righteous sad, whom I have not made sad; and strengthened the hands of the wicked, that he should not return from his wicked way, by promising him life"

This shallow Christianity never presents the sinner in the context of crying out, "God be merciful to me a sinner," realizing that he's undeserving of God's favor and knowing that it is in the mere pleasure of God to show mercy. But any expression of Christianity that puts man as the object of importance (i.e., in the driver's seat) of what he will do with Jesus, who is breathlessly waiting for His creation to "choose Him," is a false gospel. Opposition to repentance, the real issue: When a man encounters God he is immediately confronted with the holiness of God and his own sinfulness in light of that holiness (Isa. 6:5, Luke 5:8, 18:13). The natural response is godly sorrow of sinning against this good God, that leads to repentance and then he can believe the remedy. Believing in Jesus for heaven without this deep work of grace is of the devilish kind where they have never encountered Christ.

An important truth to note regarding the repentance that is spoken of when associated with God. We see this during the time of Noah (Gen. 6:7), Moses (Exo. 32:12-14), in the time of Jonah (Jonah 3:10), and other instances. When we speak of God repenting, it has a very different meaning. In Num. 23:19, God states, "God is not a man, that he should lie; neither the son of man, that he should repent: hath he said, and shall he not do it? or hath he spoken, and shall he not make it good?" God never repents within the covenant of grace of what He gives to the undeserving sinner who repents (Rom. 11:29). And there is no regret from the man who is thus infused with new life (Psa. 32:1-2). When God intends to do something, such as judge a nation, and when He chooses instead to show mercy, God is said to have repented. This has the implication where He did not do something that He intended to do (Jonah 3:10). This is a change that is not because of any inward sinfulness, for He has none; instead, it is from holiness unchanged to holiness unchanged. The God with whom there is no variableness, neither shadow of turning (James 1:17). But when we speak of man, he is affected by the revelation of truth upon inward sin, which produces a spontaneous change affecting the will, moving the offender from unrighteousness to righteousness. Though repentance does not have any merit in the works that he does, it prepares the ground for the inflow of life from above. **You don't repent to show God that you are sorry; you repent because you are sorry** (Joel 2:12-13). And you can't be sorry (of the godly sort) unless God convicts you of sin. Without the blessed Holy Spirit, there is no conviction of sin, without which there is no godly sorrow, without which there is no repentance, without which there is no salvation. The word sermonized without the Spirit is the death of many churches in America.

Believe

Many areas are taken for granted that it becomes quite easy to misunderstand and equate them to something completely different from what was intended. In that early church, they did not have the New Testament; many hearers only knew Jesus as a criminal who was put to death by Rome, disliked by the religious leaders, and accused of blasphemy. And rumors of his body being stolen by the disciples were spreading, yet when the gospel was preached, they were pricked in their hearts of the truth of it. It was the Spirit who was witnessing to the heart of the hearers of what was being preached. Paul writes regarding this in 1 Cor. 2:4-5, "And my speech and my preaching was not with enticing words of man's wisdom, but in demonstration of the Spirit and of power: That your faith should not stand in the wisdom of men, but in the power of God." And again in 1 Thess. 1:5, "For our gospel came not unto you in word only, but also in power, and in the Holy Ghost, and in much assurance; as ye know what manner of men we were among you for your sake." Where it could be said, "when ye received the word of God which ye heard of us, ye received it not as the word of men, but as it is in truth, the word of God, which effectually worketh also in you that believe." – 1 Thess. 2:13. We see other examples of this in, "Not by might, nor by power, but by my spirit, saith the

Lord of hosts." – Zech. 4:6, "kingdom of God is not in word, but in power." – 1 Cor. 4:20 and "Who also hath made us able ministers of the new testament; not of the letter, but of the spirit: for the letter killeth, but the spirit giveth life." – 2 Cor. 3:6. And this was when they did not have the New Testament or even portions of it in written form in many instances.

Jesus is not "longing" to be our friend like a redheaded stepchild who is trying to fit into the family. Though He is a friend of sinners, He is Lord, and we come to Him on bended knees on His terms, desiring His mercy. Our presentation of the gospel sometimes seems as if we are doing God a favor by accepting His Son. God is self-existent and in need of nothing, and there is nothing we do that can add to His betterment, though He has chosen to shew forth and share His love with us and desires communion with us. Jesus said, "If any man will come after me" - Luke 9:23. The gospel is not only an invitation to come, but it is a command to obey, realizing that the judgment of God is poured out on unrepentant sinners who refuse to heed the command. "when the Lord Jesus shall be revealed from heaven with his mighty angels, In flaming fire taking vengeance on them that know not God, and that obey not the gospel of our Lord Jesus Christ: Who shall be punished with everlasting destruction from the presence of the Lord, and from the glory of his power" – 2 Thess. 1:7-9. Only an awakened sinner has any awareness of his standing before God, and any choice in the matter on the part of man is displayed in his receiving the offer of free grace in humility rather than a "decision" that he takes pride or trusts in. Man is not seeking after God; God is seeking after man. Just as Adam hid from God and sewed fig leaves to cover his nakedness, man will always fill the void with anything but God (Psa. 53:2-3). Unless God initiates, man will never seek God but will go on sinning against Him (Psa. 14:2, John 6:44, 1 Cor. 2:14). "For the Son of man is come to seek and to save that which was lost." - Luke 19:10. The Son of man came to seek and save since man will never seek Him and he cannot save himself. In the case of an awakened soul, be it the Ethiopian eunuch, Cornelius, or the Macedonian vision, light obeyed begets light. And the man who loves his sin and rejects the light that he has been given *(light revealed in creation, law written in their hearts, and such)* will be given over to his lust unless he repents and believes (Luke 13:24, John 6:35, 7:37, Rev. 22:17). We realize that in all this, there is no contradiction between the sovereignty of God and the responsibility of man.

The striving of Jacob with the Angel is a beautiful picture of the truth of God's sovereignty and human responsibility. The Angel was obviously more powerful than Jacob, one who could slay an army of a hundred and eighty-five thousand overnight (2 Kings 19:35) and appear and go as commanded (Judg. 13, Luke 1). But here, Jacob is allowed to lay hold of the Angel on the promise that there was a blessing to be received and protection from being made aware of the due vengeance from his brother of certain death (Gen. 32). And he had to acknowledge that he was a deceiver (v27) before he was given a new name and a new outlook regarding life itself. He comes from that struggle changed forever, knowing that he had met God, his halt on his thigh proving it in every step he took. His life was spared, and he met Esau in peace. We see the familiar teaching of our Lord, "Then said one unto him, Lord, are there few that be saved? And he said unto them, Strive to enter in at the strait gate: for many, I say unto you, will seek to enter in, and shall not be able." - Luke 13:23-24. This human responsibility is not in the elevation of man's doing but in the humbling of man, falling on the mercy of God, and his total inability to save himself unless he hears pardon from Christ. You cannot reason someone into heaven, good morals cannot bring anyone to Christ (Matt. 19:20), and the world by wisdom knew not God (1 Cor. 1:21), it must be by the Holy Ghost that revelation is given to believe (John 3:27).

We proclaim "believe" as "take it by faith" that you already possess. What is this, to take it by faith? If a man went to get bread to feed his hungry children and was told to take it by faith without having received it from the storekeeper and goes home empty-handed and said I took it by faith, what good does that do to the starving child? Would he tell his child to take it by faith, and you will be filled? No, there must be substance. True faith will have substance where it will produce that life that is because of a transaction and not a one-sided claim to "take it by faith." It is a transaction that happens in God's way and not by man's assumption. Simon believed also and was baptized but was still in the gall of bitterness and in the bond of iniquity. It was a false profession that was lacking until it was exposed, not true salvation. He did the same thing Saul did, to ask the apostles for prayer instead of repenting toward God (1 Sam. 15:30, Acts 8:24). The power of the gospel in the word, which speaks of the grandeur of God's work, comes alive when it is illuminated by the Spirit and made effectual in the hearts of the hearers. The thief on the cross dared not "take it by faith" or claim anything when he asked for mercy in his dying moment. Christ had to finish that work where the thief heard that sweet response of Christ when He said, "Verily I say unto thee, Today shalt thou be with me in paradise." – Luke 23:43, and only after then was his salvation complete being given that full assurance.

What is the organ of faith that one can see the truth and take action upon it? The organ for receiving the truth is the mind from the senses (Prov. 20:12, 28:9, Rom. 10:17). The Person who makes the truth effectual is the Spirit through the word (John 16:13). **The organ of faith is the heart**. With the heart, man believeth unto righteousness (Matt. 13:15, Rom. 10:10). Christianity is a heart matter. Not the old heart of the natural man that is dead, but the heart which has been opened by God (Eze. 36:26, Acts 16:14, 2 Cor. 3:3). In essence, saving faith is not like sitting in a chair to hold you up, for in the scenario of the chair, the mind believes based on facts and probability, and the heart is not needed. Saving faith is supernatural, a gift of God, and exercised from the heart. Faith is not primarily based on facts, but on Truth, because of the Person.

We see a pattern in that early church that to believe was not an intellectual agreement or in a Bible verse but something much deeper that engaged all the faculties of their mind and will, counting the cost of following Christ and taking that step of faith. Such is the nature of "believe" from the heart, "That if thou shalt confess with thy mouth the Lord Jesus, and shalt **believe in thine heart** that God hath raised him from the dead, thou shalt be saved. For **with the heart man believeth unto righteousness**; and with the mouth confession is made unto salvation" – Rom. 10:9-10 *(emphasis mine)*. It does not state to believe with the mind though truth flows through the mind. This confession is the natural outflow of the proper kind of "believe" from the heart. Jeremiah 17:9 states, "The heart is deceitful above all things, and desperately wicked: who can know it?" A person growing up in a Christian home has been taught and believes with the mind and may even be convinced of the truths of the Scriptures intellectually, but when the Holy Spirit awakens him, his wicked heart is affected and transformed where he now believes from the heart. It would be the same with someone who follows another religion where they have been brought up in the teaching of their religion, and they need to be awakened by the Spirit, and they believe from the heart and not just be convinced by history or clever arguments that these things are true. It is the hearing of faith (Gal. 3:2-3) and "To day if ye will hear his voice, harden not your hearts, as in the provocation." – Heb. 3:15. Watchman Nee states, "revelation will always precede faith… revelation is always the work of the Holy Spirit, in order that, by coming alongside and opening to us the Scriptures He may guide us into all the truth."

Such gravity that the word "believe" held where Jesus said that the natural man cannot believe in that truest sense for the devils also believe and tremble; but this is a supernatural work that God does to bear witness to the reality of Christ and His atoning work, shedding His blood for our sins. The truth of the gospel is foolishness to the lost "In whom the god of this world hath blinded the minds of them which believe not, lest the light of the glorious gospel of Christ, who is the image of God, should shine unto them." – 2 Cor. 4:4. "Jesus answered and said unto them, This is the work of God, that ye believe on him whom he hath sent." – John 6:29.

To Peter, "Jesus answered and said unto him, Blessed art thou, Simon Barjona: for flesh and blood hath not revealed it unto thee, but my Father which is in heaven." – Matt. 16:17. Peter did not have that faith by his Adamic nature, but faith was imparted that he believed. The Samaritans who came and were convinced of Christ declared (to the woman), "Now we believe, not because of thy saying: for we have heard him ourselves, and know that this is indeed the Christ, the Saviour of the world." – John 4:42. Peter writing regarding this states that God "was manifest in these last times for you, **Who by him** do believe in God, that raised him up from the dead, and gave him glory; that your faith and hope might be in God." - 1 Peter 1:20-21 *(emphasis mine)*. We see Paul's admonition to the church at Corinth regarding the schisms that were present in boasting by whom they believed, Paul or Apollos, and he states, "Who then is Paul, and who is Apollos, but ministers by whom ye believed, even as the Lord gave to every man? ... but God gave the increase" – 1 Cor. 3:5-6. God gave them the ministry of the word, and they were to go weeping bearing precious seed (Psa. 126:6), but the outcome of hearts being illuminated and the word having its free course to bring the increase was God. It is one thing to say that we want to see people saved; it is another thing to say that we want to see God save people. If we focus on wanting to see souls saved, we could try to make it happen; instead, if we desire to see God save souls, then the desire becomes to pray to the God who can save souls and labor with surety knowing that He will save them and change them. It is the power of God and not the power of man's words. "For I determined not to know any thing among you, save Jesus Christ, and him crucified." – 1 Cor. 2:2. Jesus said, "And I, if I be lifted up from the earth, will draw all men unto me." - John 12:32. In Ezekiel 37, Ezekiel was to prophesy upon the dry bones which had no life. He was to say, "O ye dry bones, **hear the word of the Lord**" *(emphasis mine)*. And God brought them to life when he prophesied to the wind to breathe upon them, and they lived (v4, 9). Preaching is, in truth, raising the dead, trusting in God to open their understanding and give them faith to believe.

The natural must lead to the supernatural. They are both essential in true Christianity. What is the defining difference between Christ and Religions/Atheism. It starts with the Divine intervention of the Spirit regarding the true state of man shown by experiential conviction of sin. True conviction brings an awareness of God and not just because one agrees with what He has said. Anything else is just a form of godliness. True relationship has the end of peace with God. (Rom. 5:1)

In John 2:23-24, "many believed in his name ... But Jesus did not commit himself unto them." Their belief was from what they had seen Him do in the miracles prior and not for who He was. It was similar to my belief in Christ as God, which I had as a lost man and did many wonderful works in His name, but they were unto dead works. I did not do them to attain heaven; instead, it was something that I did as being brought up in it. The same happened in John 8:30, where "As he spake these words, **many believed on him**" *(emphasis mine)*. But was that a true "believe" as in saving faith? Later Jesus states to these who "believed" on Him in verse 44, "Ye are of your father the devil, and the lusts of your father ye will do." We see the end of their "believe" where in verse 59, "Then took they up stones to cast at him." These are the same in verses 41 and 48, which told Jesus that He was born of fornication and had a devil. Jesus rightly said that they would show their "believe" by their willingness to obey Him in continuing in His word. "Then said Jesus to those Jews which believed on him, If ye continue in my word, then are ye my disciples indeed; And ye shall know the truth, and the truth shall make you free." After that, everything went downhill, revealing what kind of "believe" theirs was; it was nothing but the belief of devils. The famous verse John 3:16, spoken to Nicodemus, is followed by verse 21, which states, "But he that doeth truth cometh to the light, that his deeds may be made manifest, that they are wrought in God." The truth that sets you free (John 8:32, 36) will also show by your deeds manifested that you have believed.

You hear all too often of testimonies such as praying a prayer for salvation at four or five and then during the teenage or as a young adult plunging headlong into sin and not caring for anything godly and living like the devil. And once they get married or have kids, coming back to church to get assurance of their childhood decision, and now they are in church. I remember that during my years as a prodigal, the desire to go to church was still there; I still read the Bible and prayed. Yes, those prayers would not have reached heaven (Psa. 66:18), and I remember with sorrow the great reproach I brought to the name of Christ, but by the grace of God, I never forsook the Lord in apostasy because His seed was in me. The prodigal never doubted that he was the son of his father. While sin can bring doubt, the grace of God sustains us from within to restore us back to Christ. Peter, who denied Christ with a curse, nevertheless went out and wept bitterly. The question is not whether a young child can be born of God; the fearful thought is that those cycles of "prayed a prayer," didn't care for God or the things of God, re-committed to Christ as an adult, all these **hang on the assumption** that as long as we believe the Scriptures intellectually and may even be convinced of them by man, **we can pray and make ourselves born into the family of God**. The devil believes that Jesus was born of a virgin, he believes that Jesus is the Son of God, he believes that Jesus died and rose from the dead, he believes in a Triune God, and he believes that he is awaiting a future judgment. Not only does he believe all this, but he also knows that it is true, and with all this, he is still the devil. The testimony service of the average church is almost at the point of mocking God; we drag it down lower and lower where instead of this radical life-altering work of God, we promote a shallow mental assent to truth, so the unsaved can feel comfortable with their sham profession and ungodly lives, thinking they are part of the Beloved.

We read this phrase in Hebrews 11:13, "but having seen them afar off, and were persuaded of them, and embraced them, and confessed that they were strangers and pilgrims on the earth." To believe is to have seen and be persuaded of the truth by the Spirit, to embrace all its implications enough to stake one's life or death on it and confess the reality of that work that God does in them. True "believe" is that which casts everything upon Jesus. Hebrews 11:6 states, "he that cometh to God must believe that he is," that He is for everything I am, His righteousness for my corruption, His holiness for my sinfulness, His life for my self-life. And to call upon Him until He saves me, knowing that "he is a rewarder of them that diligently seek him." Such is the nature of "believe." Thus, in Titus 1:1, we see "acknowledging of the truth which is after godliness" True regeneration always leads to godliness. Thus, James states that while faith is not by sight, it is proved by sight (James 2:18). To "believe" and not change reveals that you have not believed; to "repent" and not turn means that you didn't repent; to call Him as "Lord" and not submit to His commands shows that you have not submitted to Him as your God (Luke 6:46). In evangelism, the unbiblical and skewed view of the elevation of carnal man in making salvation for the happiness of man while portraying an impotent God who is subject to the whims of man is something that Americanized Christianity is guilty of.

The Lordship of Christ

When we realize the true nature of the spiritual warfare around us and the dominion of Satan that wars against the dominion of God and His truth, we quickly realize the great danger that man is in by being blinded by the god of this world. When a sinner comes to Christ and hears His command to "deny himself, and take up his cross daily, and follow me." - Luke 9:23, it is not a suggestion but a command. Jesus said, "He that is not with me is against me; and he that gathereth not with me scattereth abroad." – Matt. 12:30. There is no middle ground or what one may think of as neutral ground. Salvation is never according to man's terms of interest; it is as per God's terms. And when we realize in the realm of dominion that Jesus is Lord, it dramatically influences how we approach Him. In Peter's message on Pentecost, he declared, "Therefore let all the house of Israel know assuredly, that God hath made the same Jesus, whom ye have crucified, both Lord and Christ." – Acts 2:36. Lord is a term of authority, of a position that commands obedience, demands allegiance at the cost of denying all and following Him and acknowledge Him as Lord. In your natural life, you are the master of it, you have chosen to live apart from God but a slave to sin under the dominion of Satan. In the new life, you come to Christ realizing His dominion and becoming a willing slave to Christ by submitting to Him.

Suppose one does not submit and bow down before Him in this world. In that case, they will be forced to submit in eternity when, "That at the name of Jesus every knee should bow, of things in heaven, and things in earth, and things under the earth; And that every tongue should confess that Jesus Christ is Lord, to the glory of God the Father." – Phili. 2:10-11. Christ must reign supreme; to deny His authority over us would be to deny the faith and be Anathema. There can never be two Kings. Thus, Paul in Romans 6:18 states, "Being then made free from sin, ye became the servants of righteousness." We are servants or slaves of sin and thereby of Satan, or we are servants or slaves (doulos) from a willing heart of love to Christ, our Master, and our Kinsman. Does He rule over us in love? Yes. But it also means that we obey Him; Jesus said, "And why call ye me, Lord, Lord, and do not the things which I say?" – Luke 6:46. "and his commandments are not grievous." – 1 John 5:3. It is interesting to note that Judas, who betrayed the Lord, was with Christ for three years, performed miracles, and believed in His teachings as having moral implications, but never called Him Lord, finally denying Christ and showing his true colors. Jesus as Lord means that everything about our lives flows from Him; He is the starting point and not we ourselves. In practicality, it is not that we ask Him to bless something we are planning to do; it is submitting to Him if we should even do it or not.

We see a similar struggle with Pilate, who was desirous to release Christ but was confronted with this question by the Jews, "And from thenceforth Pilate sought to release him: but the Jews cried out, saying, If thou let this man go, thou art not Caesar's friend: whosoever maketh himself a king speaketh against Caesar." - John 19:12. And when the chief priests of the Jews complained, "Write not, The King of the Jews; but that he said, I am King of the Jews." (John 19:21), "Pilate answered, What I have written I have written" (v22). The significance of the man on the cross, according to Pilate, was that He was "a king" who was brought under the subjection of Rome, though Pilate missed the point completely. It was a similar challenge that Herod was confronted with, "Where is he that is born King of the Jews? for we have seen his star in the east, and are come to worship him." – Matt. 2:2. There can never be two Kings; one must be put to death.

It would be the height of anarchy for a subject to come to a kingdom and desire the king's protection while making known that he will always be a rebel and never submit to the laws of the land. God will never save a rebel, never, unless he lays down his sword and repents of his evil ways. I read about how when someone becomes a Christian in North Korea, it is more than a religious persuasion. In North Korea, the leader is considered lord, where absolute submission is commanded. He is seen as the provider, from food to everything needed to stay alive, so when a person becomes a Christian, it is considered treason; Jesus has become his Lord, and the North Korean leader has been dethroned. I see this doctrine is found wanting in the American church since it demands complete submission to Christ, which the typical American with his "freedom" finds hard to do. He is his own entity and has the self-dependent spirit of his forefathers, and to ask him to submit to a King is preposterous. But you will never find salvation given in any other way. "Believe on **the Lord** Jesus Christ, and thou shalt be saved" – Acts 16:31. The Philippian jailer knew what that term meant, for Caesar was lord, and to believe on the Lord Jesus Christ was to deny Caesar as lord and take Jesus Christ as Lord and submit to His commands. Additionally, the implication in acknowledging Jesus as Lord was to repent from the dominion of Satan as lord and flee to Christ for mercy (1 Cor. 12:3). We see this repeated in many other passages. "For whosoever shall call upon the name of **the Lord** shall be saved." – Rom. 10:13, "That if thou shalt confess with thy mouth **the Lord** Jesus, and shalt believe in thine heart that God hath raised him from the dead, thou shalt be saved." – Rom. 10:9, "As ye have therefore received Christ Jesus **the Lord**, so walk ye in him:" – Col. 2:6 *(emphasis mine)*. Even in John 3:16, the phrase "whosoever believeth in Him" is about what He represents; our sacrifice, Saviour, Lord, who is high and lifted up. It is the Person who bears that name, and "everlasting life" is the life of Christ in us (Col. 1:27, 3:3) and not just a future hope.

I can wear a police uniform, but I will have no authority to enforce the law. But if I am given that authority by the government and wear the uniform, then it is a whole different matter. I have the whole justice system behind me of the entire country. It was the authority of Christ that they were under when they cast the devils out and healed the sick (Acts 3:6, 9:33-34, 16:16-18). Just invoking the name is not something magical, but the Person it represents by what He represents to the kingdom of God and the kingdom of darkness. There were certain vagabond Jews who tried to use the name without the authority of the Person behind the name and got into trouble (Acts 19:13-16). No other name given under heaven for salvation (Acts 4:12) has a similar implication to Emmanuel, which being interpreted is, God with us (Matt. 1:23). It is what the name signifies, God with us as in the Person embodied. "and his name shall be called Wonderful, Counsellor, The mighty God, The everlasting Father, The Prince of Peace." – Isa. 9:6. To embrace Christ is to submit to Christ as Lord, which implies that we are to not submit to this world, its god, and its ways. This realization must be at the forefront of our minds when we confront those without Christ.

The Light of the Conscience vs. the Light of the Spirit

In John 8:3-11, the scribes and Pharisees brought unto him a woman taken in adultery in the very act. They accused her according to the law, and when Jesus responded, "He that is without sin among you, let him first cast a stone at her" (v7), we see the people being convicted by their own conscience. There is a sense in which every man has the light of the conscience, "which lighteth every man that cometh into the world." – John 1:9. But that itself is not enough, for when they were accused of their conscience, they did not run to Christ and ask for forgiveness of sins that they were convicted about; instead, the Scripture states that they "went out one by one, beginning at the eldest, even unto the last" (v9). We realize that God has given this moral compass for mankind in upholding His moral balance in this world lest mankind implodes and destroys itself. But the conscience can be trained to believe a lie by quenching the given light, and one can be left with a seared conscience. We see such at times of war or in heathen lands where through plunder and murder, men live without basic morality but are justified in their own eyes. While the light of the conscience may aid to awaken the sinner to his condition, it is the Spirit who is the one who draws the sinner to the Savior, which is the light of the Spirit. [Jesus] "No man can come to me, except the Father which hath sent me draw him: and I will raise him up at the last day." – John 6:44, "It is the spirit that quickeneth" (v63), and again in verse 65, "no man can come unto me, except it were given unto him of my Father." "John answered and said, A man can receive nothing, except it be given him from heaven." – John 3:27. The natural man cannot receive God because we have all gone astray, thus the need for the Spirit to awaken the sinner to his great need for a Savior (1 Cor. 2:11).

There is a grave danger in using the light of the conscience in showing the sinner that he has broken God's laws and asking him to pray a prayer or make a decision based on an agreement to facts of Scripture instead of waiting for the work of the Spirit to illuminate the reality of their offense toward God Himself (and not just His laws) in godly sorrow and faith toward the Lord Jesus Christ. As seen before, we need to realize that the light of the conscience can never lead anyone to Christ, for it only condemns his condition as guilty, and the text of the Bible, by itself, is insufficient. The light of the Spirit draws and bears witness since that is His exclusive office. The first one creates a proselyte; the second one regenerates; the first one can be used with human methods like faith in a chair or repeating a sinner's prayer; the second one has the supernatural work of God changing the heart of stone to a heart of flesh; the first one is intellectual, the second one is being born of God. It is the difference between damnation and salvation. The light of the word that the conscience may agree with is not enough; it is only as the Spirit empowers the word that it is made effective. As an example, someone may be tempted to think of what they have done when comparing to God's law as sinful but not consider themselves as vile. Their attitude may be, "everyone does it," or "I guess no one is perfect." It is not just what we have done but who we are which must be exposed by the Spirit. The witness of the conscience can expose what we have done, but the witness of the Spirit exposes who we are before a holy God. Sin is a spiritual issue before it becomes a moral issue.

It is not the facts of salvation or just the text of Scripture that will save lost souls; at some point, it needs to become Truth (the Person) which is revealed by the illumination of the Spirit to the listener, which will bring life. It is the Person of Scripture who saves (1 John 5:10-12). And faith is not that genuine faith, which is exercised in daily living, but faith to believe God is a gift, and not revealed because of flesh and blood but "my Father which is in heaven." – Matt. 16:17, and the rejoicing of that early church, rightfully so, was that God "had opened the door of faith unto the Gentiles" - Acts 14:27. Who could have explained the gospel or His deity better than Christ Himself, but He still states that declaration to Peter of truth given from above (Matt. 16:17). It is interesting to note that Jesus, after speaking the parable of the Sower in Luke 8, spoke of these parables as "the mysteries of the kingdom of God" (v10). The question begs to ask; if it was just an earthly story with a heavenly meaning, why is it a mystery? The key lies in verse 9, where "his disciples asked him." This speaks of the revelation that must come from above to understand the heavenly meaning and cannot be interpreted by earthly eyes that are blind. The Spirit opens our understanding when we humbly ask. "Ask, and it shall be given you; seek, and ye shall find; knock, and it shall be opened unto you" – Matt. 7:7. The Psalmist states, "Open thou mine eyes, that I may behold wondrous things out of thy law." – Psa. 119:18. The word of God gives light (Psa. 119:105, 130), but it is the Spirit who gives sight.

Using the light of conscience and showing verses from the Scripture to convince them that they are a sinner and never getting to the light of the Spirit and calling for "decisions," from kindergarten to adults, has produced a spurious wave of "converts" who show no interest in the things of God, neither bears His marks of holiness in their lives. To a Mormon, "saved" means faith, repentance, baptism, and obedience to the basic beliefs of the LDS Church; to a Roman Catholic, "saved" means that it is given through the mediation of Rome's sacraments. With our shallow declaration of calling people "saved," which means nothing more than giving assent to truth and making a "decision," we must ask for the fruits of salvation in our converts as the Scriptures command (Matt. 7:18-21, 2 Cor. 13:5, 1 John 4:1) before we call them converted.

I am horrified to be confronted with the truth that there are millions of people who think they are going to heaven who have not been given a new heart, though they have been given a new title by the church that will never hold in the bar of God's judgment. If the Holy Spirit does not save, no one can get saved, and quenching the Spirit of God where He takes flight has been the reality of what God warns of in the Old and New Testaments. *Sidenote:* To the Christian, their conscience, having been sharpened by the truths of God's word, needs to be guarded by listening to it in the matter of Christian living and not justify anything against what one has learned of the Spirit through the word.

Regeneration - A Matter of the Heart

We are confronted on every side with religion, philosophies, and cults. We saw earlier in the topic of God in the Midst that which sets us apart from all others, but what is the heart of this truth regarding how the gospel affects mankind? The gospel cannot be about taking us to heaven, for other religions have a similar concept, be it Islam, Hinduism, or Buddhism. Even in Atheism, there is a sense in which, when they die, they don't expect anything else. It is not isolated just to the facts of Christianity as in intellectual assent to truth, for the devils believe and tremble. It is not believing in a proposition about Christ, for many philosophies have propositions regarding the "divinity" of their leaders. It is not in the teachings of the Book that has no bearing on the God who wrote that Book, for other religions has "sacred" books as well. It is not in living a clean life, for many who are lost live clean lives. We see this example in the case of the rich young ruler or the five foolish virgins, who were foolish but nonetheless virgins. It is not in looking different; we have people such as the Amish who look different though they have a religion of works. It is not self-denial by the energy of the flesh; there are many monasteries worldwide where they live a life of isolation and self-denial. It is not about giving up certain things that you used to do, for many in their acts *(or even religious acts)* of self-reformation give up things that may have brought them into addiction. We see organizations like Alcoholics Anonymous that teach you to believe in a "Power greater than ourselves" to help you aid in that. It is not in supernatural acts of healing or bodily relief; we see many cults claim to heal or receive answers by praying to their false gods. It is not found in easing your conscience; religion and acts such as giving to charity have a way of helping one ease their conscience. It is not about an emotional historical event; cults have out-of-body experiences that can give them a religious "high." It is not in the sincerity of those who share the truth, for many false religions have adherents who are sincere to follow and spread their teachings even unto death.

In Proverbs 23:26, Solomon makes a plea, "My son, give me thine heart." There is so much emphasis in the Scriptures regarding the heart, for it is where the will of man is moved, and his actions take shape. If we are to realize the difference between the truth and the outflow of the gospel as opposed to the falsehood of what other religions and cults promote, we need to dig deeper. God's emphasis on being born again, where a new heart is given, speaks to the importance of dealing with this topic in greater detail. We see that there are many types of hearts that the Scripture mentions, but we will be looking at four of them.

-   The Natural Heart

In Proverbs 7:6-23, we see the picture of this natural heart of the strange woman. She has no desire for God, deceives her husband, and has a form of godliness as long as it satisfies her lust. She does not seek after God, but after sinning against God, she can wipe her mouth and can say, "she eateth, and wipeth her mouth, and saith, I have done no wickedness." – Prov. 30:20. She thinks life is without consequences, has no desire for godliness, and leads many astray. "The Lord looked down from heaven upon the children of men, to see if there were any that did understand, and seek God. They are all gone aside, they are all together become filthy: there is none that doeth good, no, not one." – Psa. 14:2-3. To say that man is seeking after God is against what God has revealed in His word. Man lost his ability to seek after God when he sinned in the garden and hid from God. God must take the first step, "No man can come to me, except the Father which hath sent me draw him" – John 6:44, "We love him, because he first loved us." – 1 John 4:19, "Salvation is of the Lord." - Jonah 2:9 for "the natural man receiveth not the things of the Spirit of God: for they are foolishness unto him: neither can he know them, because they are spiritually discerned." – 1 Cor. 2:14. We see this evidenced today where to avoid their personal accountability to a Creator, man embraces evolution. He finds an avenue to declare that there is no God. He is glad to worship the creature more than the Creator

(Rom. 1:25), even trying to worship "Mother Earth," not realizing that this planet as we know it today God will destroy in the coming judgment (2 Peter 3:10). When God has used natural calamities to awaken His people or warn a nation, man blames it on prevalent teachings of his day, such as global warming, while failing to take the time needed for a deeper understanding of the real reason for the issue. While we understand that there are cycles of weather patterns and climate variations that the world goes through as ordained by God, and we are to be good stewards of what He has provided for us, we also realize that God has used specific events in the past to bring awareness to His judgments. To this person, their need is the **existence of God**. We see this displayed in the life of the apostle Paul when he preached on Mars Hill (Acts 17:22-23). This is where everyone begins and where America is, where God is nothing more than Santa Claus, and those who call themselves "Christians" see Christianity as nothing more than fitting an imaginary "God" into their lives as long as it suits them. A pseudo-Christian religion of convenience, whereas God calls us to sweat, blood, and tears, and the way of the cross is narrow.

-   The Hardened Heart

In Romans 1:18-32, we see the depravity of man's heart that rejects the call of God and is given over to a reprobate mind, to do those things which are not convenient. This person is unwilling to believe though they may be convinced of the truth by the Spirit. In Prov. 1:24-25, we see the call of God, "Because I have called, and ye refused; I have stretched out my hand, and no man regarded; But ye have set at nought all my counsel, and would none of my reproof:" We see the fearful response of God who gives them over to their sin in v26-30, "I also will laugh at your calamity; I will mock when your fear cometh; When your fear cometh as desolation, and your destruction cometh as a whirlwind; when distress and anguish cometh upon you. Then shall they call upon me, but I will not answer; they shall seek me early, but they shall not find me: For that they hated knowledge, and did not choose the fear of the Lord:

123

They would none of my counsel: they despised all my reproof." To this person, their need is to **repent**. We see this in the life of Peter, who preached at Pentecost (Acts 2:14-38) and of the early church (Acts 3:19, 20:21).

Opposition to repentance, the real issue: When a man encounters God, he is immediately confronted with the holiness of God and his own sinfulness in light of that holiness (Isa. 6:5, Luke 5:8, 18:13). The natural response is godly sorrow of sinning against this good God, which leads to repentance and then he can believe the remedy. Believing in Jesus for heaven without this deep work of grace is of the devilish kind because they have never encountered Christ.

-   The Broken and Contrite Heart

In Luke 18:9-14, we see the Publican who "standing afar off, would not lift up so much as his eyes unto heaven, but smote upon his breast, saying, God be merciful to me a sinner" (v13). This heart has been convicted of sin by the Spirit, realizes that God is good and that he is evil, that God is holy and that he is sinful; he realizes that God is just in preparing him for judgment since he is guilty of his offense toward this good God and not just His laws. He is gripped by the fear of God, where he is bowed down. He hates his sin and hates who he is, a sinner who hates God and loves his sin. He asks for mercy, knowing that God is merciful though he does not deserve it; he knows he has no claim to the mercy of God by anything he can do. He is shown the way of escape, by the Spirit, through the blood of Christ. The call to this person in a state of repentance is to **believe** on the **Lord** Jesus Christ. We see this in the life of Paul and Silas, where the jailer came trembling and asked, "Sirs, what must I do to be saved?" (Acts 16:25-31). This jailer was convinced of the truth, convicted of sin, and constrained by the Spirit.

- The Regenerated Heart

This is the pivotal place where Americanized Christianity has pronounced many as Christians where they have neither met the living Christ nor heard His voice. They have been baptized and sent as missionaries and become pastors, evangelists, and laymen but have never experienced the transaction of a changed heart. We have movie stars claiming they are born again but continuing to live a life of sin or those who live a lifestyle that God hates in LGBTQ+ yet claiming to be born again. God came to save us from our sin (Matt. 1:21), yet they want to live in what God calls an abomination and that which put Jesus on the cross; and claim to be His child while living in sin, having no desire to turn from it. Acceptance of sin in the name of "love" or "tolerance" is not, in truth, loving, for it sets the sinner on the path to destruction. The sinner is to be told the truth to repent from his evil ways and seek forgiveness from a God who is gracious and will show mercy to the repentant sinner.

To give proper attention to this, we need to discuss some key areas beginning with what it is not: (John 1:10-13)
- It is not an Intellectual agreement to truth (James 2:19)
- Not in a human decision derived from facts
- Not praying a sinner's prayer or signing a decision card
- Not self-preservation as fire insurance from hell
- Not one-sided (believe it and claim it)

What it is: (2 Cor. 5:17)
- It is a Person (new REVELATION)
  - o The revelation of the truth of the deity of Jesus Christ by the Spirit (Matt. 16:15-17, Col. 1:27, Eph. 2:1)
- It is a transaction (new HEART)
  - o The Holy Spirit is the only agent given to draw sinful man (John 6:44). He uses the word, but it is as He uses the word where the word is made effectual.

Being born of water and the Spirit (John 1:12-13, 3:5, Titus 3:5)

o This transaction is not one-sided; Jesus is always in the beginning, center, and finishing the work (Luke 7:48-50, to the Jews - Acts 2:37-42, to the Gentiles - Acts 10:43-44). There is a grave danger to consider the work of Christ on the cross as an event of the past that I believe with no implication of waiting for the active response needed by God when uttering, "God be merciful to me a sinner." Those who said, "Lord, Lord," and went on with their wonderful works found out that He never knew them. This "knowing" is a two-sided exchange of relationship, being born into the family of God (Matt. 7:22-23). It is repent, flee to Christ for mercy, trust in Him and ask the Spirit to renew you; instead of making a decision based on facts and claiming you are saved. It is the difference between being born of God vs. being born of the will of the flesh.

o No one is a Christian by birth; they become one by the work of the Spirit and are given a new heart (Eze. 36:26)

- It is an inflow (new LIFE)

o The inflow of Faith: Faith is the organ that is not found in the cause and effect of the fallen realm by the natural man; it is an outcome that is based upon a supernatural dependence upon a God who has been reckoned with by Divine illumination. Thus, when Jesus rose from the dead, He didn't try to prove to the Pharisees that He was alive; instead, the Spirit bore witness where those who were convicted turned to Him by faith, not having seen Him, and it is precisely the same with us. The Scripture says faith "cometh" by hearing (Rom. 10:17) since man lacks this faith in himself. Furthermore, we see that this "hearing by the word of God" is the essential Word, the Lord Jesus Christ, who was in the beginning (John 1:1). Paul has been speaking of Christ in the previous verse (Rom. 10:16) from that prophetic chapter of Jesus Christ, Isaiah 53:1 and following "Who hath believed our report? and to whom is the arm of the Lord revealed?" We see Peter's grand declaration after that lame man was healed to those wondering, "And his name through faith in his name hath made this man strong, whom ye see and know: yea, **the faith which is by him** hath given him this perfect soundness in the presence of you all." - Acts 3:16. "And be found in him, not having mine own righteousness, which is of the law, but that which is through the faith of Christ [who is the author and finisher of our faith – Heb. 12:2], the righteousness which is of God by faith" – Phili. 3:9 and repeated in Romans 3:22. Paul writes to the church in Galatia, "Knowing that a man is not justified by the works of the law, but **by the faith of Jesus Christ, even we have believed in Jesus Christ, that we might be justified by the faith of Christ**, and not by the works of the law: for by the works of the law shall no flesh be justified." – Gal. 2:16. "But the scripture hath concluded all under sin, that **the promise by faith of Jesus Christ might be given to them that believe**." – Gal. 3:22, and further clarified in verses 23-25 *(emphasis mine)*. Thus, we see more clearly how faith is a gift from God. And in Hebrews 4:12, we see the same essential Word, where he continues on to speak of the Person in verses 13-16. Thus, Jesus said, "My sheep hear my voice, and I know them, and they follow me" - John 10:27. The Father draws the sinner by the Spirit, the Spirit illuminating the written word to point to the essential Word, and the essential Word by the Spirit imparting faith to believe and brings in the lost sheep who has been redeemed by His blood, where heaven rejoices over one sinner that repenteth. And salvation is a work involving all three Persons of the Triune God. It is interesting to note that faith is mentioned both as a gift of the Spirit and a fruit of the Spirit (1 Cor. 12:9, Gal. 5:22). Abraham was called when God spoke to him (Gen. 12:1-4), and faith was imparted to him, and he believed (Rom. 4:3-5). And from that belief, his faith (that proved itself by the action he took in leaving the Ur of the Chaldees) was counted for righteousness because it was of the right kind. The gospel is foolishness to the natural man (1 Cor. 1:18), for he has been blinded by the god of this world (2 Cor. 4:4); he needs Divine intervention (Heb. 12:2)

- o The inflow of Hope (John 6:29, Rom. 5:5)
- o The inflow of Love (Rom. 5:5, 1 John 4:19)
- It is an outflow (new DESIRES)
  - o We see this in the life of the apostle Paul, where what he once hated but now, he loves; once a rebel but now a slave of Jesus Christ; was filled with pride, but now he is willing to suffer all for the sake of Christ in humility. In God-centered regeneration, God declares man's lostness, and man's pride is broken, and he comes through God's way, through the cross, in submission to the Lord Jesus Christ.
  - o On John Newton's tombstone, it states, "John Newton, once an infidel and libertine, a servant of slaves in Africa, was, by the rich mercy of our Lord and Savior Jesus Christ, preserved, restored, pardoned, and appointed to preach the faith he had long labored to destroy!" He stated it well when he wrote, "Amazing Grace, How sweet the sound, That saved a wretch like me. I once was lost, but now I am found, Was blind, but now I see. 'Twas grace

that taught my heart to fear, And grace my fears relieved"

- o True regeneration will produce a radical change of degrees to those professing that they have believed (Acts 19:17-20)
- It can be proved (new LIFESTYLE)
    - o He has a new desire for holiness because of the seed of God implanted in him (reflecting the character of the new Spirit); he has a new hatred toward sin. "O wretched man that I am! who shall deliver me from the body of this death?" – Rom. 7:24 (Matt. 22:37-40, 1 Cor. 6:9-10, 1 John 1:5-7, 1 John 4:19, 2 John 1:9, Heb. 12:14, Gal. 5:24). He has that inward primary witness of the Spirit (Job 32:8, Rom. 8:15-16, 1 Cor. 2:11, 2 Cor. 5:5, Gal. 4:5-6, 1 John 5:6) and the secondary witness of the word (1 John 5:13)
    - o He does not see salvation as just a past event but realizes that it is a lifelong process of change in sanctification, taking up his cross daily and following Christ. "For therein is the righteousness of God revealed from faith to faith: as it is written, The just shall live by faith." – Rom. 1:17. A life of repentance, growing from faith to faith. A true believer realizes the struggle of sin in continuously trying to bring him under bondage and resists sin at all costs. At times of faltering, he rises again. (Prov. 24:16, 1 John 1:6-10, 2:15, Jude 1:23)
    - o He experiences new victories (Eze. 36:26-27, Rom. 6:14, 1 John 2:15, from habitual sin: 1 John 3:1-9, he is bothered by sin and its pull upon his longing for holiness). Is corrected: When a child of God strays away from God, God as a loving Father brings him back by His goodness that leads to repentance (Rom. 2:4), putting thorns in his path (Prov. 13:15, Hos. 2:6), and correction that brings him to himself (Luke 15:17, Rom. 2:4, Heb. 12:5-8)

o He has a new inward willingness to obey Christ by the Spirit through the word (Rom. 6:17-18, 2 Tim. 3:16-17, 1 John 5:3). He does not need to say that he is a Christian. Instead, he shows by his life that he is a follower of Christ. "But wilt thou know, O vain man, that faith without works is dead?" – James 2:20

o Produces fruit unto good works: A true believer produces good works because of salvation and not for salvation (Matt. 7:18-19, Rom. 8:14, Gal. 5:19-23, 1 John 2:3-4). One of the fruits is his love for the brethren: A Christian has a genuine love for those of the faith, knowing the common bond in Christ and witnessed by the Spirit's assurance (John 13:35, 1 John 2:9-11, 3:14). Jesus plainly said, "Wherefore by their fruits ye shall know them." – Matt. 7:20. Someone may say that the passage is talking about false prophets, yes, but the principle is the same. What you possess is what you will produce (Luke 6:43-45, Titus 1:16). John the Baptist deals with this in Luke 3:9, and James speaks of this principle when he writes to believers in James 3:11-12

o It is a steadfast faith: He draws his strength from an ongoing walk with God. He clings to the old-rugged cross through times of darkness and when the world assaults him to sift him like wheat. He can identify with George Bennard from the hymn, **On a hill far away stood an old rugged cross**, the words "So I'll cherish the old rugged cross, till my trophies at last I lay down; I will cling to the old rugged cross, and exchange it some day for a crown." (Luke 22:31-32, 1 Thess. 4:1-4, 2 Tim. 4:6-8)

The promise is that "For whosoever shall call upon the name of the Lord shall be saved." – Rom. 10:13. The encouragement to the person who has seen their need is to keep calling until God saves them and bears witness in their heart that they are the children of

God. And to the claim that God would not ask us to do something such as "whosoever shall call upon the name of the Lord shall be saved" unless we had saving faith within ourselves is not a valid argument. That call is true, but the whole freeness of salvation is preceded by the truth that man must be awakened to his condition because he is dead and is unable to take a step to righteousness. He lost his will to choose right in the garden and being darkened he became dead in sin unable to choose righteousness, instead rejects and rebels against it. We see the same when Jesus dealt with the woman at Samaria. While John 4:10,14 is a fact, the woman's response in verses 11 and 15 speaks of her natural response, like Nicodemus in John 3. Thus, Paul states that his commission from Christ was, "To open their eyes, and to turn them from darkness to light, and from the power of Satan unto God, that they may receive forgiveness of sins, and inheritance among them which are sanctified by faith that is in me." - Acts 26:18. And this opening by revelation in Divine intervention is by the Spirit alone in His exclusive office of conviction of sin, repentance, faith, believe, regeneration, and assurance. "Strive to enter in at the strait gate: for many, I say unto you, will seek to enter in, and shall not be able." - Luke 13:24. He uses means such as preaching, praying, spiritual warfare, and such to accomplish His work. He that hath an ear let him take heed how he hears, with reverence and godly fear or with arrogance and indifference. But we are to try the spirits (1 John 4:1), to make sure we don't pluck unripe fruits. And since anyone can get saved and the need is there to open their blinded eyes through Divine illumination, prayer being the key and the power of the gospel being the means, the reliance is upon God to do that work instead of relying on man to decide; where we can then preach with power calling men to repent and believe the gospel. Hence, the imperative and profound importance of the Great Commission (Mark 16:15, Rom. 10:13-15).

Sidenote: What is the relationship between faith, believe, and repentance? We see in the ministry of Christ, "When Jesus heard it, he marvelled, and said to them that followed, Verily I say unto you,

I have not found so great faith, no, not in Israel... And Jesus said unto the centurion, Go thy way; and as thou hast believed, so be it done unto thee. And his servant was healed in the selfsame hour." - Matt. 8:10, 13, "Then Jesus answered and said unto her, O woman, great is thy faith: be it unto thee even as thou wilt. And her daughter was made whole from that very hour." - Matt. 15:28, "Then touched he their eyes, saying, According to your faith be it unto you." - Matt. 9:29, or in the case of the father with the possessed child, "Lord, I believe; help thou mine unbelief." - Mark 9:24. We see it in the ministry of the apostle Paul, "The same heard Paul speak: who stedfastly beholding him, and perceiving that he had faith to be healed, Said with a loud voice, Stand upright on thy feet. And he leaped and walked." - Acts 14:9-10. On the contrary we also see that, "many believed in his name, when they saw the miracles which he did. But Jesus did not commit himself unto them, because he knew all men" - John 2:23-24, "Nevertheless among the chief rulers also many believed on him; but because of the Pharisees they did not confess him, lest they should be put out of the synagogue: For they loved the praise of men more than the praise of God." - John 12:42-43, and the familiar passage in John 8 where many believed but ended up trying to stone Christ in the end. We also see in James 2:19 that, "Thou believest that there is one God; thou doest well: the devils also believe, and tremble." In the ministry of the apostle Paul and Peter, "King Agrippa, believest thou the prophets? I know that thou believest." - Acts 26:27, "Then Simon himself believed also" - Acts 8:13. In all this there is a pattern that is seen. There is such thing as a belief of devils, which Judas Iscariot had and there is a belief which produces saving faith unto eternal life which the Samaritan woman had. From these examples and others, we infer that true faith always has an element of believe (Heb. 11:6,13) which has been imparted by the truth of God (John 17:17) to an open heart that has received it (John 1:12-13), one that has been plowed and made ready by the Spirit of God (Luke 8:15). True faith always produces obedience out of love, the will being affected by it. It also gives an assurance that He is mine and I belong to Him (Song. 6:3). On the contrary one can believe but not have that true saving faith, but it will be the belief of devils regarding the truth about God and its implications, but which has not been received to act based on that revelation. Thus, repentance speaks of the nature of the soil, whether they see their sin as God sees it, are they are willing to take sides with God against their sin, which clears the way having believed and now looks to Christ in the eye of faith.

To the person who has been regenerated, the call is **obedience**. We see this in the witness of Philip when the Ethiopian eunuch asked to be baptized in obedience to Christ (Acts 8:26-39). We realize that terms such as believe, repent, and obedience are not about using the proper phraseology but rather the realization of the full weight of its implication. A good time to count your converts *(if there is such a thing)* is after six months to one year when they show credible evidence of regeneration. You cannot tell a person that he is whole when he had not realized that he was lacking, that he is clean when he didn't think himself to be unclean, be declared innocent when he did not even see himself as being guilty, or that he is healed when he did not know that he needed a physician. And only the Spirit can bring him to that place of godly sorrow which worketh repentance to salvation. There is a rebuke that God speaks of regarding the false prophets and priests, "They have healed also the hurt of the daughter of my people slightly, saying, Peace, peace; when there is no peace." – Jer. 6:14. We are so quick to pronounce peace when they have not even experienced their guilt. In. Luke 7:47 Jesus spoke of the woman as, "Wherefore I say unto thee, Her sins, which are many, are forgiven; for she loved much: but to whom little is forgiven, the same loveth little." Why don't we let them wallow in their misery until they come to themselves instead of offering a superficial covering? Have they not offended a good God? have they not crucified the Saviour? have they not blasphemed His name? Let the Spirit bring light and peace instead of us trying to produce it.

Plucking unripe fruits is one of the main reasons we have so many professions of faith but no fruits of their faith in our converts.

133

Would it be a surprise if half the congregation of the average Bible-believing church does not show up in heaven? They have no desire for a life of holiness or for reaching others; they warm the pews on Sunday mornings, have no desire to grow in Christ, never show up to the prayer meetings, nor show any love of Scriptures; nor would it be a surprise if many who preached in the pulpits of America or went as missionaries don't show up in heaven either. That is not being unkind but the reality of what the Scriptures teach of the life of God in the soul of man and the reality of what is seen. Instead of singing the song "When we all get to heaven," we should sing it as "If we all get to heaven." Not because God is unable to keep those He saves, and our eternal security rests on Him, but because we have deluded many into thinking they are saved when the supernatural inflow of life has never happened. John states in 1 John 2:19, "They went out from us, but they were not of us." These were thought to have believed but were not. We like to see quick results, so we try to sow, water, and reap a harvest in one sermon, and we end up plucking unripe fruits. We pronounce peace to the many who will go thinking they are saved, convinced in their delusion, unable to be reproved otherwise. They are still lost in their sin.

The Puritans called their preaching deep ploughing. Only the ground that has been broken up can receive that good seed of the word. John Wesley stated, "Before I can preach love, mercy, and grace, I must preach sin, Law, and judgment. Preach 90% Law and 10% grace." But having said that, we realize that **the Holy Spirit is sovereign in the call He uses to reach hearts of stone** (John 3:8). Everyone we read of in the Scriptures had a different conversion experience. Our responsibility is to be truthful to preach the gospel in its entirety and leave the way the Spirit works to Him (1 Cor. 3:6-7). Jesus began His ministry by saying, "repent and believe," the Pharisees and Sadducees who came to John the Baptist heard John thunder, "bring forth therefore fruits meet for repentance," to the Philippian jailer who came trembling, it was "believe." And even others, as Jesus said, "Strive to enter in at the strait gate: for many, I say unto you, will seek to enter in, and shall not be able." – Luke 13:24. That is the Spirit's work, but we cannot use that as an excuse to share a portion of the gospel as the entirety of the gospel. If we do so, we will not be truthful to the Person of the gospel in what He has given us in His word. Who is the greater danger? The person who preaches half-truths or the person who denies them altogether. I believe it is the person who preaches half-truths to multitudes who believe him and follows his teachings into hell. Hear Count Zinzendorf as he prays for a few girls ranging in age from ten to thirteen whose spiritual education had become his care. "He observed that though their demeanor was blameless, and their intellectual grasp of the truth was satisfactory, yet no evidence of a heart knowledge of God appeared among them. This weighed on his soul and led him to earnest intercession for them. Cultured, wealthy young noble man that he was, he was not above taking thought for the spiritual welfare of a few girls. More intense grew his concern, culminating at last in a season of such truly energized prayer as produced a most extraordinary effect."

In all this, we see a progression to "receive." Men loved darkness - John 3:19, and the natural man receiveth not the things of God for they are foolishness unto him - 1 Cor. 2:14, that the revelation must come from above – Matt. 16:17, where salvation is a gift that God will impart - John 3:27, 1 Cor. 4:7. There is a quickening – Eph. 2:1. "For the wages of sin is death; but the gift of God is eternal life through Jesus Christ our Lord." – Rom. 6:23. It is a gift that is given when you ask, being awakened to your condition *(the spontaneous response of an awakened heart)*. When the gift has been given and thus received, "as many as received him, to them gave he power to become the sons of God, even to them that believe on his name: Which were born, not of blood, nor of the will of the flesh, nor of the will of man, but of God." In its summary of as many as received Him, as in the nature of this work in those who are born of God - John 1:12-13, realizing that it is by grace through faith – Eph. 2:8-9. A gospel that caters to the carnal man in making it acceptable to his flesh cannot be subject to the law of God and deal with the true spiritual need of the man, for Christ did not come to save us from hell or even to take us to heaven, which are fringe benefits, but to save us from ourselves (Matt. 1:21). We are giving a gospel that is attractive to the sinner and have removed the offense of the cross. Sure, he wants to go to heaven, but he has no sorrow for that which has offended God. Thus, making the focus on heaven in the presentation of the gospel is foundationally misrepresenting God, for the sinner will see God as a hindrance to going to heaven because of his sin, and having the desire to avoid hell would allow himself to pray to Jesus to be able to get there; while in his innermost being have no desire to submit to the authority of Christ, or needing God in any aspect of his life; and he will continue in his sin for which Christ died for, to be damned forever.

We cannot close this topic of regeneration without realizing what we have been made for when God gave us a new heart and put His Spirit inside us when He regenerated us. We were in bondage to sin, slaves of sin before being born again, but now we have been freed, and our will has been freed, as it was in the garden before the fall, to love God willingly. But what does that mean? We are spiritual beings, and there are things that we were made for which were corrupted due to sin and must be reckoned with to live the full spectrum of the Christian life. Here are a few of them:

- We were made for worship. We see the lost man worshiping whatever he can, except God (stones, sun, animals, intellect, science, philosophies, sex, etc.), since that is the natural response of the fallen man. So, when the hindrances are taken away in the new man, and the truth of God is meditated upon, the Spirit renews our spirit, and worship is the spontaneous response of that inner man.
- We were made for love. We see the lost man confuse love with lust and stagger, blinded by the stimulus of his body. So, when the new man desires Christ above all things, his love for God is the natural outflow of the Spirit, bringing him in tune with His Creator.

- We were made for desires. We see the lost man desiring material things, friendships, and such. So, when the new man realizes that the things that hinder his desires toward God are the beggarly elements of this world, he willingly stops desiring them because he realizes he is made for something greater. To desire God Himself and what a glorious life it is to desire our Beloved, and to know He is mine.

- We were made for a union. We see the lost man desires union in marriage and tries fulfillment in that relationship. So, when the new man realizes his sacred union with Christ, he willingly becomes His slave and divorces from everything this world has to offer and is espoused to Christ.

- We were made for longing. We see the lost man longing after things he cannot attain and trying to gain them by sinful methods. So, when the new man comes at times in his life when the face of his Beloved is hidden, he longs after Christ being sick of love, to find Him and sets his sail for that day when the dark clouds will be dispersed, and Christ will be revealed once again to his yearning heart.

- We were made for beholding beauty. We see the lost man being attracted to beauty in art, sceneries, someone he loves, and such. So, the new man fixes his eyes upon Christ and, through His word and by His Spirit, beholds the loveliness of Christ where he is taken in an ecstasy of joy in enraptured gaze upon Him.

- We were made to reflect the glory of God. We see the lost man giving glory to himself, to his achievements, and desiring to fulfill that wish to be a god unto himself. So, the new man, once freed to abide in Christ, loses interest in the glory of man and responds willingly in heart worship to give and live to the glory of God alone.

- We were made to be at peace with our Maker. We see the lost man trying everything he can to bring peace to his soul with religion, materialism, denying the existence of God, drugs, pleasure, and so forth. So, the new man, having now come to the place of his position in Christ, is already at peace with his Maker and is freed to enjoy that peace while maturing and experiencing the fruits of the Spirit.

- We were created for holiness. We see the lost man who loves his sin and is bound by the sway of sin, living unholy lives. He takes pleasure in them, for he is naturally dispositioned to sin. So, the new man, having been set free from the chains of sin that have brought condemnation and made a new creature, is now freed to desire after the nature of God in the indwelling Spirit residing in him.

- We were made for service. We see the lost man having noble thoughts when doing service for others. In doing works of charity, he goes about trying to establish his own righteousness. So, the new man, now seeing this world in light of what God made him to be, goes about in selfless love to spend and be spent for the betterment of another in their misery of sin and woe to point them to the Savior, and then to help their physical needs as the situation affords. He cannot stay silent, for he realizes his calling to be a servant of all as his Master was when He washed His disciples' feet and told them to do likewise. He employs the gifts of the Spirit that he is given for the edification of the body of Christ.

- We were made to bring God pleasure. We see the lost man desiring pleasure for himself and portraying others as objects of pleasure for his selfish wants. So once the new man is brought to seeing the earthly pleasures as temporal and for a season, he is freed to turn his heart and his innermost being to worship God and enjoy fellowship with God and bring Him pleasure.

- We were made for communion. We see the lost man trying to get at peace with his inner self, following his heart, trying to find a connection with his dog, communicating with the dead, and such. So, the new man, now cleansed of guilt, under no condemnation, and rightly related to God, sees the goodness of God and enjoys intimate communion with his

Maker. From such heights of regeneration, the new man abhors his sin that breaks his communion with God, hating even the garment spotted by the flesh. And if he falters, he rises again in repentance and tears, seeking God to create in him a clean heart and to renew a right spirit within him.

Though what God created us for is not sinful when applied properly, such as marriage, enjoying God's creation, and such, the ultimate focus that must be upon Christ is the context of what is being discussed here. Man is created as a multi-faceted individual, unique and precious in God's sight. Only God values man accurately, that he is made in the image of God, that he is not an animal or just an evolved creature with no purpose, and that his soul is priceless. Only the Christian gospel values the true worth of man, for it brings the sinful man who is under condemnation to a right relationship with His Creator. **The greatest help** a preacher can give to the regenerated man is to bring him to the place where he realizes his position in Christ, what he was created for, and to help put away the hindrances from him by the word of God and applied by the Spirit of God, so he can be freed to be one with his Creator. He can shine as jewels in God's crown when he is liberated to live in the position Christ created him for. And so, we see how we love His appearing where in physical death we lay down this body of flesh and are freed from the presence of sin; our soul finds her rest in God. My greatest joy is to be with Christ, where even the prospect of heaven by itself does not matter anymore.

We see Paul writing to the church at Corinth and, in his first epistle, under the inspiration of God, brings many grievous sins into account, knowing that the Spirit who indwells them will bear witness and bring about conviction and change. He knew that if that did not happen, then the question was to examine yourselves, whether ye be in the faith; prove your own selves (2 Cor. 13:5) unless they had believed in vain (1 Cor. 15:2). Thus, he goes on to speak of the hindrances and to forsake them, which bears fruit when he speaks of God's work in their hearts in his second epistle.

To bring this crucial topic of regeneration to a close, we must ask ourselves, **what is the gospel?** One can quote 1 Corinthians 15:3-4 or state it as "good news" and such. Yes, while those may be considered elements of the gospel, we are still confronted with the question, "What is the gospel?" I like to borrow what Henry Scougal put as the title of his book, "The life of God in the soul of man," as displayed in full force in Romans 1:16-17 (For I am not ashamed of the gospel of Christ: for it is the power of God unto salvation to every one that believeth; to the Jew first, and also to the Greek. For therein is the righteousness of God revealed from faith to faith: as it is written, The just shall live by faith). If we truly grasped that, what would our response be, of what we expect that to look like in those who profess faith in the Lord Jesus Christ? If regeneration is by the power of God, to bring us to repentance and faith, in essence, God getting hold of us instead of us getting hold of God, Divine conquest of fallen man, the supernatural birthing into the natural man which cannot be explained, that which we call as being born again. It is through that power of changing us from the inside out that the righteousness of God Himself is revealed in us and lived through us to this world; if such is the grandeur of God's work, then how would that change us to view so great salvation? The apostle Paul writes, "Ye are our epistle written in our hearts, known and read of all men" - 2 Cor. 3:2. The Thessalonians "were ensamples to all that believe in Macedonia and Achaia." - 1 Thess. 1:7. Would we say that of our converts, if a lost man doesn't believe in God, they can observe this convert's life and know the existence of God and what it means to live a holy life? My heart is crushed to see how degraded our view of so great salvation has been brought to, which is nothing more than fulfilling the carnal desire of man for heaven, desiring the benefits of Christ but not submitting to the commands of Christ, to leave the regenerated man impoverished and not knowing the riches that Christ has for them in this life, and being a pauper where they are strangers to the abundant life. Any degraded representation of the gospel cannot be called the gospel, but it is, in truth, another gospel.

The Witness of the Spirit

There is a way to get quick results by using human methods and things that are within our control. If someone can be told to read a verse and give assurance based on that, it is easily accomplished rather than having to desire the witness of the One who does the regenerating. The same Spirit who birthed Christ in the womb of Mary is the same Spirit who births us into the family of God through Christ. He creates new life where there was no life. Jesus describing the uniqueness of His work, spoke, "The wind bloweth where it listeth, and thou hearest the sound thereof, but canst not tell whence it cometh, and whither it goeth: so is every one that is born of the Spirit" – John 3:8. If the Spirit has to illuminate the word to blinded hearts and bring them to a realization of the truth, would it not be treason to take His exclusive office of bearing witness to our spirit that we are the children of God and attributing it to something we can produce? A sizeable Christian youth camp that has been in the ministry for decades and has seen thousands of young people make professions over the years had this in their worker's guide for those who come forward to trust Christ. "Remember that the source of assurance is the Bible," with no mention of the Spirit and His work in the matter. Not only is this grossly unbiblical, but it is also something we were never given the authority to do. It is one thing to say, "here is what God says if you believe," when seeking the Lord, it is an entirely different thing to take that person and say, "now you have believed, so you are saved." Our place can be to point them to the Scriptures to help them find truths that the Spirit can give assurance to, but not the other way around. **Pronouncing one's assurance by the word of God without the express witness of the Spirit of God is spiritual suicide**. And there will be many church members, missionaries, pastors, evangelists, and workers who gave intellectual assent to the truth of the Scriptures who will hear on that great and terrible day, "I never knew you: depart from me, ye that work iniquity."

Not one of the disciple's presumed God was working until they saw the evidence of the Spirit before they gave any promise from the Scriptures. Peter at Pentecost said, "Repent" to the unaided response from the people who cried, "Men and brethren, what shall we do?" – Acts 2:37. Saul said, "Believe" to the jailer who was already under conviction and said, "Sirs, what must I do to be saved?" – Acts 16:30. And to Phillip, the Holy Ghost said, "Go near, and join thyself to this chariot." – Acts 8:29. Just asking why someone came forward does not prove anything, they could have come forward because the preacher told them to, because their friends came, or to go to heaven with no desire to submit to Christ, they may not have any sorrow for their sin that they have offended a good God and deserve hell.

It is easy to say, "Do you believe? Then the Bible says if you believe, you are saved," and call him a Christian. But we cannot read the hearts of men; we don't have the capacity to know the condition or intent of their hearts. They may be still "in the gall of bitterness, and in the bond of iniquity" (Acts 8:23). I have seen people profess Christ and get baptized, later to find out it was for marrying someone or professing Christ and never darkening the doors of a church. My wife testified that before she was genuinely born again, she professed Christ and got baptized to study in a Christian school since they required it. It is easy to produce assurance from the word, and we can do it; the witness of the Spirit only God can produce. Are you able to look back and see that it was the life of God in you and proven by the Scriptures for the continual ongoing change in your life, or was it the instructions from the Scriptures that you applied that changed your life without any inward constraining force?

We have seen earlier how the Spirit has manifested His work of regeneration in the earlier topic on the heart, and are we able to go to an audience of a thousand and think that they all need the same 4-step method? Some may need repentance, some may need to believe, some may need to be told to submit to the Lordship of

Christ and humble themselves, and some may need to be told to bring forth fruits meet for repentance to see the genuine work of God before they can be told to believe. And like Lydia, some may be where "whose heart the Lord opened" (Acts 16:14). No one had to prove to me that I was converted, my life was transformed in an instant, and there was nothing to prove or get assurance of from the Bible; it was right there for all to see. Looking back, I can see how it is spoken of in the Scriptures and bore witness to what happened in my life, but that was not my starting point to get assurance from the Bible before I knew God had saved me.

Think about those early believers receiving John's letter in what we have as 1 John. Here were believers who were already experiencing the victory of freedom from sin, having the witness of the Spirit, wondering at times on the matter of sin in the life of a believer and such, now receiving this letter from John by the Spirit, and as they read can testify of its reality in their own lives. In 1 John 5:9, John writes the witness of the Father about the Son, "If we receive the witness of men, the witness of God is greater: for this is the witness of God which he hath testified of his Son." This is a legal term similar to someone testifying in a court of law to make a solemn declaration under oath for the purpose of establishing a fact. And goes on in verses 10 and 11 to speak of this record that God states of His son, "He that believeth on the Son of God hath the witness in himself: he that believeth not God hath made him a liar; because he believeth not the record that God gave of his Son. And this is the record, that God hath given to us eternal life, and this life is in his Son." The "record" given here is not speaking about the written text of the Scriptures that someone can blindly claim without the witness of the Spirit spoken of earlier in v6; instead, it is the record (declaration) of the binding nature of what God declares to those who have been born of God. We see this clarified in 1 John 5:13, where he states, "These things have I written unto you that believe on the name of the Son of God; that ye may know that ye have eternal life, and that ye may believe on the name of the Son of God." What things? All the prior chapters and verses. They were able to identify its truths in their lives and are greatly comforted to persevere. We put the cart before the horse to state to the lost, "these things," to ask them to "make a decision," where they are not even evident in their lives even after they have made a profession of faith.

How about those who were converted before they had the written word of God? How about Job or Noah or Abel or Enoch? How about a pagan nation like Nineveh who only heard, "Yet forty days, and Nineveh shall be overthrown" (Jonah 3:4) with no talk of remedy; but they believed God. How about those in the early church where the preaching of the cross was seen as a new doctrine? Or Paul in Athens preaching the gospel to the stoics and philosophers? He did not have to say, "now close your eyes, raise your hand, come to the altar, pray this prayer, and believe in the Bible for assurance." You can throw a person in jail like Richard Wurmbrand and have no access to the Bible during his 14 years in the communist prisons and be brainwashed days upon days, be broken physically and emotionally, and still come out stronger for Christ. How? It is the blessed Spirit who can sustain us in our worst conditions.

There is something beyond mental knowledge or convincing ourselves; the spirit of man in us tells us that we are who we are and not someone else. It is not a birth certificate that proves to us that we are human; we know it. We see some things that are beyond the intellectual, where Paul writes about the love of Christ in experiential witness, "And to know the love of Christ, which **passeth knowledge**, that ye might be filled with all the fulness of God." – Eph. 3:19 *(emphasis mine)*. We have quenched the office of the Spirit bearing witness in our hearts and have produced multitudes of people who don't know why they are saved, what they are saved from, or if they are saved other than a passage of Scripture, not having that inward witness which is the surest proof of Christ in you, the hope of glory (Col. 1:27). A good way to deal with someone coming forward for help would be to start with the basics. Are you saved? *Yes.* What are you saved from? *Not sure, but I am going to heaven because I prayed a prayer.* Does your life show it by your holy living of what God is doing in your heart? *No.* Then let's talk about salvation before any other help can be provided. To preach the outcome or the fruits of new life where there is no life is to preach death.

This was the same challenge that John Wesley had to deal with, where the majority of the people had a form but lacked that inward witness that he longed for in his own life before he was born again. He states, "The testimony of the Spirit is an inward impression on the soul whereby the Spirit of God directly witnesses to my spirit that I am a child of God; that Jesus Christ hath loved me and given himself for me; that all my sins are blotted out, and I, even I, am reconciled to God." And he goes on to conclude, "The manner how the divine testimony is manifested to the heart I do not take upon myself to explain. ... But the fact we know: namely, that the Spirit of God does give a believer such a testimony of his adoption that while it is present to the soul he can no more doubt the reality of his sonship than he can doubt the shining of the sun while he stands in the full blaze of his glory."

What saith the Scriptures? "But there is a spirit in man: and the inspiration of the Almighty giveth them understanding." – Job 32:8, "For ye have not received the spirit of bondage again to fear; but ye have received the Spirit of adoption, whereby we cry, Abba, Father. The Spirit itself beareth witness with our spirit, that we are the children of God:" – Rom. 8:15-16, "For what man knoweth the things of a man, save the spirit of man which is in him? even so the things of God knoweth no man, but the Spirit of God." – 1 Cor. 2:11, "To redeem them that were under the law, that we might receive the adoption of sons. And because ye are sons, God hath sent forth the Spirit of his Son into your hearts, crying, Abba, Father." – Gal. 4:5-6, "And he that keepeth his commandments dwelleth in him, and he in him. And hereby we know that he abideth in us, by the Spirit which he hath given us." – 1 John 3:24,

"Now he that hath wrought us for the selfsame thing is God, who also hath given unto us the earnest of the Spirit." - 2 Cor. 5:5. "This is he that came by water and blood, even Jesus Christ; not by water only, but by water and blood. And it is the Spirit that beareth witness, because the Spirit is truth." – 1 John 5:6, and then in v13, he goes on to comfort them (written to those who were already redeemed) that "These things have I written unto you that believe on the name of the Son of God; that ye may know that ye have eternal life, and that ye may believe on the name of the Son of God." It was a call to persevere more than a call of assurance. The witness of the word comes after the Spirit, where the Spirit bears witness (through various times) to their spirit that they are God's child and cry out, "Abba, Father."

The Grandeur of the Work of God

We see many beautiful and glorious passages that touch on God's work in bringing sinners to Himself, such as Eph. 2:8-9, Matt. 1:21, John 1:12-13, and Col. 1:27. We must realize that salvation is all of grace by the sovereignty of the Holy Spirit on how He calls. While we recognize the sovereignty of God in salvation, we also see man's responsibility in what he will do with Jesus Christ.

We must realize that the work of seeing sinners born of God must bring us to our knees to have that high view of God, and the absolute impossibility of man to be able to produce it, but the great possibility with God to intervene. To realize the need to be clean vessels God can take and use. For some to water, some to plant, but God alone to give the increase, that He alone might be glorified.

Though we realize that God uses various means to draw men and women to Himself, and the steps themselves may be combined in some instances as the Holy Spirit works, the table below hopes to shine some light on the depth and beauty of regeneration.

State	Indicators	Outcome
DEAD IN SIN	Man covers his sin with anything but God. Gen. 3:7, Deut. 32:35 - Does not seek God: Psa. 14:1-3 - Rejects light: 1 Cor. 2:14 - In total darkness: Matt. 6:23, John 3:19	God preserves him with prevenient grace. Gen. 20:6, Gal. 3:24. *(God delights in costly prayers that are offered unceasingly by believers for Divine intervention, sharing the gospel, and such)*
REVELATION	John 16:8-11, 1 Tim. 3:16, Matt. 1:23	Divine illumination. John 3:27, 6:44, Matt. 16:17. Person of Christ revealed, Eph. 5:14
CONVICT OF SIN	The holiness of God, The law of God. Rom. 7:7-8, 11, 13	Conscience awakened by the Spirit. John 8:9, 16:8-11

REPENTANCE	The sinfulness of sin. It produces a response of the heart which has been affected by the mind (godly sorrow) and makes them willing to action (an act of the will to turn from sin). Acts 11:18, 2 Tim. 2:25, Luke 13:3, 5	Turn from sin. Isa. 55:7, 2 Cor. 7:10, Acts 20:21, 26:20. - Toward God: Matt. 3:8 - Lordship of Christ (Authority, submission to Him, surrender to God's terms) Matt. 6:24, Acts 2:36, 16:31, John 13:13, Acts 9:6, Phili. 2:9-11
FAITH TO BELIEVE	Responsibility of man. Titus 1:1	John 6:29, Rom. 10:17. God be merciful to me, a sinner, Luke 18:13-14. Faith being the channel imparted by the Spirit
REGENERATION	Justification. New creation. 2 Cor. 5:17	Rom. 4:6-8, From death to life. Evident change: Eph. 2:1, Eze. 11:19. A new heart and a new Spirit: Eze. 36:25-27
ADOPTION	Sonship. Gal. 4:6, Abba, Father	- The primary witness of the Spirit: Job 32:8, Rom. 8:15-16, 1 Cor. 2:11, 2 Cor. 5:5, Gal. 4:5-6, 1 John 3:24, 5:6 - The secondary witness of the word: 1 John 5:13, 2 Tim. 3:14-17

SANCTIFICATION	Ongoing work of God in conforming us to the image of His Son. Rom. 8:35-39.	- Mind of Christ: Phili. 2:5-6 - Correction when needed: Heb. 12:8 - Spiritual maturity: Rom. 12:1-2 - Looking unto Jesus: Heb. 12:2

In expanding on the means of grace to bring about this work, we mentioned a couple of them in the matter of costly prayer and sharing the gospel. But we also have the matter of Spirit-anointed preaching, "For after that in the wisdom of God the world by wisdom knew not God, it pleased God by the foolishness of preaching to save them that believe" - 1 Cor. 1:21. We also see the times when God moved into a community with His manifest presence to bring sinners unto Himself. Duncan Campbell, during the Hebridean Revival, said, "Seventy-five percent (of the people) were gloriously saved before they came near a meeting." We must never limit God to how we perceive the work of God must happen; if we do so, we will bring this so great salvation into a formula or human-derived method which gets packaged and sold like cheap wares in a flea market.

So Great Salvation

What does it mean to be saved? We have cheapened the gospel to the point of such shallowness that it is nothing more than a cliché to respond to this question of enormous depth. In the Scriptures, we see salvation as this grand work of God performed upon the soul of man. And through the Scriptures, we see the four stages of man. Everyone born of Adam's race is born dead in sin (Eph. 2:1). They are all, as it were, in this river of existence that flows one way. They have the reasoning power to know what to do or not to do, to belong to a certain religion, or oppose certain causes, but they all are heading the same way. They are doctors, teachers, workers,

149

religious, speak the name of Christ, atheists, etc. Their heart is a stone and is dead, and it will continue to eternal death, which means that there is no internal force that opposes the external forces that everyone faces "For all that is in the world, the lust of the flesh, and the lust of the eyes, and the pride of life, is not of the Father, but is of the world." - 1 John 2:16. This is the state of the natural man, and he has no desire to change it since it fits well with the internal persuasion though he may do things to better himself. He follows or accepts the rules imposed by external teachers to profit himself and tries to save his life, maybe religion, philosophy, art, science, and so forth. He is even affected by it, but it is always based on what he has been raised with, along with the light of his conscience (if it is not seared as in 1 Timothy 4:2).

Then comes the Divine intervention, light from above revealing Truth, his sin condition brought to light, cries for mercy knowing he does not deserve it, a new life imparted, a new heart transacted, and now there is a heart of flesh (Eze. 36:26) with life given to this man, which will continue on to eternal life. He is saved from the penalty of sin (Col. 2:14), to be condemned no more (Rom. 6:7, 8:33-39). Life has been imparted, which means that instead of "I made a decision," it is "God saved me." Something external got a hold of him. This is the first stage of this new man, who is now a new creature "Therefore if any man be in Christ, he is a new creature: old things are passed away; behold, all things are become new." - 2 Cor. 5:17. He realizes that something pure and holy resides inside him, and what he does and does not do is not an independent decision anymore but rather impacts that Person within. He is still in the world but not of the world any longer (John 15:19). Regeneration, when we look back as when it happened, is **past tense**, as in, "Even when we were dead in sins, hath quickened us together with Christ" – Eph. 2:5.

As a Christian, he is immediately thrust into the process of sanctification (1 Thess. 4:4, 2 Thess. 2:13). And this is not optional. "And we know that all things work together for good to them that love God, to them who are the called according to his purpose. For whom he did foreknow, he also did predestinate to be conformed to the image of his Son, that he might be the firstborn among many brethren." – Rom. 8:28-29. We are to be conformed to the image of His Son, and what a glorious thought that this call goes all the way to glorification until the very end (v30). This is the next stage of "being saved" from the dominion and power of sin, where this new life of Christ is starting to consume Him more and more, the One who started this life is now doing what He promised, to present him faultless before the throne of His Father (Jude 1:24). To this man, though victory has been secured, sin is not the same when committed, though it gave pleasure for a season. Now he sees that there is something that makes sin less attractive and drives him progressively forward to find freedom from it. A person who was dead in sin may give to consensual sex and not be bothered by it, but now he abhors such a thought. Now he realizes that there is a contradiction that is raging inside of him. He starts being taught that he needs to yield to righteousness, make progress on holiness, put away things that will hinder him, put on the whole armor of God and fight, exercise in prayer, the renewed mind, the crucified life, the exchanged life, etc. As he is faithful, he now has that opposing force (the Holy Spirit) that continues to make His presence known, which not only opposes his old man's influence but also is in stark contradiction to that external river that he was flowing along quite peacefully before his regeneration experience. He realizes that he has to cooperate with God to ensure he can live a full and victorious Christian life and such "For I delight in the law of God after the inward man: But I see another law in my members, warring against the law of my mind, and bringing me into captivity to the law of sin which is in my members." – Rom. 7:22-23. He is comforted, given tokens of assurance by the Spirit to cry "Abba, Father," constantly pushes to yearn after a life of holiness in learning to be dead to sin, at times broken but never in despair; he falls but rises again and starts plunging deep into Christ to build his house upon that Rock. It is by grace we are saved and grace by which we live the Christian life. This process of sanctification of "being saved" is in the **present continuous tense**, as in, "work out your own salvation with fear and trembling." – Phili. 2:12.

A person who says that he is just saved from the penalty of sin but has no desire for the other steps is just lying to himself, for God never starts a work that He doesn't finish. He may try to excuse it by saying he is quenching the Spirit and such, but in reality, this man is lost. Though quenching the Spirit is a real state, it is never an acceptable and allowed state that God will leave the sinner to be in for long. God confronted David with His prophet, even though it was after nine months. The problem we have is that we want God and everything else the world has to offer, even good things that may not be sinful but that will never work, for there is nothing better than God, and you can either have Him or the world. While doing things necessary to live in this world should be in our peripheral view, God should be like the noonday sun and should always be in full view before us. Our lives must revolve around Him.

As he continues the journey, as he learns to possess his vessel, purify himself in desiring and having the mind of Christ (1 Cor. 2:16), learning whatsoever things are true to think on these things (Rom. 6:6-14, Phili. 4:8), he starts yearning for purity in working out his salvation in fear and trembling knowing that God is the grand Master, executor, and completer of this work (Phili. 2:12-13), he even hates the garments that are spotted by the flesh (Jude 1:23), longing for the day when he is freed from the presence of sin. The promises of His appearing become sweeter (2 Tim. 4:8). In his yearning, he realizes, "For which cause we faint not; but though our outward man perish, yet the inward man is renewed day by day. For our light affliction, which is but for a moment, worketh for us a far more exceeding and eternal weight of glory" - 2 Cor. 4:16-17. In finality, he crosses the river of death and is now freed from the presence of sin. Where he saw darkly through a clouded glass and was constantly beholding Christ through it, he now sees Him face to face and enters his final resting place with God Himself. This is the final stage of salvation from the presence of sin. "So when this corruptible shall have put on incorruption, and this mortal shall have put on immortality, then shall be brought to pass the saying that is written, Death is swallowed up in victory. O death, where is thy sting? O grave, where is thy victory?" - 1 Cor. 15:54-55. This expectation "to obtain salvation" from the presence of sin is in the **future tense**, as in, "For God hath not appointed us to wrath, but to obtain salvation by our Lord Jesus Christ" - 1 Thess. 5:9 and "But now being made free from sin, and become servants to God, ye have your fruit unto holiness, and the end everlasting life." – Rom. 6:22.

So, in essence, all of mankind is in one of these four positions. They are either dead in sin, which is the natural man; saved from the penalty of sin as in regeneration, which is the Christian's starting point with fear of no condemnation; being saved from the power and dominion of sin, to make it the reality of what his position in Christ is; and finally saved from the presence of sin, which is to lay down this mortal body in death and sleep in Christ.

Such sacred glory of salvation is cheapened into someone who lives carelessly, stating they were saved 30 years ago, and it has done nothing to his life since then. What a tragic and fearful place to be in. And so, Paul, writing to the Hebrews, states, "How shall we escape, if we neglect so great salvation" – Heb. 2:3. Americanized Christianity has not only cheapened salvation by its method but polluted its beauty by its application.

Fellowship of the Saint

I was reading a little booklet about this young lady in the Russian prison camp in the 1960s for her faith, speaking to a Christian friend who came to visit her. The author states, "Only those who have suffered for Christ's sake know the preciousness of the fellowship of the saints." My understanding of fellowship was about eating hotdogs and talking about anything and everything you could do, similar to a social club. You hear people talk about their pets, entertainment, politics, whine about their persecution of watching their favorite football team lose, and other inconsequential events. I am reminded of Christ's warning to the church at Laodicea, "So then because thou art lukewarm, and neither cold nor hot, I will spue thee out of my mouth." – Rev. 3:16. Americanized Christianity has tried to marry prosperity and worldly interests to "consider one another to provoke unto love and to good works." And then I read about the Macedonians "that in a great trial of affliction the abundance of their joy and their deep poverty abounded unto the riches of their liberality." - 2 Cor. 8:2. I read Paul's exhortation to "endure hardness" and Peter exhorting those early members with, "Beloved, think it not strange concerning the fiery trial which is to try you, as though some strange thing happened unto you: But rejoice, inasmuch as ye are partakers of Christ's sufferings; that, when his glory shall be revealed, ye may be glad also with exceeding joy." - 1 Peter 4:12-13. And Paul's desire to be identified with "the fellowship of his [Christ's] sufferings, being made conformable unto his death;" – Phili. 3:10 *(emphasis mine)*. Can we imagine the fellowship of the saints who met in the catacombs fearing for their lives and not having seen each other for days and being able to enquire one another of their faith in Christ and how God has ministered to them, and in that dark, damp, smelly place in the black of night join their hearts in worship toward God, not knowing if that may be the last time they may see each other alive on earth?

Americanized Christianity expects to get the same reward when they stand before God next to someone who has lived scarred for life because they were burned for their faith. Fellowship has a different meaning when we realize the exhortation in Hebrews 10:24, "And let us consider one another to provoke unto love and to good works:" and follows with "Not forsaking the assembling of ourselves together" - v25. Provoking someone in their spiritual walk means inciting or "pushing them" unto good works in working out their salvation with fear and trembling. Americanized Christianity has emphasized the "rights" of the "American" where no one, including their preacher, can tell them what to do; they are happy taking some suggestions if it suits their jaded appetites. And they stop coming to church because they were "offended" that no one shook their hand, and you have to attract them back with dinners and Easter bunnies. They sing "Soldiers of the cross, arise!" but scurry off to watch their favorite show or refuse to attend church because they are afraid of catching a virus. We are happy to give money so someone else can suffer. Paul's exhortation was to "Remember them that are in bonds, as bound with them; and them which suffer adversity, as being yourselves also in the body." – Heb. 13:3. We ought to pray that their faith fail not, that we gladly consider a life of sacrifice in light of their poverty, to consider their needs as our needs, help where needed as led by the Spirit of God, weep with them that weep, and so forth.

When Christ at the last supper said, "this do in remembrance of me" (Luke 22:19), it was to be taken as a solemn command where the depth of Christ's sacrifice must be pondered at length and given to weeks of contemplation by the messages preached before partaking of the Lord's supper, lest we forget the price that was paid, similar to a child who carelessly toys with a priceless jewel not knowing it's costly value. True Christian fellowship always produces or increases faith, for the life of Christ is manifested through the life of the believers in fellowship. The preaching of the word that the Spirit empowers will produce faith, for Jesus is the author and finisher of our faith. This is a self-evaluation that I had to do in realizing the decades of going to church and being active in the fellowship; did it increase my faith, or was my growth stunted, or did it seed unbelief in me instead?

Militant Christianity

C. T. Studd wrote a book called "The Chocolate Soldier" that rightfully describes our soft-spoken inoffensive Christianity. C. T. Studd states, "Christ's call is to save the lost, not the stiff-necked; He came not to call scoffers but sinners to repentance; not to build and furnish comfortable chapels, churches, and cathedrals at home in which to rock Christian "professor" to sleep using clever essays, stereotyped prayers, and artistic musical performances, but to capture men from the devil's clutches and the very jaws of hell. This can be accomplished only by a red-hot, unconventional, unfettered devotion, in the power of the Holy Spirit, to the Lord Jesus Christ." Furthermore, he stated, "Some wish to live within the sound of church or chapel bell; I want to run a rescue shop within a yard of hell." These were men of a different kind who were accustomed to a different type of Christianity and served another Christ who said, "He that is not with me is against me; and he that gathereth not with me scattereth abroad." – Matt. 12:30.

Americanized Christianity is soft-spoken, sentimental, non-judgmental, spineless religion. You don't hear leather-lunged John the Baptist preach a soft message but thundered, repent and bring forth therefore fruits meet for repentance, and "now also the axe is laid unto the root of the trees: therefore every tree which bringeth not forth good fruit is hewn down, and cast into the fire." – Matt. 3:10. You don't hear Elijah on mount Carmel burning with holy anger saying, "I am sorry, I apologize, I have to do this thing." He mocked them (1 Kings 18:27); for true love "Rejoiceth not in iniquity, but rejoiceth in the truth" – 1 Cor. 13:6. And after the event, he took the prophets of Baal, all four hundred and fifty of them, and put them to death. Did Peter say to Ananias and Sapphira, "well now, you have lied to the Holy Ghost, but no one is perfect; God loves us anyway in spite of what we do, so just claim 1 John 1:9" or other catchy and uplifting one-liners? No, he was seeing what God saw in their lives of hypocrisy and their great deception, and like Joshua with Achan, he pronounced the judgment of God upon their lives. Jesus, when speaking to the scribes and Pharisees, did not use flowery statements of sentimental nonsense; instead, He cried out "woe" with statements such as "hypocrites," "ye blind guides," "Ye fools and blind," "whited sepulchres, which indeed appear beautiful outward, but are within full of dead men's bones, and of all uncleanness." When He began

His ministry, He made a scourge of small cords and drove the money changers out, tipped over the changers' money, overthrew the tables, and cleansed the temple. What does Paul instruct a young Timothy who was called to be a Pastor? Does he give sentimental titbits on how to be popular with the world and get along? How to write sermonettes that will tickle the ears of the people? He was told in 2 Timothy 2:3 to "endure hardness, as a good soldier of Jesus Christ." There is grave danger when the world speaks well of us (Luke 6:26), but it takes hand-to-hand combat in the trenches against the enemy to receive scars. Leonard Ravenhill stated, "He [God] is not looking for medals; He is looking for scars." We read, again and again, terms such as fight the good fight of faith; we wrestle against principalities, against powers, against the rulers of the darkness of this world, against spiritual wickedness in high places; put on the whole armor of God; and having done all, to stand, and other passages.

We see gross sentimentalism during the time we celebrate Christmas. It seems to be a time for pitying baby Jesus while keeping Him in the crib. Do we also remember the eternal existence of Christ, who had no beginning? While He took on humanity as what we celebrate as the Advent, Jesus Christ always was and is the great I AM in human flesh (John 6:46, 8:58, 10:30, 14:9), the Second Person of the Trinity. It was Christ who created heaven and the earth (Col. 1:14-17). It was the pre-incarnate Christ that Moses saw in that burning bush and was afraid to look upon God (Exo. 3:2-6). It was Christ whom Isaiah saw in his vision of the Lord sitting upon a throne, high and lifted up, and His train filled the temple (John 12:41). Joshua saw and fell to the ground and worshipped Him (Josh. 5:13-15) along with Abraham (Gen. 18:1-3), and Daniel (Dan. 10:5-10), and it was He who walked in the midst of the fire during the reign of Nebuchadnezzar (Dan. 3:25). This great and terrible God that John fell at His feet as dead (Rev. 1:17). It is Christ who dwells in everlasting past to present to everlasting future, "Who only hath immortality, dwelling in the light which no man can approach unto; whom no man hath seen, nor can see" (1 Tim. 6:14-

16). The world is happy to celebrate the child of Christmas, but one day they will submit to Him as Lord. Today, heaven does not celebrate His birth, for He came, died, and is already risen and seated upon the throne glorified, on Jehovah's right hand. While we ought to remember His reason for coming, we must do so considering His glory and the worship due unto Him.

It is easy to address sin from a third person's point of view or even in a general sense where it does not affect the listener. We hear phrases of generalization such as "we all have done something wrong" and "none of us are perfect," with no arrows pointing to the hearts of men or individuals by calling into account their sins by the Spirit through the word. But Jesus did not mince words. He was clear and pointed when He addressed those Jews standing in front of Him, "Ye are of your father the devil, and the lusts of your father ye will do." - John 8:44. Neither was Peter when he spoke with authority, "Jesus, whom ye have crucified" - Acts 2:36 and Stephen who addressed the council and said, "Ye stiffnecked and uncircumcised in heart and ears, ye do always resist the Holy Ghost: as your fathers did, so do ye. Which of the prophets have not your fathers persecuted? and they have slain them which shewed before of the coming of the Just One; of whom ye have been now the betrayers and murderers:" - Acts 7:51-52. In contrast, our preaching is tailored to offend no one. Truth is offensive to those who live in error, and **the true gospel is not seeker friendly for having dialogues; rather, it thunders the immutable requirements of God upon those in rebellion against His authority. In essence, the gospel is non-negotiable**. The book of Acts has no mention of the word love. They were confronting sin and the kingdom of darkness head-on to bring those perishing to God. Compassion can become an excuse for sloppy evangelism that neither has the blessing of God nor the power of God. What would happen to your church if God killed some Ananias and Sapphira in your church this Sunday? We must realize that love towards God and the glory of God comes first, after which comes the love for people.

We are in a bloody war. "Must I be carried to the skies on flowery beds of ease, While others fought to win the prize and sailed through bloody seas?" - Isaac Watts. I read some of the writings from the early days of the Salvation Army by the General. They used a different language; blood and fire, war cry, fire a volley, and so forth. It was not just words; in their early days, they set derelicts and neighborhoods on fire and faced the enemy head-on. They proved their mettle; someone said they went into ninety countries in seventy years. Their message was to preach repentance towards God, as well as faith in Jesus Christ, a life of obedience to God, relying on the power of the Spirit to transform lives. The devil is not too concerned with Christianity in America because it is powerless. There are a few trickle drops here and there, but for the most part, there is no call to war among the redeemed of the Lord. General William Booth gave a series of addresses in 1889 on "The requirements of Jesus Christ's service." He stated regarding the battle for the souls of men, "There is only one way, and that is by fighting. We cannot bow, or notice, or persuade the devil out of this his favorite citadel and stronghold. If polite requests, and eloquent persuasions, and logical arguments addressed to his majesty would have done it, he would have departed long ago. Nay, if indolent or even fervent and believing prayers to the Divine Spirit to drive him out would have effected this purpose, we should have had our Eden back again a long time ago. But, no, there is only one way-a way, alas! most unpalatable to indolent and selfish humanity; and that is to drive him out by actual persevering, self-sacrificing warfare. There is nothing for it but to fight, and to fight to the death. Who is willing for this?"

What is our motivation for serving Christ? It cannot be sentimental. A soldier does not join the military for sentimental reasons. He is there with a singular focus, to carry the banner of his country high, to fight the good fight, to be able to please his master, to kill or be killed. Do we see what Christ suffered and died for? Should we not be grieved as He was when He groaned at the tomb of Lazarus? He saw what sin had done to mankind and broke the power of death in bringing Lazarus back to life. He "having spoiled principalities and powers, he made a shew of them openly, triumphing over them in it." – Col. 2:15. Our motivation can be fear "Heb. 11:7," it could be for compassion "Jude 1:22," it could be for love "1 Cor. 13." In all these, there is an underlying desire that Christ be known in all His glory and is worthy of it. Can we see the desire of the Father to glorify His only begotten Son, whom He had to bruise? Jesus said, "And this is life eternal, that they might know thee the only true God, and Jesus Christ, whom thou hast sent." – John 17:3. But though we may be motivated for various reasons, we must realize that we are in warfare and the enemy is in this for keeps. Satan has come to steal, kill and destroy while our Captain has given the battle cry to resist, fight, endure hardness, pull down strongholds, and such. And we desire all things for His glory and die for His cause with gladness that He might be lifted up.

Calling a spade a spade: More than ever, we need to discern truth from darkness. Catholics (baptismal regeneration, believe Mary as a co-redemptrix, immaculate conception, purgatory, works-based salvation, Pope as the vicar of Christ, etc.), the Mormons (believe Jesus was the half-brother of Lucifer, deny His eternal Godhead, works-based salvation, etc.), the Jehovah's Witness (deny Christ as God, deny the bodily resurrection of Jesus Christ, works-based salvation, etc.), Christian Science (deny the Trinity and the deity of Jesus Christ,) Scientology (denies the deity of Christ and the Trinity, believes in re-incarnation like Hinduism, etc.), Seventh-Day Adventist (believe in the extra-Biblical inspiration in the book of Ellen G. White, works based salvation, etc..), Free Masons (follow a Masonic god, believe in the ability of man to save himself, etc.), Judaism (works-based salvation), and others with similar teachings, are NOT Christians. True Christianity has always been based on the foundation of the word of God alone, salvation is by the grace of God alone without man's works, Christ alone as the all-sufficient Saviour, Faith alone in the meritorious works of Christ alone, Glory of God alone to seek and save the lost. "For by grace are ye saved through faith; and that not of yourselves: it is the gift of God: Not of works, lest any man should boast." - Ephesians 2:8-9. "Not by works of righteousness which we have done, but according to his mercy he saved us, by the washing of regeneration, and renewing of the Holy Ghost" - Titus 3:5.

Why are we afraid of the world and have to skirt around the bare word of God? Why can't we just state the truth instead of going around the issue? Why don't we declare from the pulpit what God says? It could be a sin of any proportion or maybe glamorized by the world like booze, gambling, and entertainment, but sin is still sin, even in this Century. Preach the truth that Homosexuality is a sin and brings the judgment of God; transgenderism is a sin for it destroys the image of God and His authority over us in how He created us, male and female; all lives are precious to God; there is only one Human race, and God is no respecter of persons. Militant Christianity has one goal, to listen to their Commander and plunder the enemy pulling those in bondage out of the fire (Jude 1:23). "the people that do know their God shall be strong, and do exploits" – Dan. 11:32. It does not say "the people that know the Bible." Knowing God takes time and militant effort; God uses His word, but He also uses trials, prayer, thorns in the flesh, mountaintops, and valleys to bring it about. Militancy is what is required, for we are in spiritual warfare. It is a fight to the end. Yes, God has His seven thousand who have not bowed their knees to Baal; **what we need today are a thousand Elijah's among us declaring the word of the Lord in the power of the Holy Ghost until we have repentance, riot, or revival instead of this rut that we are rotting in**. At the end of his journey, Paul declared, I have fought a good fight, he knew what he faced in the world, the flesh and the devil, and it was until the very end. Do we hate men? Quite the contrary, true love feels the heart of God and sees the danger man is in; the natural man is an enemy of God; true love goes against the forces of darkness and rescues the perishing, carrying the blood-stained banner of Jesus Christ.

It was Militant Christianity when evangelists used to come in the past and cities were swept by the power of God where saloons closed down, and places of ill-repute were abandoned, so much so that the business owners would oppose such a meeting knowing the aftermath that their places of evil would face. Such was the testimony of that early church in the book of Acts. We have hundreds of evangelists in our generation, but not even one who can shake a city for God. Our "revival" services go unnoticed by the world and get forgotten by the congregation within a week. Nothing more than a glorified week of meetings. They don't need instructions from the Bible that may have moved them temporarily to take some action; what we need is the demonstration of Spirit and of power. Anything else is just running on fumes that breed unbelief and produces proselytes. If all our expectation is to have a good meeting and not have any expectations of the breaking forth of God upon a meeting (1 Chr. 14:11), then we are doomed to continue the degeneration of truth that we are in.

Sidenote: There is a tragedy in what we have become used to as "scheduled revival meetings." J. Edwin Orr speaks of seeing a church sign that stated, "Revival, every day this week except Friday." While wondering what that meant he passed by another church sign that said, "Revival, Friday only." Charles G. Finney had the wrong understanding of being able to produce "revivals" using the proper means instead of revival being a sovereign act of God to a prepared people. He stated in Lectures on Revival, "A revival of religion is not a miracle, nor dependent on a miracle in any sense. It is a purely philosophical result of the right use of the constituted means--as much so as any other effect produced by the application of means." This was unknown in history past from the Evangelical Awakenings to the Lewis Awakening among others. Do opponents of this new theology believe in being idle and just "wait" upon God? The proper context would be that [1]people are awakened to the need around them of the apathy in the Church, [2]the powerlessness of God's people, [3]the explosion of sin, and their inability to stem its tide are all reasons why the church would hold meetings in the past (such as the Hebrides Revival with Duncan Campbell) on seeking the Lord for a fresh outpouring of His Spirit. They realize that they need Divine intervention, and instead of working up means to "make it happen" (which we have been trying to do every year with our scheduled revival meetings) the realization was that judgment would begin in the house of God (1 Pet. 4:17) and repentance in the church was the means needed to see why God was grieved and had withdrawn His Spirit. This was the case with Elijah at Mt. Carmel or at Pentecost when they were in one accord before the glory of the Lord filled the place. It was not an assumption, but rather a manifestation of God in His time to a prepared people "being in the way" (Gen. 24:27) when God sends times of refreshing from the presence of the Lord (Acts 3:19). Today in mainstream Christianity we have come to the apathetic place of being able to hold revival meetings that never affect the community and go on our way self-content that we have "seen" revival because a big-shot speaker came and preached. And our young people go home thinking there is nothing more to Christianity or anything supernatural that happened in the services. They see no difference between what happens in their "prayer" meetings as compared to when they go to a lecture at their secular college. While God used Finney in response to the needs of his day, building a doctrine and church practice based on incidentals is dangerous, and over a period of time, it becomes idolatry in following a pattern of mechanical repetition. We see similar frills in practices such as the sinner's prayer, Roman's road, "decisions," altar calls, etc. There is no Biblical example or practice that has even a hint of such methods. Now we are reaping the fruits of it with the Spirit grieved and a nation in peril.

We have our Bible colleges spit out thousands of students year after year like a cookie-cutter machine and a nation that is continually moving further and further into depravity. Our colleges talk about fulfilling the Great Commission in equipping their students for the gospel; what does that really mean? What percentage of those who come for full-time ministry end up doing it? Or do they end up in Chick-fil-A?

The Scriptures state, "No man that warreth entangleth himself with the affairs of this life; that he may please him who hath chosen him to be a soldier." – 2 Tim. 2:4. Timothy was told to "Fight the good fight of faith, lay hold on eternal life, whereunto thou art also called, and hast professed a good profession before many witnesses." - 1 Tim. 6:12. What does the One who has called us command us to do? "No man, having put his hand to the plough, and looking back, is fit for the kingdom of God." – Luke 9:62, "Whosoever therefore shall be ashamed of me and of my words in this adulterous and sinful generation; of him also shall the Son of man be ashamed, when he cometh in the glory of his Father with the holy angels." – Mark 8:38. When Jesus comes back *(with whatever eschatology you believe regarding the book of Revelation)*, He is not coming as a Lamb but as a conquering King to destroy His enemies, where from His judgment, blood runs even unto the bridles of horses from the slain bodies of those who opposed Him. Sentimental love that overlooks sin is not of God, for God hates sin, and He is not mocked. Reaching others in love and compassion must be done from the viewpoint that we are here to set captives free from an enemy who has blinded and bound them. And we war not against flesh and blood but against the god of this world, the world system, that has them captive. It is the same in our fight against the lust of the flesh, lust of the eyes, and the pride of life, realizing that we are called unto holiness (2 Tim. 2:19). In so doing, we boldly take a stand for Christ without compromise in the power of the Spirit.

Worship

In expanding on the theme of worship, one is confronted with the regular worship service of pre-planned order of service, the shouts of "amen" to the display of talent, the emotionally charged stage with the beats and moving to tears with sentimental songs, the temporary elevation in portraying the God of the impossible and leaving people just as empty as they came when they go back to their homes. To truly reflect on this matter of worship, I had to come to the place of grasping in some small way the loveliness of Christ. We read, "yea, he is altogether lovely" in Song of Solomon 5:16. Lovely has the meaning of an object of affection or desire, a beloved. We see reflections of the loveliness of Christ in many facets of life itself, for it came from the heart of God when it was untouched before sin and remains to declare the glory of God even today. We see Him lovely in the beauty of creation, lovely in salvation and its execution into the heart of a sinner; in His beauty as the great Shepherd of our souls; we see that He is all the more lovely in His compassion toward unworthy sinners, in loving the unlovable, in obedience to the Father, in calling us His friends, and in unending majesty and glory. And then you turn from what you see darkly in these reflections as a clouded glass and face the altogether lovely One, and you stay spellbound and silent as you are unable to grasp in beholding His beauty. Yet it pleased the Lord to bruise Him, and He was not comely to look upon, which makes Him incomparably lovely (Isa. 53).

True worship is not found in the noise and emotional beginnings of a sentimental thought, though emotion can be involved. Jesus said that it must be in spirit and in truth (John 4:24). One can worship with their faculties purely from their emotions, feeling, and such (soulish), or it can be from the spirit of man, which has been regenerated by the Spirit of God, and where God indwells. We will see more on this in the topic of The Exchanged Life. True worship draws us deeper into silence as we gaze on His beauty with speechless adoration, one who is consumed with Him. And from such depths, we utter songs of praise from our innermost being, which has been touched by the purity of its expression. Thus, what is sung as a special is done as unto the Lord, where it does not entertain the audience; instead, it moves the audience to desire Him above all in His nearness, where the person is hidden, and Christ is revealed. The song should change us before we expect it to change others. And it is amplified when we sing unto Him in joyous adoration as a congregation. It may be appropriate, as the Spirit leads, to pause the singing of a choir and have the congregation join in the worship and adoration to God, so it is not a show of performance; instead, it is an act of interjoined worship to God. Worship also could be during times of stillness of the soul that has the hindrances of the cares of this life removed and allows the focus to be wholly upon Christ. Mary Peckham, who was converted during the Hebrides Revival with Duncan Campbell, states, "when we would come near the church, the conversation would die; when we would enter into the church, there was that stillness, that silence." **Worship is the spontaneous love-response of the heart to the Being of God because of the revelation of God's glory**.

Think of the woman in Luke 7 who came to anoint Christ, who was a sinner. In the audience of that day where she was found adoring Christ, she had come to that home where she was not welcomed, was criticized, and shunned. Her one focus was Christ, and she gave her undivided attention to Him in unhindered worship. Amidst all the noise, she was in stillness as she took her time to break the box and, in one uninterrupted motion, began to wash His feet with her tears, with great care wipe it with her hair, giving Christ her crown of splendor. In such captivated attention, she gave a multitude of kisses to those tired feet and, with a silent throb, poured out that precious ointment and anointed the precious feet of Christ. This is from a heart moved with the truth of who Christ was and a love that embraced her God, where truth reigns supreme and heartfelt emotions bear witness. It was true worship from the heart displayed by her actions. The fragrance that was poured upon Christ rested upon her as she went out in joyous gladness, her sins which were many forgiven, a changed life, and devotion to Christ. In our rushed services, pre-planned order of meetings, and keeping in check with time, so we don't go over the schedule, in such an atmosphere, there is little possibility to gaze upon His beauty and worship Him in spirit and in truth. We can become so time-conscious that we can miss out on being God-conscious.

Adoration *(definition from a dictionary):* the act of worship, profound love, or regard, paying honors to a divine being; worship addressed to a deity; the supreme worship due to God alone.

Sacrifice

We see the glorious time of Solomon's dedication of the temple where "the priests could not stand to minister by reason of the cloud: for the glory of the Lord had filled the house of God." - 2 Chr. 5:14. But we also see that just before that happened, there was a great price that was paid in preparation where they brought the vessels (v1) and the Ark (v2-5) as instructed by the Lord and were of one accord in their worship (v13). But in the middle of that, we see this record, "Also king Solomon, and all the congregation of Israel that were assembled unto him before the ark, sacrificed sheep and oxen, which could not be told nor numbered for multitude." - 2 Chr. 5:6. **Calling the people to pray before special events and not willing to pay the price of sacrifice in consistent weeks of prayer for desiring His manifest presence is an insult to God.** Unless we are willing to sacrifice, nothing will happen. God does not care for token prayers but prayers that are birthed from the depth of our soul (innermost being), which yearns after God in groanings unutterable where the heart of God is moved. In Judges 10:16, we see the response of God when Israel put away strange gods and served the Lord where "his soul was grieved for the misery of Israel."

As long as we think we can go along without God and continue our routine without too much inconvenience, God will let us do so. One may have heard of the familiar observation by a Chinese Christian who visited America. After attending churches observed, "it is amazing to see what the American church can do without the Holy Ghost." Sacrifice has always been the precursor to God's moving, for it prepares us to receive what God has for His people in the imagery of what the Welsh divines called revival as "God visiting His garden." Jesus said, "Howbeit this kind goeth not out but by prayer and fasting." – Matt. 17:21. Unless we see God come once again and visit His garden, the state of current affairs will not get any better. People are willing to give time as long as it can fit into their schedule; anything that inconveniences them is seen as a hindrance. It is easy to stay in the superficial and not pay the price of sacrifice, but the superficial always breeds unbelief no matter how sincere we are. We can have a big church, financial soundness, and visitors attending the meetings, but what will be the spiritual depth of a church that does not sacrifice in nights of corporate prayer, making time to examine herself, etc.? It will be as that member of the church who said when asked the question, "How big is your church?" responded, "Our church is five miles wide and one inch deep." Sacrifice is hard on the flesh, time schedules, and family, but there is no other way if we are to be a soldier of Jesus Christ. God did not call you to be a sissy taking a cowardly stand. Put your head into the fire and say, "Lord, either you save me or let me die in the fight for the glory of God" (Dan. 3:16-18).

Trial by Fire

There is no assurance in the Scriptures that if we are right with the Lord, God will always respond with reviving grace as per our request. While there is validity in the Scripture of James 4:8 to "Draw nigh to God, and he will draw nigh to you." many of the people God used in the Scriptures were lonely men. Joseph was forgotten in the slave markets of Egypt before being raised second in command over all of Egypt, Moses in the backside of the desert for forty years, Elijah was unknown until he was sent to Ahab, and John the Baptist was over thirty years before his shewing forth and spent many of those years in the wilderness, The apostles were told to "tarry ye," Paul went to Arabia for three years before commencing his ministry, and others. There are periods when God will test our faith to prove us before He can use us. He may remove people from our lives who may be hindrances; for Abraham, it was Lot, with a love for God that superseded his love for his only son Isaac (Gen. 13:14, 22:16). While the Christian life is a life of repentance, during those times of testing, we may be right with God and not have willfully sinned against Him; still, we realize that **God at times hides His face from us** for us to know what needs we have in growing into the vessel that God is shaping us to be. We can become discontented with God when following the American dream and getting things our way, which is antithetical to how God works. And to preach that God will always respond because you are right with Him is simply not true. God responds according to His plan and schedule and not according to our "priorities." And such is the requirement for seeing God send His gracious work among us, where costly prayers are uttered, and the faith to believe must be met with the patience that has been bred in stillness and, at times, in loneliness. Such prayers are costly because "as Zion travailed, she brought forth her children." – Isa. 66:8.

We see Abram's patience when he had to wait upon God while having to chase off the birds that tried to come down upon his sacrifice (Gen. 15:11-12). James states, "Knowing this, that the trying of your faith worketh patience. But let patience have her perfect work, that ye may be perfect and entire, wanting nothing." – James 1:3-4. We see the vessel unto honor, that is meet for the Master's use, and the vessel is not ready until it is sent into the crucible of fire to harden it where it can be strong enough to hold what is poured into it and take the external forces that may desire to break it. In Judges 2, we see the beginning of the sad plight of Israel, which plunged into sin after those Judges that God raised to deliver them died. And so it states, "And the anger of the Lord was hot against Israel; and he said, Because that this people hath transgressed my covenant which I commanded their fathers, and have not hearkened unto my voice; I also will not henceforth drive out any from before them of the nations which Joshua left when he died: That through them I may prove Israel, whether they will keep the way of the Lord to walk therein, as their fathers did keep it, or not." – Judg. 2:20-22. They were to be proved by God. Speaking of Joseph, "Until the time that his word came: the word of the Lord tried him." – Psa. 105:19.

Job spent many a night in loneliness and had to abandon himself to God when he went through such great suffering before God met him in a whirlwind. When faced with solitude and sorrow, Job in 23:8-10 uttered, "Behold, I go forward, but he is not there; and backward, but I cannot perceive him: On the left hand, where he doth work, but I cannot behold him: he hideth himself on the right hand, that I cannot see him: But he knoweth the way that I take: when he hath tried me, I shall come forth as gold." We are encouraged by God's great promises, "But they that wait upon the LORD shall renew their strength; they shall mount up with wings as eagles; they shall run, and not be weary; and they shall walk, and not faint." – Isa. 40:31. "Wait on the LORD: be of good courage, and he shall strengthen thine heart: wait, I say, on the LORD." – Psa. 27:14. We see a similar exhortation from 1 Peter 1:7, "That the trial of your faith, being much more precious than of gold that perisheth, though it be tried with fire, might be found unto praise and honour and glory at the appearing of Jesus Christ:"

Americanized Christianity is found wanting where it has convinced impatient Christians, young and old, that God is primarily after their interest, and if He does not answer, there must be sin in their lives. While sin hides His face from us, the true nature of God's dealing could be His plan of breaking us and remaking us into a vessel He can use and not what we imagine ourselves to be. "Who is among you that feareth the Lord, that obeyeth the voice of his servant, that walketh in darkness, and hath no light? let him trust in the name of the Lord, and stay upon his God." – Isa. 50:10. We see Habakkuk, who saw the judgment of God and barrenness around him, said, "Although the fig tree shall not blossom, neither shall fruit be in the vines; the labour of the olive shall fail, and the fields shall yield no meat; the flock shall be cut off from the fold, and there shall be no herd in the stalls: Yet I will rejoice in the Lord, I will joy in the God of my salvation." (3:17-18) and spoke with confidence that "The Lord God is my strength, and he will make my feet like hinds' feet, and he will make me to walk upon mine high places." (v19).

The desire of Christ for Peter, who was to be sifted as wheat by Satan (Luke 22:31), was not deliverance; instead, it was, "But I have prayed for thee, that thy faith fail not: and when thou art converted, strengthen thy brethren." – Luke 22:32. If we are to maintain our vitality, it must be of God, by the Spirit through the word. Having said that, we ought to learn to desire His appearing (2 Tim. 4:8), looking for that blessed hope (Titus 2:13). Whether through His return or by death, we desire to be with Christ. I think of times when those who died for the faith went through extreme persecution and faced their end with joy. The early Christians in Rome under Nero, Perpetua made herself ready for her Beloved until the last thrust of the blade that killed her. We can think of the many Martyrs who kissed the stake where they were to be tied to and burned. What was their secret? While the grace of God is able to keep us when sealing our testimony in blood (Acts 7:55-60), I believe that there is also the desire that wells up within the child of God who has been living for the world to come; they lay their treasures in heaven where their heart is (Matt. 6:19-21), and they desire to be with Christ more than life on earth. "For I am in a strait betwixt two, having a desire to depart, and to be with Christ; which is far better" – Phili. 1:23. **If you are in love with this world, then you are in bondage to it** (1 John 2:15-16). "Remember Lot's wife." - Luke 17:32. While yearnings for their family were there, like, John Bunyan, who exclaimed, "Oh! the parting with my wife and children is as the pulling of the flesh from my bones. What hardships, and miseries, and wants, my poor family are likely to meet with, if I am taken from them; especially my poor blind child, who is nearer to my heart than all beside. Oh! the hardships this poor blind one will have to undergo will break my heart to pieces!" nevertheless encouraged a fellow prisoner with, "I find, my brother, the best way to go through suffering is to trust in God, through

Christ, as touching the world to come; and as touching this world, to count the grave my home, to make my bed in darkness; to say to corruption, Thou art my father; and to the worm, Thou art my mother and sister."

Jesus said, "These things I have spoken unto you, that in me ye might have peace. In the world ye shall have tribulation: but be of good cheer; I have overcome the world." - John 16:33. Not "overcome the world" so we won't have trouble; instead, being able to go through tribulation with Christ's victory as our own, setting our affections on things above (Col. 3:2). A way to prepare ourselves for going through such times, in addition to what has been discussed, would be to cultivate a spirit of humility in all things no matter where God takes us. In the mountaintops and in the valleys, always being humble, realizing that "every branch that beareth fruit, he purgeth it, that it may bring forth more fruit." - John 15:2. **Knowing God cannot be attained in a theological seminary or by knowing the Bible**; instead, it is forged in the crucible of suffering, the hidden closet of prayer, and the illumination of the Spirit about the God of the word. And such deep work takes time.

Making Provision for the Flesh

The constant call of God is to live a holy life. We see it in multiple places, such as in Leviticus 11:45 "For I am the Lord that bringeth you up out of the land of Egypt, to be your God: ye shall therefore be holy, for I am holy." And repeated in 1 Peter 1:15, "But as he which hath called you is holy, so be ye holy in all manner of conversation;" We are called to "be partakers of his holiness." – Heb. 12:10. When one strays from the nature of who God is because of a low view of God then one must make provision for things seen which do not align with the Scriptures. Americanized Christianity allows sin to be accepted since its converts do not prove otherwise. In those who have no desire to live for God, we have come up with the term "carnal" Christian. To someone living like the devil but may have made a profession as a child, the response is, "they are just quenching the Spirit." **There is no such thing as a carnal Christian**; he is just displaying what is in his heart by what he desires after or the lack thereof. It is an excuse for bankrupt Christianity to make provision for false converts to continue in their sin. "The Lord knoweth them that are his. And, let every one that nameth the name of Christ depart from iniquity." - 2 Tim. 2:19.

The word carnal in Romans 8 (sarx) is the whole man who is dead and has no struggle of righteousness except the accusation of the conscience, which could become seared and pervert the truth (Titus 1:15). This is similar to the natural man in 1 Corinthians 2:14 (psychikos). The passage in Romans 8 speaks of the effect of the natural man (carnal) who is in enmity against God and is not and cannot be subject to the law of God (Rom. 8:7), and only the spiritual man (the new man) can have the righteousness of the law fulfilled in him (v4). And no good can come from the heart of flesh, for it is in enmity against God (v5-8). In verse 9, he switches from this natural man to the spiritual man, "But ye are not in the flesh, but in the Spirit, if so be that the Spirit of God dwell in you. Now if any man have not the Spirit of Christ, he is none of his." Now that the transaction has been made, he continues on to state the position of the new man. You are either backslidden and need to repent like the prodigal, or you are lost. There is no middle ground of being able to continue in sin while justifying yourself as a "carnal Christian" (v13). To those redeemed, all things have become new because He saved us. We love him because he first loved us and changed us (2 Cor. 5:17, 1 John 4:19). God is in the business of changing us from the inside out. In contrast, Americanized Christianity is in the business of allowing the sinner to continue in his sinful behavior as long as he has made some intellectual assent to the truth.

The word carnal in 1 Corinthians 3 (sarkikos) is one who is in contradiction with himself (the new man). Paul in Romans 7:14 uses the same word when he states, "For we know that the law is spiritual: but I am carnal, sold under sin." And he further speaks of this in Romans 7:15-23 speaks of the war of the inward man against the law of sin in his members. This is the one who, though at times commits and has pleasure in sin for a season, cannot be at peace with himself, for a contradiction is raging inside him. Thus, the word carnal here, in the truest sense, is the influence of the old man who is constantly desiring to usurp control over the new man. "For the flesh lusteth against the Spirit, and the Spirit against the flesh: and these are contrary the one to the other: so that ye cannot do the things that ye would." – Gal. 5:17. And this does not mean as is perceived sometimes as being able to live in sin without having any desire to submit to God while professing a belief in God. God will bring him back with tokens of love (Rom. 2:4), chastisement (Prov. 13:15, Heb. 12:8), suffering (Hos. 2:6-7), etc. If one persists in their rebellion as a child of God, they will be destroyed by God (Prov. 29:1, 1 Cor. 3:17). To make provision for the flesh and justify the practice of sin further hardens the heart of a proselyte against any sincere Christian who desires to see him come to Christ in true repentance and faith.

Zealous in Love

There is a skewed view of showing the love of Christ and excluding the responsibility of submitting to the Lordship of Christ. Zeal without knowledge can be dangerous, for it will soon change into another christ. The Jews were those who had a zeal for truth but forgot the spirit of the truth that was given in the Law. Jesus had to dig deeper in saying, "Ye have heard that it was said by them of old time, Thou shalt not commit adultery: But I say unto you, That whosoever looketh on a woman to lust after her hath committed adultery with her already in his heart." – Matt. 5:27-28. Paul recalls, "For I bear them record that they have a zeal of God, but not according to knowledge." – Rom. 10:2. Zeal is needed, agape love is to be manifested, warmth is crucial, compassion is essential, but we are at a stage where truth has been forgotten at the altar of sincerity and "good" intentions. Those well-intended in leading many to raise the hand and pray a prayer to lead folks to Christ so that they can "go to heaven" may do it in sincerity but may be plucking unripe fruits. It is the Spirit that regenerates and not a one-sided call to believe; it must be a work that God does in drawing and saving them, using earthen vessels to proclaim His truth. **Yet there is a warning**. The place of learning these truths intellectually to make sure I have every dot and tittle checked can bring me to a place of barrenness and sterility where I become technically correct but spiritually powerless. The opposite is just as valid as well; to be sentimental and sacrifice doctrine and lead people into a false belief system that is very similar to what is real but, in reality, is far from the truth is a deadly poison. To those, the dreaded words "And then will I profess unto them, I never knew you: depart from me, ye that work iniquity." (Matt. 7:23) will be heard on that last day. We sadly see the tremendous success of the sincere cults who lead multitudes to a devil's hell in making devoted proselytes.

Is God the embodiment of love? Is He touched with the feeling of our infirmities? Did He say, "Come unto me, all ye that labour and are heavy laden, and I will give you rest"? Is He the Beloved in the Song of Solomon? Yes, yes, and a hundredfold times, yea, and Amen to that. But even in that context, we don't divorce God's nature to embrace God's identification in human suffering; the greater the love, the greater the awareness of dealing with sacred things and an awareness that we are on holy ground.

There is no place for flippancy and trivial representations of soothing the wounds before they see their need. "For they have healed the hurt of the daughter of my people slightly, saying, Peace, peace; when there is no peace." – Jer. 8:11. We see this even in times of revivals where there is great joy in the presence of God but also great soberness, great rejoicing but also great awe, great fellowship with the Divine but also great searchings' of one's standing before Him, great thanksgiving but also great enjoyment

175

of Him in the beauty of holiness. If anyone went through the crucible of suffering, we must say it was Job. But when God met him in the whirlwind, Job said, "Behold, I am vile; what shall I answer thee? I will lay mine hand upon my mouth. Once have I spoken; but I will not answer: yea, twice; but I will proceed no further." – Job 40:4-5; Jacob running for his life and meeting with God, responded, "And he was afraid, and said, How dreadful is this place! this is none other but the house of God, and this is the gate of heaven." – Gen. 28:17; Peter, hearing Christ, "fell down at Jesus' knees, saying, Depart from me; for I am a sinful man, O Lord." – Luke 5:8; Isaiah in seeing the vision of God said, "Woe is me! for I am undone; because I am a man of unclean lips, and I dwell in the midst of a people of unclean lips: for mine eyes have seen the King, the Lord of hosts." – Isa. 6:5; John who lay in the bosom of Christ and being in the Spirit on the Lord's day was in an ecstasy of His presence, "fell at his feet as dead" – Rev. 1:17; "the voice of many angels round about the throne and the beasts and the elders: and the number of them was ten thousand times ten thousand, and thousands of thousands" in uninterrupted and joyous worship cry out, "Worthy is the Lamb that was slain to receive power, and riches, and wisdom, and strength, and honour, and glory, and blessing." (Rev. 5:11-12). Does our love for God lift us up with enraptured worship with those who have gone before us, along with those who adore and worship Him in heaven day and night even now, to proclaim, "for the Lord God omnipotent reigneth"? – Rev. 19:6.

A false representation of love can stem from what man can produce in what he deems "love." Thus, in his definition of "love," he can make provision for the flesh, where what God calls an abomination, such as the sin of homosexuality, man can define as "all that matters is love," ultimately bringing God into the harsh scrutiny of what he deems as just. Homosexuality is more than a lifestyle or preference, it is sexual rebellion promulgated by the spirit of this world. The Scriptures give us the definition of true love, that it "Rejoiceth not in iniquity, but rejoiceth in the truth;" – 1 Cor.

13:6, and that "love is the fulfilling of the law." – Rom. 13:10. We are at a stage in America where even our sincerity needs to be evaluated in light of the truth of God's word. When God brings us back to His definition of love, compassion, and joy, then the promise is true where "He that goeth forth and weepeth, bearing precious seed, shall doubtless come again with rejoicing, bringing his sheaves with him." – Psa. 126:6, "And of some have compassion, making a difference:" – Jude 1:22. He realizes that he is preaching to dead people and, while knowing the reality of his inability to bring life, relies on the Spirit to "reprove the world [the hearers] of sin, and of righteousness, and of judgment:" – John 16:8 *(emphasis mine)*. Genuine compassion sees where the sinner is headed in denying God the rightful place as his Creator and weeps for their sin, desires them to repent knowing that they are on their way to destruction; it desires that the audience hears an accurate representation of God; of love, judgment, truth, and holiness. He has sorrow of the heart, knowing the heart of Christ.

Sorrow of the Heart

Our knowing the word of God but not knowing the God of the word has bred colleges, camps, and congregations that have no realization of the burning holiness of God and the wretched sinfulness of sin, the wrath of Almighty God, and the eternal torments of hell for the dammed; where we are found preaching another christ. I had to come to the place of sorrow that the heart of Christ is grieved over Her Bride, who is to be spotless and blameless as a chaste and pure virgin to be presented to the Lord. Instead, the church is in step with the world in its practice of sin and ignoring God's desire for her to repent and turn to Him. The command to be blameless in Philippians 2:15 was the same command given to Abraham in Genesis 17:1 to "walk before me, and be thou perfect." We also see God's displeasure when Solomon turned to other false gods and, "his heart was not perfect with the Lord his God, as was the heart of David his father." - 1 Kings 11:4. In the painful recovery of Biblical Christianity and re-learning the truths of the heart of Christ, I was confronted with the subject of grief that does not bring bitterness to the soul but sorrow to the heart. In realizing this, there are many reasons to be sorrowful when dealing with eternal souls and the consequences of a nation rejecting God; below are a few.

- The reproach on the name of Jesus: There is a reproach on the name of Christ because people don't believe our salvation "decisions," for there is no abiding fruit of holiness for the most part. We have no power that the world must reckon with. A pagan king named Darius declared Daniel a "servant of the living God," he knew that Daniel served a different God who was alive than all the gods that he went to worship (Dan. 6:20). But Christianity today has become just another religion, and Christ has become just another "holy man" like Buddha or others.
- Someone rejecting Christ: They are trampling the precious sacrifice of Christ and rejecting the only way of escape, not knowing the danger they are in. You groan and grieve, seeing what sin has done and can do in an individual's life and what it can lead to.
- The laugh of Satan: The devil laughs at our blindness, the destruction, and mayhem that sin is causing in this world, and as a promoter of it with religion, slaves of sex, sports, and entertainment, evolution, destruction of the home, and marriage. He laughs at our blind Americanized Christianity that is powerless to stop the tide of sin, spreading a false gospel, destruction of the mind through drugs, destruction of the body through venereal diseases, and churches thinking they met God but go back blinded by their own teachings and denominational pride. The Bible preached but the God of the Bible who is never present but is grieved over His harlot Bride. A church praying for revival but never repenting of her evil ways. And Jesus is not going to come back for a harlot Bride, but one that has purified herself as a pure and chaste virgin (more on this will be

discussed under the topic of The Church Aflame). He will purify her no matter what, even if it takes persecution to do that work.

- Those following idols: Glory and service that rightfully belongs to God being given to something that cannot talk, changing the glory of the invisible God to creeping things and beasts.
- Deficient theology or doctrine of devils: Leading many astray with a false peace when there is no peace.
- Making portions of the gospel call as the entirety of the gospel: Polluting the Bride of Christ, the world thinks low of the gospel since it does not work according to what they hoped, thus bringing the gospel down and as nothing useful. If I, as a minister, attract the attention of the Bride of Christ to myself, then I am playing the harlot by drawing her away from her true Bridegroom, Jesus Christ, who gave Himself for her. The church is in bed with the world and has brought reproach to her Groom to whom she has been unfaithful.
- Will of man to "decide" as a "believe it and claim it by faith or take it by faith," which removes the reproach of the gospel and the elevation of man: Making a proselyte that makes them a twofold child of hell, powerless to live in victory and failing to see the victorious Christian life, bringing shame to the name of Christ. There was a time where when someone became a Christian, they were expected to be different, but we cannot expect that anymore in Americanized Christianity. Our coverts have not encountered God; they just believed a proposition. And the world does not believe in Christianity because it does not believe in our coverts.
- Lack of prayer meeting: The grief of God to see our self-sufficiency without Him to run His church (Rev. 3:20).
- Eclipsing the glory of God: The grief that the purest motive of God being glorified is not accomplished because man is too much in view.

179

- When seeing the church opposed to having a balance of both sovereignty and responsibility: Robbing the riches of God's truth and subjecting it to a low view of God that is worthy of man but unworthy of God.

Our sorrow should be because we love. From such sorrow comes the need for righteous anger, where to "Be ye angry, and sin not: let not the sun go down upon your wrath:" – Eph. 4:26. You see this in the life of Paul when he was in Athens "Now while Paul waited for them at Athens, his spirit was stirred in him, when he saw the city wholly given to idolatry." – Acts 17:16. The word "stirred" is to arouse to anger, to burn with anger or to make angry. Jesus, in righteous anger, condemned the Pharisees with sharp terms such as "Woe unto you, scribes and Pharisees, hypocrites! for ye are like unto whited sepulchres, which indeed appear beautiful outward, but are within full of dead men's bones, and of all uncleanness." – Matt. 23:27 and cleansed the temple with a whip driving the moneychangers out. We read the sobering statement, "God is angry with the wicked every day" – Psa. 7:11. Though we ought to have righteous anger, we do not respond in anger but in humility and truth; and we turn to God, who is the righteous judge, "Dearly beloved, avenge not yourselves, but rather give place unto wrath: for it is written, Vengeance is mine; I will repay, saith the Lord." – Rom. 12:19. What did that early church do when they were threatened and sent away in Acts 4, they prayed and saw God plunder the enemy. Yes, we see the wrath of God that is about to be poured out because of what we truly deserve, but we also see and should feel the heart of God in grief, in the misery of the soul, over the sin of His people. To share in His burden.

Victorious Christian Living

I remember a few years ago listening to a Christian audio drama. The context was this runner, representing Christian, who was running this race and facing obstacles. But at the end of the race, you see this runner depicted as a beat-up individual, having no strength, crawling on the ground and dragging himself to finish the race. This pathetic depiction was supposedly the picture of our Christian race. Not only is that picture grossly deficient, but it is also depicted in the general mindset of where Americanized Christianity is today. Struggling to make it to the next day and living in defeat, angry at God. I shared the gospel with a Hindu a while back, and when talking about salvation, her question was, "do we still sin after we become a Christian?" I responded, "yes, we do, but God will forgive us," her response (rightfully so) was, "if you are still going to sin, then what is the point of becoming a Christian?" You see, I had gotten used to the teaching that sin was normal in the life of a Christian, and Christianity was not something where we could have consistent victory over sin. I did not know that the normal everyday Christian life is a life of victory.

Have we considered what it means to come to the truth that in Christ we have died already and that our sin was crucified on the cross, never to have dominion over us anymore? "For sin shall not have dominion over you: for ye are not under the law, but under grace." – Rom. 6:14, and that, "Whosoever is born of God doth not commit sin; for his seed remaineth in him: and he cannot sin, because he is born of God." – 1 John 3:9. We realize the nature of habitual sin to enslave us, but in regeneration, the grip of sin has been destroyed (just as Egypt was destroyed where it was never to be a threat to the Israelites in the wilderness, and our life is hid with Christ in God, spoken of in Colossians 3:3), never to have sway over us. **Jesus Christ did not come to save us just from the penalty of sin or the guilt of sin but also from the dominion, corruption, and power of sin** (Matt. 12:28-29, Rom. 6:14, 6:17-22, Gal. 1:4, Eph. 5:27, Col. 2:13-15, Titus 2:11-12, 2:14, 1 John 4:4). A gospel message that only deals with the penalty of sin is a false gospel. Only a repentant sinner who has been convicted of sin by the Spirit of God is desirous for a Savior who can save him from his sin, all of it. And without holiness, no man shall see the Lord (Heb. 12:14), For God hath not called us unto uncleanness, but unto holiness (1 Thess. 4:7). "But as he which hath called you is holy, so be ye holy in all manner of conversation" – 1 Peter 1:15, because of salvation. The command "be ye holy" ought to be a progressive term where we are constantly desiring after and pursuing after, to be in the likeness of Christ, who is perfect in holiness. The five wise virgins proved that they were born of God by their response in being prepared for their bridegroom (Matt. 25:1-12). We realize that we still have the body of flesh, and while the inner man is renewed day by day, the influences of the flesh and our weakness of the past cause us to be tempted with the pleasures of Egypt, but victory is already ours through Jesus Christ our Lord who was victorious. As a faithful High Priest, "he is able to succour them that are tempted." – Heb. 2:18. Our rest is in heaven, and the more Satan tempts us where we flee to Christ, the more God shapes us into the image of the Lord Jesus Christ, where Satan will mean it for evil, but God will bring good from it (1 Peter 1:7). "Beloved, think it not strange concerning the fiery trial which is to try you, as though some strange thing happened unto you: But rejoice, inasmuch as ye are partakers of Christ's sufferings; that, when his glory shall be revealed, ye may be glad also with exceeding joy." - 1 Peter 4:12-13.

We know that regeneration does not eradicate sin, and while the possibility to fall is there, the ability of God to keep us from falling is greater (Jude 1:24). And "if" we sin (with the possibility of not sinning) when we quench the Spirit and yield to the flesh, "we have an advocate with the Father, Jesus Christ the righteous:" – 1 John 2:1, thus when we do wrong (as in already committed) 1 John 1:8 states, "If we say that we have no sin, we deceive ourselves, and the truth is not in us." It does not state, "If we say that we *do* no sin." And he goes on to encourage those who are thus saddened by their sin "If we confess our sins, he is faithful and just to forgive us our sins, and to cleanse us from all unrighteousness" (v9) and reprimands those who would try to hide it since he is addressing those who "walk in darkness" in v6, "If we say that we have not sinned, we make him a liar, and his word is not in us" (v10). The sacrifice of Christ provides a covering for sin, with its finality in eradication when we are glorified in physical death. In this pilgrimage on earth, we still have the influences of the old nature in this body of flesh. However, the new inner man cannot sin (1 John 3:9), and sin cannot have dominion over us (Rom. 6:14) because "Knowing this, that our old man is crucified with him, that the body of sin might be destroyed, that **henceforth we should not serve sin**. For he that is dead [as in died with Christ, when He was crucified – past tense] is freed from sin." – Rom. 6:6-7 *(emphasis mine)*. Positionally, in regeneration, our old man has been crucified with Christ, and having risen with Him and seated in heavenly places (Eph. 2:5-6), we are freed from the law of sin and death (Rom. 8:2, Gal. 2:20). Paul further makes the argument, "So then with the mind I myself serve the law of God; but with the flesh the law of sin." – Rom. 7:25. Thus, in regeneration, the fallen state from Eden is restored, our will freed, where we obey God out of love willingly rather than when we were lost and followed the god of this world as slaves to sin. You could almost feel the weight of this statement when Paul exclaims, "What shall we say then? Shall we continue in sin, that grace may abound? God forbid. How shall we, that are dead to sin, live any longer therein?" – Rom. 6:1-2. This is our everyday Christian life and what God expects of us. By letting Christ live through you and not having any confidence in your own flesh to live it, **you can live the victorious life of Christ as your own life**. *Sidenote:* When living this victorious life, there is a difference between obedience and law-keeping. In obedience, you want to obey because you love the Lord having a proper fear of God. The fear of sinning against God is seen for what it does; it brings sorrow to the heart of your Father coupled with a reverence for the greatness of God and what He represents in His holiness and majesty. In law-keeping, you do it in bondage because you feel forced to keep it. In Christ, the law has been fulfilled, and you have fulfilled the law in Christ as His child (Rom. 8:4), and now you have been set free to obey in love, and the Spirit who resides in you will direct you no otherwise. The law only produces fear, but in Christ, having fulfilled the law, faith is produced and a clean conscience toward God (Heb. 10:22). It gives us the confidence to come boldly to the throne of grace in time of need (Heb. 4:16). And in so doing, you will fulfill the law of Christ, "Teaching us that, denying ungodliness and worldly lusts, we should live soberly, righteously, and godly, in this present world;" – Titus 2:12, which is the "the grace of God that bringeth salvation hath appeared to all men" – Titus 2:11. And to such belongs the joy of "Looking for that blessed hope, and the glorious appearing of the great God and our Saviour Jesus Christ" (v13).

In coming to grips with realizing that when we are tempted, we need to remember our position in Christ that His victory is our victory, and I don't "have" to sin, and it is possible to live in victory; this truth to me was liberating. Christ is our High Priest "For in that he himself hath suffered being tempted, he is able to succour them that are tempted." – Heb. 2:18. In submitting to His victory as ours, we reject the temptation, and God gives us the victory. We see this in Ephesians 4, the command to "put off the old man" (v22) and to "put on the new man" (v24), and the key is given in verse 23, "be renewed in the spirit of your mind." A "renewed mind" is not in thinking about victory but in **living in the reality of what is already true**. It is like saying, "Don't live like a beggar in the king's palace as his son." There are areas that we are responsible for in ensuring that we do not put ourselves in compromising situations that can feed the flesh (Rom. 6:16, 1 Cor. 10:13, 2 Cor. 6:14, James 1:12-15). Still, our remembrance of the greatness of Christ in us, the hope of glory (Col. 1:27), should cause us to go from victory to victory. And in our moments of weakness, though we fall, we rise again (Prov. 24:16). We ought to pray for discernment where we recognize any thought which is of the flesh which must be rejected before it is accepted and becomes an action (2 Cor. 10:5). And don't let the devil deceive you into thinking that you thought something vile, which was nothing but the fiery darts of the wicked one (Eph. 6:16). Reject it by faith that in Christ you are pure, before that dart lodges in your heart and you accept it and ponder on it and give into sin. Temptation is not sin, but yielding to it is (James 1:12-15). Yes, it is a battle, and we are to "Put on the whole armour of God, that ye may be able to stand against the wiles of the devil." – Eph. 6:11, that God's command is for us to "Be sober, be vigilant; because your adversary the devil, as a roaring lion, walketh about, seeking whom he may devour:" – 1 Peter 5:8. But we also realize that with the grace of God, we can run the race in the triumph of Christ, where we can say in humility, "I have fought a good fight, I have finished my course, I have kept the faith: Henceforth there is laid up for me a crown of righteousness, which the Lord, the righteous judge, shall give me at that day: and not to me only, but unto all them also that love his appearing." – 2 Tim. 4:7-8. He has given us all things in Christ, the precious Holy Spirit to lead us, the word to light our path, and the voice of God that does not return void. To live in victory by faith and not by sight.

When dealing with past failures, something to remember with the apostle Paul, who said, "Brethren, I count not myself to have apprehended: but this one thing I do, forgetting those things which are behind, and reaching forth unto those things which are before, I press toward the mark for the prize of the high calling of God in Christ Jesus." – Phili. 3:13-14. There is a higher calling than to live in the past, to look behind. One needs to seriously consider this lest they be discouraged in their Christian journey and are stunted in their growth, giving Satan an advantage. Have you been convicted, have you confessed, have you repented, have you made restitution where possible, have you sought mercy, have you received assurance of cleansing? Then don't look back. Stop reminding God what He has chosen to forget. "I, even I, am he that blotteth out thy transgressions for mine own sake, and will not remember thy sins." – Isa. 43:25.

The abundant life: We think of the various commands that have been given to us, such as, "Go ye into all the world, and preach the gospel to every creature." – Mark 16:15, "Every man according as he purposeth in his heart, so let him give; not grudgingly, or of necessity: for God loveth a cheerful giver." – 2 Cor. 9:7, "Wherefore come out from among them, and be ye separate, saith the Lord, and touch not the unclean thing; and I will receive you." – 2 Cor. 6:17, and so forth. But these all are to come as an overflow from within. Let me explain. We have often been told from the pulpit that we ought to give the gospel, give tithes and offerings, go to church, live a holy life, separate from the world, love our neighbors, sacrifice, pray, and so forth. But we forget that living the Christian life is not what we can do; instead, it is to live in the reality of the example Christ has shown, who lives in us (Col. 1:27) and can live through us (Col. 3:3). When He prayed "Our Father," it was addressed in the way that through Christ, His Father has become our Father. The unbroken communion that Christ had with His Father is an example for us to live that righteous life as He did. What a beautiful picture of living that holy life in an unholy world. And this is to be done by the abundant life or the Spirit-filled life, a life that is completely controlled by the Spirit. Once we come to that place, all the other commands will fall into place. His commandments will not be grievous (1 John 5:3). So instead of emphasizing singing, preaching, witnessing, giving, etc., which are all secondary, the primary focus becomes that sacred inflow of that abundant life so the outflow will naturally take care of the others that are needed to be done as the Lord directs us.

This was true of that early church, where they ventured or were restrained as the Spirit moved them. It is from being *(as in a continuous inflow)* filled with the Spirit (Eph. 5:18) and abiding in Christ (John 15:4-5) that we receive the sustenance where "out of his belly shall flow rivers of living water." - John 7:38, to be a blessing to many. Jesus said in John 10:10, "I am come that they might have life, and that they might have it more abundantly." They might "have life" in regeneration since we were dead in trespasses and sins and followed by the "more abundantly" of this abundant life. And prayer becomes twofold where it is for maintaining that inflow that we pray where it outflows to what God desires to do among us. Living the Christian life can be a struggle when lived in the energy of the flesh, but the abundant life should be a life of joy and trust. Even in times of sorrow, and it seems as though His face is hidden from us, we continue in the assurance that we are secure in Him (Rom. 8:35, 38-39). What a liberating truth is ours when we realize that our life is hid with Christ (Col. 3:3); we can experience His perfect life in us and lived through us (Phili. 4:13). We must venture further into this matter of the self-life exchanged for the Christ-life which will allow us to see more fully the victorious Christian life.

The Exchanged Life

Jesus stated, "If any man will come after me, let him deny himself, and take up his cross daily, and follow me." - Luke 9:23. Our life which has been redeemed is now under our Creator, our loving heavenly Father who hath begotten us again unto a lively hope through Christ (1 Peter 1:3-4) to become children of God and join-heirs with Jesus Christ (Rom. 8:17). And with such privilege comes the joyous desire to be a bond slave to Jesus Christ and **willingly take up our cross and follow Him**. The disciples had a gross underestimation of the worth of Christ when the woman broke the alabaster ointment of spikenard very precious on Him, that she was wasteful (Mark 14:4). Still, Christ is more precious than all the world can offer. Our lives poured out to Him lavishly is not enough, even if we do it for infinite lifetimes. "And Jesus said, Let her alone; why trouble ye her? she hath wrought a good work on me… She hath done what she could: she is come aforehand to anoint my body to the burying." - Mark 14:6, 8. She gave everything of that which cost her the most. We do well to remember the hymn, **Is Your All on the Altar?** by **Elisha Hoffman**.

> You have longed for sweet peace,
> And for faith to increase,
> And have earnestly, fervently prayed.
> But you cannot have rest,
> Or be perfectly blest,
> Until all on the altar is laid.

Refrain:
Is your all on the altar of sacrifice laid?
Your heart does the Spirit control?
You can only be blest,
And have peace and sweet rest,
As you yield Him your body and soul.

Would you walk with the Lord
In the light of His Word,
And have peace and contentment alway?
You must do His sweet will
To be free from all ill–
On the altar your all you must lay.

Oh, we never can know
What the Lord will bestow
Of the blessings for which we have prayed,
Till our body and soul
He doth fully control,
And our all on the altar is laid.

Who can tell all the love
He will send from above,
And how happy our hearts will be made,
Of the fellowship sweet
We shall share at His feet
When our all on the altar is laid!

public domain

But what is this life? Is it to be lived in the strength of what we possess? our talents that we desire to use for the Lord, our ability that God may have fitted us with in a particular area? Though our old man has been crucified with Christ, never to rise again, the new man has members that must be given over to God for His service now. Romans 12:1 speaks of our reasonable service as this exchange of presenting our bodies as a living sacrifice upon the altar. A living sacrifice is not something that God has complete control over to take and use; it is to put to death. That is what a sacrifice does. The high priest killed it before he presented it to the Lord. Thus, a sacrifice is putting to death of something. And if we ought to put something to death, we don't just desire it; we take the action of doing it. This is where the cross comes in. The cross is not only a symbol of death but an instrument of death. When one gets on the cross, there is only one reason for it, which is to die. Paul states in 1 Corinthians 15:31, "I die daily." And what is this death? It is the faculties of the old man under the new dominion of Christ.

God cannot use the faculties of the old man, for they are of the flesh and must have the cross bear upon it and be put to death. Our talents, our abilities, our intellect, our tongue, our reasoning capacity, our minds, our hands, our feet, and all must have the cross laid upon it, that no flesh should glory in His presence (Exo. 30:32, 1 Cor. 1:29). And this is a joyous thing where we daily take up our cross and put to death anything of ours and give it to God to use or not to use as He pleases and follow Him. Not follow our abilities and talents but Him. Thus, looking unto Jesus in Hebrews 12:2 is not just looking to Him for strength but looking solely to Him where we look away from our own selves or others, and letting Christ be our only desire and not look back. Jesus said, "No man, having put his hand to the plough, and looking back, is fit for the kingdom of God." - Luke 9:62, "Remember Lot's wife." - Luke 17:32. To echo with Paul, "For to me to live is Christ, and to die is gain." – Phili. 1:21. Not just surrender but putting it to death, to have no life of our own. To come to the place where we can state with no reservations, not my will but Thine be done.

To help with this, we need to pause and delve a bit deeper. As a created being, we have the body (faculties of the body, senses), soul (reason, emotion, desire, volition/will, mind, etc.), and spirit (conscience, communion/worship, intuition). In Creation, the spirit had its dependence and continual life that flowed from God; the soul was under subjection to the spirit, and the body was under the

189

control of the soul. He was an entity under complete dependence upon God, who created him. When Adam sinned, it was his soul (which Satan appealed to) that reasoned outside the will of God, desired to become a god in league with Satan (Gen. 3:5), and thus sinned against God, violating the spirit, and Satan became his lord and father (John 8:44). At this moment, the spirit died (Eph. 2:1) and came under the bondage of the soul, which controlled the body on the actions taken. The wrath of God now abideth on him (John 3:36). The conscience helps in the area of moral light (Prov. 20:27, John 1:9) but can become seared (1 Tim. 4:2). The conscience is always accusing or excusing but never approving (Rom. 2:14-15). In all this; fallen man (the natural man) completely lost his ability for spiritual things, neither can he know them (1 Cor. 2:11, 14); he has no inclination to the true God (Gen. 3:7-8, 6:5, Psa.14:1-3, Rom. 3:11); he loves his sin and wants to continue in it (John 3:19). He has become altogether dead, taken the image of Satan against God in joint rebellion to dethrone God, deaf to the voice of God and blinded by the god of this world (Acts 26:18, 2 Cor. 4:4). This soul life does everything it can to please self (self-life/ego/flesh). When he is awakened by Divine illumination (John 3:27, 6:44), the word of God by the Spirit divides the soul to reach the deadened spirit (Heb. 4:12). The spirit now in the full blaze of the holiness of God sees the depravity of sin and cries out for mercy (Luke 5:8, 18:13). Where in the past he may have had remorse (soul life), now he truly repents from the heart that has been affected in godly sorrow that is toward God (2 Cor. 7:10). When the Spirit imparts the faith to believe, the word of God used in the call, he sees the way of escape and believes (Matt. 16:17, Mark 1:15, Acts 20:21, Rom. 10:13, 17, Gal. 3:22). The Spirit regenerates the spirit of man, removes the heart of stone, and puts a new heart of flesh (Eze. 36:26, 2 Cor. 5:17). It is all of grace, not of works, not the will of the flesh, or the will of man (John 1:12-13, Eph. 2:8-9). Now man (the spiritual man) can worship God in spirit and in truth (John 4:24). From the new heart, new desires flow for holiness and righteousness, and he is made altogether new (Eph. 4:24). The regenerated spirit (where Christ indwells and reigns) is back in control as it was in the garden before the fall, with dependence and continual life that flows from God. But the temptation is there to go back to the soul life, dethrone Christ and enthrone self (Rom. 7: 22-23, Gal. 5:17). God wants the new man to live the "spirit life," where the yielded spirit controls the soul and, in effect, directs the faculties of the body. The exchanged life puts the cross to do its work on the soul (Luke 9:23), so it can put to death fleshly thinking while **intentionally engaged in the "spirit life" daily**; and when faced with circumstances. When Satan tempts us with a thought, he is appealing to the soul; we reject it by listening to the Spirit and not accepting his accusation through the shield of faith (Eph. 6:16). And this is enabled by the Spirit of God, the word of God used in the process (John 15:5, 2 Tim. 3:16-17). Thus, yielding to the Spirit (Rom. 6:12-14), renewing your mind (Rom. 12:2, Eph. 4:23), putting on the whole armour of God (Eph. 6:10-18), not quenching the Spirit (1 Thess. 5:19), and such are all part of this. "But God forbid that I should glory, save in the **cross of our Lord Jesus Christ, by whom** the world [which appeals to the soul life] is crucified unto me [put to death], and I [spirit life] unto the world [to its pulls]." – Gal. 6:14. "I am [natural man] crucified with Christ: nevertheless I live; yet not I [soul life], but Christ liveth in me: and the life which I now live in the flesh I live [spirit life] by the faith [gift and fruit of the Spirit] of the Son of God, who loved me, and gave himself for me [impetus]." – Gal. 2:20 *(emphasis mine)*.

The temptation of Christ (Matt. 4:1-11) speaks to this. Satan tempted Christ in the matter of provision to protection to worship, to live the soul life independent of God. Where the first Adam failed and gave in to Satan, Christ, the final Adam, was victorious in rejecting to live as directed by the soul and rather recognizing the preeminence of the Father upon Him. Think about this statement from Christ, "But I say unto you, Love [agapao] your enemies, bless them that curse you, do good to them that hate you, and pray for them which despitefully use you, and persecute you;" – Matt. 5:44 *(emphasis mine)*. This is only possible in the spirit life. The agape love that is often mentioned, which is the love that the Holy Spirit produces (Gal. 5:22), lives in the spirit realm (spirit life) and not in the soul life. The soul life can produce phileo (friendship love), storge (family love), and eros (romantic love), but only the Spirit can produce agape love, and flows from the spirit life of those born of God. The same agape love is mentioned in this command, "Husbands, love your wives, even as Christ also loved the church, and gave himself for it;" – Eph. 5:25. Such love is not about what I have heard stated, "love is a choice," instead, it is an outflow of the fruit of the Spirit. And as the Spirit works the mind of Christ into the soul that is in subjection to the Spirit (Phili. 2:5), we can experience the life that God created us for in the garden before the fall. The answer to "O wretched man that I am! who shall deliver me from the body of this death?" is "I thank God through Jesus Christ our Lord. So then with the mind [soul that is in submission to the Spirit] I myself serve the law of God [spirit life]; but with the flesh the law of sin [soul life]." – Rom. 7:24-25 *(emphasis mine)*. When the soul life is not in subjection to the Spirit, it receives wisdom that is earthly, sensual, and devilish. But when received from the Spirit where the soul is in subjection, the soul can use that and take action (volition/will) and apply it. (James 3:14-17). With the spirit life, we can bring every thought into captivity to the obedience of Christ (2 Cor. 10:4-5). We can think about dealing with pride, jealousy, anger, etc., and how the soul life desires to usurp authority over the spirit life. The implication of such consequential truths is far-reaching.

We will now continue to see how this applies. God does not need the talents of our old man (soul life controlling the body), He may not even use them, but He does need our death (on the altar of sacrifice as in Romans 12:1) by letting the cross do its work on us, so He can use us (spirit life) as He sees fit and not how we think we can do (soul life), even in our sincere zeal for the Lord. God only uses the vessels that are consecrated (after it has been put to death) to Him, and the cross does that. In the Old Testament, after the animal was sacrificed and the work done by its preparation, it was considered holy to be offered unto the Lord (Exo. 29). When Isaiah saw that vision (Isa. 6), it was after the live coal was placed in his lips (which kills and cauterizes the flesh) that he was asked to go and tell (v6-9). This **taking up our cross daily** has the same meaning as willingly accepting the death of what we perceive as our rights (soul life) and not looking back, and letting the Spirit control the soul and body (which has been given over in consecration). The cross is not something that happens to us (health issues, death of a loved one, financial troubles, etc.); sickness and such are the reality of living in this sin-cursed world that the lost go through as well. It is something we take and daily crown Him as Lord of our life. "I [soul life] die daily" - 1 Cor. 15:31. Paul is pointed when he speaks to this matter of mortification and bringing his body under subjection. Here is one in context of what the cross can help us with, "Mortify [put to death through the cross] therefore your members which are upon the earth [soul life]; fornication, uncleanness, inordinate affection, evil concupiscence, and covetousness, which is idolatry:" – Col. 3:5 *(emphasis mine)*. It was a reproach to carry one's cross, and a man who went on the cross had only one end, death. "Let us go forth therefore unto him without the camp, bearing his reproach." – Heb. 13:13. We take up our cross willingly with the understanding of what Jesus said; we will face tribulation (John 16:33), not being ashamed of Christ (Mark 8:38), identification by baptism (Rom. 6:3-5), bearing His name in identification with what He represents (Acts 11:26), and so on. People who bore their cross and followed Christ, at times, lost loved ones; such was the case of Jim Elliot and the others who died, with their families having to continue the work alone. And you do it willingly because you were "made willing" through the new birth transaction, and you love Christ with all your heart, soul, mind, and strength (Mark 12:30-31).

He wants to bring us to the place where we have absolutely no confidence in the flesh (Phili. 3:3). Once we die as a corn of wheat in this crucified life (John 12:24-26), it is then that God gives life to it. And this new life is not sustained by us but by the Vine Himself, where we realize in practice what Jesus said, "I am the vine, ye are the branches: He that abideth in me, and I in him, the same bringeth forth much fruit: for without me ye can do nothing." - John 15:5. And it is losing our lives for His. Thus we live the exchanged life; our death for His glory, our shame for His exaltation, our obscurity for Him being made known, our self-mind for His renewed mind, our fears for His strength, our impotence for His omnipotence, our bearing His reproach for His victory, dying to our way of living for self and instead living for His way in the power of His resurrection, our spirit subjected for His Spirit outpoured, our giving up our life in exchange for Him living His life in us and through us, our likes and wants for His will and purpose, our impatience for His compassion, the praise of man in exchange for the approval of God. Not rushing to do the next "service" for the Lord, but instead abiding in Him to let the sap from the Vine flow through us and His love constraining us into action (2 Cor. 5:14). When tempted to sin or have an impulse to do something, we should ask the question, "What saith the Spirit?" He will use the word; He will use prayer, and so forth. At times, instead of letting the soul life overcome the spirit life, an appropriate response would be to reject it and "Stay in the Spirit." – Gal. 5:16. And this is not automatic but an action on our part to take up our cross daily and follow Him. We can then echo with Paul, "I am crucified with Christ: nevertheless I live; yet not I, but Christ liveth in me: and the life which I now live in the flesh I live by the faith of the Son of God, who loved me, and gave himself for me." – Gal. 2:20. "For to me to live is Christ, and to die is gain." – Phili. 1:21.

Americanized Christianity has emphasized talents and someone's ability (maybe what they had when they were lost or seen in their service) as an asset that can be used in the kingdom of God, but anything that is not put under the cross has the stench of the flesh which cannot be used by God or be pleasing in His sight. Submitting to the Lordship of Christ and taking up our cross daily is not an option; it is an absolute necessity of every Christian without exception. Without this, we cannot make any progress toward maturity in our devotional life, Bible reading, and such. Yes, God gave His life for mine at Calvary, but now requires our life for His as a follower of Him. That's the trouble we have; we are happy that He died for us but don't want the cost of following Christ. A Christianity that requires nothing in return is a false religion (Luke 9:23-24, Matt. 25:34-40). *Sidenote:* There is a grave danger in dealing with a lost man as just an intellect (soul life of the natural man) to reason with him using facts (apologetics), trying to prove scientifically about God, emphasizing good feelings, and such, to come to a conclusion about God. The **Scriptures deny that man by himself can come to enlightenment about God as a Person, a living Being**. "Canst thou by searching find out God? canst thou find out the Almighty unto perfection? It is as high as heaven; what canst thou do? deeper than hell; what canst thou know? The measure thereof is longer than the earth, and broader than the sea." - Job 11:7-9. To appeal to the soul life and have him make an intellectual "decision" to go to heaven without the Divine intervention of the Spirit has been the cause of multitudes who think they are saved but continue to live dominated by their fleshly appetites or monastic lifestyle while having no miracle of the new birth transaction. The soul life desires happiness at the expense of anything that will harm itself. Thus, when he is confronted with hell from a pure self-preservation perspective, the soul life will accept whatever proposition he is shown. It could be nirvana in Buddhism or Hinduism; it could be heaven in the Christian or Islamic faith; it could be anything. But reaching the innermost being (spirit of man that is dead) has to be of God, or there is only darkness. To "be ready always to give an answer to every man that asketh you a reason of the hope that is in you with meekness and fear:" – 1 Peter 3:15 must be done with the prayer that **the Spirit must bring them from truth shared from the text to life imparted (revelation) by the Spirit** (1 Cor. 2:9-10, 2 Cor. 3:6). I am aghast that evangelical Christianity has used carnal methods to reach the soul (self-life/ego/flesh) but never got to the spirit (which is dead), calling multitudes saved by the word alone, where the Spirit never bore witness to their sonship.

The exchanged life is about sacrifice; it is death; it is a daily putting of our talents, abilities, strengths, and assets, putting them to death on the cross and living in weakness to gain His strength. His strength, which is made perfect in our weakness, and His grace to be sufficient for us. "And he said unto me, My grace is sufficient for thee: for my strength is made perfect in weakness. Most gladly therefore will I rather glory in my infirmities, that the power of Christ may rest upon me." - 2 Cor. 12:9. God did much more with the apostle Paul when he put to death his intellect and his self-life, and God resurrected it and used it for Himself. And from such a life, you can have the triumph of the Spirit, a broken and a contrite heart, in which God is pleased to dwell.

Spiritual Warfare

What is this life of Christ in us when dealing with the enemy? When Christ came, He was immediately confronted by the kingdom of darkness of this world due to the nature of who He was. In His birth, Herod tried to kill Him; in His life, the Pharisees and others tried to trap Him, and finally, they put Him to death. And Jesus said to His disciples, "The servant is not greater than his lord. If they have persecuted me, they will also persecute you; if they have kept my saying, they will keep yours also." - John 15:20. When dealing with spiritual blindness or someone who needs to be awakened to their need, our prayer must be specific to direct it at the heart of the issue. Instead of a general prayer for them to be saved, it would be proper to pray for desiring the communion of the Spirit to guide us into what to pray for; to remove the hindrances that are as towering walls on the heart which have been blinded by the god of this world (2 Cor. 4:4). We may have to pray for hindrances such as friends, substance abuse, relationships, etc., for them to be removed before they can be awakened to their need. When we realize that our life is hidden with Christ (Col. 3:3) and that Christ is in us (Col. 1:27), we resist the enemy on the basis of the victory of Christ and the authority He has given us as His children (Luke 9:1-2, Matt. 28:18-19).

How does this look from being able to apply this in our daily living? "For we wrestle not against flesh and blood, but against principalities, against powers, against the rulers of the darkness of this world, against spiritual wickedness in high places." – Eph. 6:12. And taking the armor of God, we stand, "for we are not ignorant of his devices." - 2 Cor. 2:11. We have no strength of our own, but we fight "from" victory and not "for" victory availing the blood of Jesus Christ. When Christ presented His own blood to the Father, He was initiating what was to become the position of His redeemed children. What a proclamation of victory it was when Christ conquered the finality of sin and "by his own blood he entered in once into the holy place, having obtained eternal redemption for us." – Heb. 9:12.

In the book **War on the Saints** by **Jessie Penn-Lewis** and **Evan Roberts**, we read, "Stand daily on Romans 6:11" - what does this mean? It has reference to the attitude of the believer: reckoning himself "dead unto sin...in Christ Jesus." It is a declaration of death—a gulf of death—to evil spirits as well as sin. To resist the enemy on the ground of the blood of Christ means wielding the weapon of the finished work of Christ, by faith: believing that Jesus' death for sin frees the trusting believer from the guilt of sin; that Jesus' death to sin on the cross, and the believer's death with Him, frees the Christian from the power of sin; and that Jesus' death-victory on Calvary frees the believer also from the power of Satan.

Plead the blood of Christ to cover you and your entire family by name and go against the enemy in the name of Jesus who has already declared His victory, "having spoiled principalities and powers, he made a shew of them openly, triumphing over them in it." – Col. 2:15. To those who thus appropriates Christ's blood we read Isaiah's proclamation, "No weapon that is formed against thee shall prosper; and every tongue that shall rise against thee in judgment thou shalt condemn. This is the heritage of the servants

of the Lord, **and their righteousness is of me**, saith the Lord."
— Isa. 54:17 *(emphasis mine)*.

Living in this World for Eternity

Man is inherently tied to this world system, and though being born again, he is not at liberty to live outside of it. But there are certain things he can do to help set his eyes upon Christ to get a better understanding of where he is, what he should be doing, and what can benefit his spiritual growth. The American philosophy of living the American dream, making money, rights, conservative voting, etc., is but a vapor. Did God give us "unalienable rights"? yes; did God bless us with the freedom to spread His kingdom with the means He has provided? yes; did God bless America because she was founded under the principle of Psalm 33:12, "Blessed is the nation whose God is the Lord"? a resounding yes. But our dependence upon what this nation can offer for the betterment of spiritual growth stops there. In this world, you have the **essential** part of the God-ordained institutions in what is needed, such as the home, government, and spiritual foundation of truth. And then you have **non-essential** but very much visible such as sports, entertainment, news media, religions, denominations, ideologies, philosophies, eschatology, conspiracy theories, titles, accolades, and political parties such as conservative, liberal, etc. What is to be the viewpoint on these two matters? The essentials are closely linked together, whether they are functioning as they are supposed to or dysfunctional. And for the essentials, we ought to learn to submit where appropriate "that we may lead a quiet and peaceable life in all godliness and honesty." - 1 Timothy 2:2. It could be in the home (Eph. 5:22-25, 6:1) and work (Eph. 6:5-9), the government (1 Peter 2:13), or the church (Heb. 13:17).

Jesus, when giving instructions to His disciples and at times of praying during those last days before His crucifixion, shared two key areas that He was focusing upon. One was His instruction that they were chosen out of the world (John 15:19). The second is His prayer for them to be kept from evil even though they were to be in the world and living in the midst of it (John 17:15). To realize the extent of the world system we must come to the proper alignment that "all that is in the world, the lust of the flesh, and the lust of the eyes, and the pride of life, is not of the Father, but is of the world" (1 John 2:16). So, the non-essential activities that we (generally) spend most of our time in is the place where we need to be kept from evil (John 17:15). When we give ourselves to (the pull of this world) arguing with religions, supporting someone who may agree with us maybe in social media or entertainment, giving our lives to campaigning for political parties, moral majority, etc. we are, by the nature of it, sitting inside the ideology of the world system and trying to better it by throwing rocks against those who oppose us. It is like someone who is in a large stadium and battling with others opposing them, and we will get nowhere. "No man that warreth entangleth himself with the affairs of this life; that he may please him who hath chosen him to be a soldier." - 2 Tim. 2:4. If we are seated in heavenly places in Christ (Eph. 2:6) and are asked to set our affection on things above, not on things on the earth (Col. 3:2), then we must change our viewpoint.

Our viewpoint should be one of seeing everything as it were (from the earlier example), sitting outside that stadium with Christ. All the non-essentials that were mentioned should be something that we extremely limit our attention to and see it as competing for our attention and pulling us away from Christ. The more I realize the fullness of Christ, the more I am confronted with the need to lay aside every weight that hinders me and run the race with my eyes upon Him (Heb. 12:1-2). We live to shine as lights to the glory of God (Matt. 5:16, 1 Cor. 10:31), and this can be done only by living outside that stadium, to be able to look at all the distractions of this world and count them as dung and having no eternal value (Phili. 3:7-9). We ought to live daily with the interests of this world put to death in living that exchanged life (Gal. 6:14, 17). And being useful is not by living the American dream but by having the mind of Christ knowing that the world is not a friend of Christ (John 15:19), but God has chosen us to bring forth fruit, and that our fruit should remain (v16), and accepting the fact that "The servant is not greater than his lord" (v20). Jesus stated, "But I say unto you, That every idle word that men shall speak, they shall give account thereof in the day of judgment." – Matt. 12:36.

"Two things have I required of thee; deny me them not before I die: Remove far from me vanity and lies: give me neither poverty nor riches; feed me with food convenient for me: Lest I be full, and deny thee, and say, Who is the LORD? or lest I be poor, and steal, and take the name of my God in vain." – Prov. 30:7-9. Here is a man who had everything this world had to offer, tried it all to see what would be profitable for man and what he could indulge in to find contentment and happiness from what the world system had to offer; instead, he got fed up with it and spoke wisdom by saying, "Let us hear the conclusion of the whole matter: Fear God, and keep his commandments: for this is the whole duty of man." – Eccl. 12:13.

Someone may justify non-essentials as just weights, but before you know it, you end up spending hours of wasted time that have not been profitable, and at most times, it leads to sin. There are some non-essentials, such as buying a home, the proper use of technology, investing wisely, and such, which have their place, but they all must be held loosely so they don't tie our hearts down to earthly things (and bring us back into that life lived inside that stadium). They all need to be seen from the temporal nature of them while heeding the warning from Christ, "Lay not up for yourselves treasures upon earth, where moth and rust doth corrupt, and where thieves break through and steal: But lay up for yourselves treasures in heaven, where neither moth nor rust doth corrupt, and where thieves do not break through nor steal: For where your treasure is, there will your heart be also." – Matt. 6:19-21. I want to hate anything that ties me down to be earthbound. It could be family, friendships, even what I may consider as "blessings" which may in truth be a hindrance to following God. "If any man come to me, and hate not his father, and mother, and wife, and children, and brethren, and sisters, yea, and his own life also, he cannot be my disciple." - Luke 14:26.

Enduement of Power for Service

When I read the book of Acts and go through that early history of the church, I read of two consequential things again and again. One was the result of their witness, "Now when they heard this, they were pricked in their heart, and said unto Peter and to the rest of the apostles, Men and brethren, what shall we do?" – Acts 2:37, "And with great power gave the apostles witness of the resurrection of the Lord Jesus: and great grace was upon them all." – Acts 4:33, "And when they found them not, they drew Jason and certain brethren unto the rulers of the city, crying, These that have turned the world upside down are come hither also" - Acts 17:6, "And many that believed came, and confessed, and shewed their deeds. Many of them also which used curious arts brought their books together, and burned them before all men: and they counted the price of them, and found it fifty thousand pieces of silver. So mightily grew the word of God and prevailed." – Acts 19:18-20. Not just grew but made an impact and plundered the kingdom of darkness.

And the second was the source of that power to witness. It began with Jesus giving the Holy Spirit in that upper room, "And when he had said this, he breathed on them, and saith unto them, Receive ye the Holy Ghost:" – John 20:22, and the future promise of power, "And, behold, I send the promise of my Father upon you: but tarry ye in the city of Jerusalem, until ye be endued with power from on high." – Luke 24:49. They were instructed **by the Holy Ghost before He ascended**, "Until the day in which he was taken up, after that he through the Holy Ghost had given commandments unto the apostles whom he had chosen." – Acts 1:2.

Jesus said in John 14:17 said that the Spirit of God would dwell with you and "in you." While we realize the office of the Holy Spirit regarding His indwelling presence, in Acts 1:8, Jesus emphasizes this other work of the Spirit coming "**upon you**." "But ye shall receive power, after that the Holy Ghost is come upon you: and ye shall be witnesses unto me both in Jerusalem, and in all Judaea, and in Samaria, and unto the uttermost part of the earth." – Acts 1:8. The word "witnesses" in Acts 1:8 has the ethical sense of "martyr," which is to mean "those who after His example have proved the strength and genuineness of their faith in Christ by undergoing a violent death." Were the disciples who fled before His crucifixion ready for that? Was Peter, who denied Christ, ready for that? Were the disciples who fell asleep when Jesus prayed with sweat as it were great drops of blood at Gethsemane ready for that? They needed something more than what they possessed. This coming upon was the same way that God had worked in the past. We see it in the life of Othniel, "And the Spirit of the Lord came upon him, and he judged Israel, and went out to war" – Judg. 3:10. We see the same manifestation in other instances, such as Gideon (Judg. 6:34), Jephthah (Judg. 11:29), Samson (Judg. 14:6, 19, 15:14), David (1 Sam. 16:13), Azariah (2 Chr. 15:1), Zechariah (2 Chr. 24:20), and many other instances. We see the results not only in the exploits of those men of God but also mentioned in Isaiah 32:15-16 of the result. "Until the spirit be poured upon us from on high, and the wilderness be a fruitful field, and the fruitful field be counted for a forest. Then judgment shall dwell in the wilderness, and righteousness remain in the fruitful field."

Then we see the fulfillment of the prophecy of Joel 2:28-29 at Pentecost in Acts 2, but it was not limited only for that time, since this was for them to bear witness, and was repeated again and again in the same word used, "filled," in other instances as in the day of Pentecost. We see Paul in Ephesians 6:19 asks for prayer that utterance may be "given," he knew he didn't have what it takes and did not assume that it was in him, but that God will endue him again with unction from above for boldness to declare the mystery of the gospel. In times prior when this happened, we see supernatural results, the time of Moses (Exo. 28:3, 31:3, 35:31, Num. 11:25-26), Elisha asking for a double portion (2 Kings 2:9) and proved that he had it when "he took the mantle of Elijah that fell from him, and smote the waters, and said, Where is the Lord God of Elijah? and when he also had smitten the waters, they parted hither and thither: and Elisha went over." (v14), etc. "Then he answered and spake unto me, saying, This is the word of the Lord unto Zerubbabel, saying, Not by might, nor by power, but by my spirit, saith the Lord of hosts." – Zech. 4:6, and in the New Testament before Pentecost, in the life of Elizabeth (Luke 1:41), John the Baptist (Luke 1:15), Zacharias (Luke 1:67), and others. But from the day of Pentecost, these touches of the Spirit's enduement were not just limited to those few that were seen prior, but "in the last days, saith God, I will pour out of my Spirit **upon all flesh**" – Acts 2:17 *(emphasis mine)*. Acts 1:8 is just as applicable for us today.

This was continued with subsequent fillings similar to Pentecost in Acts 4:8, 31 (Then Peter, filled with the Holy Ghost, said unto them, Ye rulers of the people, and elders of Israel, ... And when they had prayed, the place was shaken where they were assembled together; and they were all filled with the Holy Ghost, and they spake the word of God with boldness), regarding Stephen in Acts 7:55 (But he, being full of the Holy Ghost, looked up stedfastly into heaven, and saw the glory of God, and Jesus standing on the right hand of God), Acts 10:44-45 (While Peter yet spake these words, the Holy Ghost fell on all them which heard the word. And they of the circumcision which believed were astonished, as many as came with Peter, because that on the Gentiles also was poured out the gift of the Holy Ghost), and further in Acts 4:31, 13:9, 13:52, 19:6. Here were men and women who did not have the New Testament, had to contend with the mighty machinery of Rome, spiritual blindness of the Jews, intellectual might of the Greeks, the lies that were spread regarding the body of Jesus being stolen, no completed canon of Scripture, no archeological evidence, apologetics and such, but just their bare word had to take root in the hearts of men who were to receive it as the word of God. Because of this enduement of power, they were able to spread the gospel to the whole world in a single generation (Rom. 1:8, Acts 17:6, 28:22, Col. 1:6, 23).

This filling was not something they already had when they got saved or about yielding to the Spirit (which is valid in the proper context of Romans 6:16, Ephesians 4:30, and 1 Thessalonians 5:19). We see this in the lives of these men and women who were **given this unction as an inflow of power by the Spirit**. They not only had this power, but they knew it when they received it and were able to know the difference since it was not a gradual filling but in full measure and immediate. "Then Saul, (who also is called Paul,) filled with the Holy Ghost, set his eyes on him." – Acts 13:9. We see Paul asking those believers in Ephesus, "Have ye received the Holy Ghost since ye believed?" - Acts 19:2. They had believed earlier (v2) and got re-baptized under the authority of the Lord Jesus Christ (v5) which meant that they had been saved and had the Spirit of God dwelling inside of them before they could be baptized, and during this encounter with Paul they were filled with the Spirit (v6). This was normal and expected in that early church to have that enduement of power for service and to live the full Christian witness. We see this pattern repeated when Paul was converted (Acts 9:5-6) and was addressed as "Brother Saul" (v17) by Ananias, who was sent so that "thou mightest receive thy sight, and be filled with the Holy Ghost" (v17). In a day where words have little meaning of their depth as given in the Scriptures, we need to consider the truth that there is a difference between having the liberty to preach the word where people have prayed and sought God contrasted to the anointing that is from above with the power of the Holy Ghost (*dynamis*) which breaks hardened hearts, and the mountains flow down at His presence.

Throughout the Scriptures, we see that there is always an outburst of power seen immediately after this enduement. We see Samson in Judges 15, where it states, "the Spirit of the Lord came mightily upon him" (v14); what was the outcome? He did not have to work up what he already had or try to "yield a little more to the Spirit," but "the cords that were upon his arms became as flax that was burnt with fire, and his bands loosed from off his hands." (v14) and "he found a new jawbone of an ass, and put forth his hand, and took it, and slew a thousand men therewith" (v15). A thousand full-armed and trained men against an unarmed man with a jawbone. He knew when the Spirit came and was moved to action in supernatural strength. We see that in Acts 4, where it states, "the place was shaken where they were assembled together; and they were all filled with the Holy Ghost" (v31); what was the result of that? "and they spake the word of God with boldness" (v31). It was natural, and there were always exploits against the forces of evil.

This Baptism of power (*dynamis*) is God's power manifested for fulfilling God's purpose and for God's glory. If there is any motive of Simon (Acts 8:18-19) or Lucifer (Isa. 14:14) to desire it for selfish reasons, a bigger church, getting respect, pride, or such, this power will not be given. And persecution immediately follows it. Satan is alerted that power has gone from the throne of God to a person or a group of people, and he attacks them to try to stem the tide of truth. You see this pattern in that early church. Thus, Paul writes in Philippians 3:10, "That I may know him, and the power of his resurrection," and immediately follows it up with "the fellowship of his sufferings, being made conformable unto his death." But it is well worth living for six months and getting beheaded while having this power than living a thousand years without it.

One can observe, in general, many references that are made in the Scriptures to help understand a given truth in the context of what it represents. We see references in the parables of Christ regarding the kingdom of heaven, a Roman soldier for the spiritual armor we are to wear, the Christian life as a runner running the race, etc. One of the phrases used for this enduement by the Spirit is given in Ephesians 5:18 "And be not drunk with wine, wherein is excess; but be filled with the Spirit." Those who have been under the intoxication of alcohol *(before they were converted)* understand in some small way what that means. There is a felt possession by this external force quite beyond the ability of the one who drinks alcohol. It could be a (false) boldness, fearlessness, and such. One would do things they would not imagine doing when they were in their sane mind. A mind that has been affected by a force behind that intoxication. So, when we read of the boldness that the disciples had after they were filled with the Spirit of God, it was not that they were occupied with the Spirit; it was something beyond their natural ability, affected by an external force similar to how Samson was influenced. While "the spirits of the prophets are subject to the prophets" (1 Cor. 14:32), this is something that everyone around them notices, that they are different and clothed with a mantle from God. What was once spoken as truth when they shared God's word now penetrates the hearer like a knife into their heart where they are confronted with the living "Word." You don't look for an experience, but you don't receive it without an experience, and this outward flow of God's power that is seen by all is unto holiness.

We read of testimonies of those whom God has used, such as D. L. Moody, A. W. Tozer, W. P. Nicholson, David Brainerd, and others who were already born again but sought God for this specific work of the Holy Spirit to have power with God and man, for the glory of God. They could testify of a time or multiple times when this happened. There was no manifestation of "tongues" but the supernatural ability to bear witness to the truth with power. This is the normal Christian life. It was not just limited to preachers but also others such as John (Praying) Hyde, Hudson Taylor, Frances Havergal, a fisherman named Jock Troup, and so on. Anyone who will ask and pay the price for it. We see this illustrated in the life of Jesus, who, after the depiction of this as a dove descending upon Him during His baptism, "immediately the spirit driveth him into the wilderness." – Mark 1:12, and after the victory in the wilderness against the devil He began His earthly ministry in the temple by reading from Isaiah, "The Spirit of the Lord is upon me, because he hath anointed me to preach the gospel to the poor;" – Luke 4:18

and onwards, and then stated, "This day is this scripture fulfilled in your ears" (v21). Jesus cast out devils by the Spirit of God (Matt. 12:28). We see Peter's declaration of Christ, "How **God anointed Jesus of Nazareth with the Holy Ghost and with power**: who went about doing good, and healing all that were oppressed of the devil; for God was with him." – Acts 10:38 *(emphasis mine)*. In Matthew 12:18-21 we read the prophecy of Isaiah 42:1-4 being fulfilled in Christ. It is interesting to note that the same phrase of "put my spirit upon him" is used in both passages. We see this specifically references the anointing that came "upon" Him, which is further spoken of regarding Christ in Acts 10:38. Surely, we can agree that Jesus already had the Holy Spirit in Him before that day.

We see it in the life of John Wesley, George Whitefield, and others gathered for a prayer meeting on Jan 1, 1739. Quoting from John Wesley's journal:

> Mr. Hall, Kinchin, Ingham, Whitefield, Hutchins, and my brother Charles, were present at our love-feast in Fetter Lane, with about sixty of our brethren. 'About three in the morning, as we were continuing instant in prayer, the power of God came mightily upon us, insomuch that many cried out for exceeding joy, and many fell to the ground. 'As soon as we were recovered a little from that awe and amazement at the presence of his Majesty, we broke out with one voice, 'We praise thee, O God; we acknowledge thee to be the Lord.'

George Whitefield, writing of the same occasion, said, 'O that our despisers were partakers of our joys!' And looking back on that brief season after returning from America, as friends gathered in London to pray, he writes:

> Sometimes whole nights were spent in prayer. Often have we been filled as with new wine. And often have we seen them overwhelmed with the divine presence and crying out,

'Will God indeed dwell with men upon earth? How dreadful is this place! This is none other than the house of God and the gate of heaven!'

We see this in the life of Jonathan Edwards before that great sermon "Sinners in the hands of an angry God" preached on July 8, 1741. In the book "The Works of Jonathan Edwards: Volume I & II," he writes:

"Once, as I rode out into the woods for my health, in 1737, having alighted from my horse in a retired place, as my manner commonly has been, to walk for divine contemplation and prayer, I had a view, that for me was extraordinary, of the glory of the Son of God, as Mediator between God and man, and his wonderful, great, full, pure and sweet grace and love, and meek and gentle condescension. This grace that appeared so calm and sweet, appeared also great above the heavens. The person of Christ appeared ineffably excellent, with an excellency great enough to swallow up all thought and conception — which continued, as near as I can judge, about an hour; which kept me the greater part of the time in a flood of tears, and weeping aloud. I felt an ardency of soul to be, what I know not otherwise how to express, emptied and annihilated; to lie in the dust, and to be full of Christ alone; to love him with a holy and pure love; to trust in him; to live upon him; to serve and follow him; and to be perfectly sanctified and made pure, with a divine and heavenly purity. I have several other times had views very much of the same nature, and which have had the same effects."

We read of John Sung, who was greatly used in the revival movement among the Chinese in Mainland China, Taiwan, and Southeast Asia during the 1920s and 1930s states, "The Holy Spirit poured onto me, just like water, on top of my head," then "The Holy Spirit continuously poured onto me wave after wave."

We think of the Yarmouth Revival in England among the fisherman in the 1920s, where God used fisherman Jock Troup to bring scores into the kingdom. His wife recollects that the secret to all of her husband's ministry was the mighty experience that took place in 1920 in the Fisherman Mission at Aberdeen. Something glorious happened there that made him the man he became. He entered into a definite experience with the blessed Holy Spirit. The experience was so sacred to him that he did not mention it often and then only to a few intimate friends. He would have called it "a baptism of power for service." One of his favorite verses was, "But ye shall receive power, after that the Holy Ghost is come upon you: and ye shall be witnesses unto me both in Jerusalem, and in all Judaea, and in Samaria, and unto the uttermost part of the earth." – Acts 1:8. *(Compiled from the book, Our Beloved Jock by James A. Stewart)*

We can reflect on the difference this made in the life of Peter, who was already saved and had the Spirit before the book of Acts: He did not understand spiritual things (Matt. 15:15-16), hindered the Lord (Matt. 16:22-23), was earthly-minded (Matt. 17:4, Mark 9:5), fell asleep when he was supposed to be praying (Matt. 26:40, Mark 14:37), denied the Lord three times (Matt. 26:75), doubted the resurrection (Mark 16:11, 13, 14), went back to fishing after the resurrection (John 21:3) though he saw the resurrected Christ and had received the Holy Ghost earlier (John 20:22). In contrast, **after the baptism of the Holy Spirit** (Acts 2:4), he was imprisoned (Acts 12:5), persecuted for the faith (Acts 5:17-40), went all over the world, and boldly preached the gospel (Acts 2:14, 4:3-22, 8:14), wrote part of the canon of Scripture, and as per church tradition eventually died as a martyr being crucified with his head downward, at his request during the reign of Emperor Nero. It was an outburst of what was poured into him that flowed out in rivers of living water, and it moved them to act in the power of the Spirit with an unstoppable force. Not something he possessed when he was regenerated.

We see Paul in the accounting of this states, "And my speech and my preaching was not with enticing words of man's wisdom, but in demonstration of the Spirit and of power: That your faith should not stand in the wisdom of men, but in the power of God." – 1 Cor. 2:4-5. "For our gospel came not unto you in word only, but also in power, and in the Holy Ghost, and in much assurance; as ye know what manner of men we were among you for your sake." – 1 Thess. 1:5. Holy Ghost and power are two different things; the mind of Christ is by the Spirit, and the power of His resurrection is the power; of bringing the dead to life. You can have liberty in the Spirit to preach, and you can come back with the assurance that that is what the Spirit wanted you to preach, but it may not be assisted with power that comes from God with "much" assurance, which penetrates the heart as it did at Pentecost. Not just life, but life more abundantly (John 10:10). In being convinced of these truths by God from the Scriptures, in church history, and in Christian biographies, **the lack of power in our pulpits and our witness is not because of a lack of the word of God being preached, but the lack of God manifesting His power as a result of this enduement that is not sought after**. Having heard that we have everything we need and nothing else to strive for has put us in a place of barrenness in trying to work up what we don't have, power with God and man, which only comes from this specific work of the Spirit that is separate from His indwelling work. Thus, we are left to our own devices. "For I will pour water upon him that is thirsty, and floods upon the dry ground: I will pour my spirit upon thy seed, and my blessing upon thine offspring:" – Isa. 44:3.

I am afraid that we, as a church in America, are nothing more than a class of kindergarteners playing with blocks of intellectual truths, running in circles, tooting our horns, and having a good time. Christian warfare is spiritual, and we are trying to instruct people on God, how to live, and how to fight without the supernatural element of the battle. And instead of the supernatural power of Pentecost, we are trying to logically and with instruction trying to accomplish that which can only be done by the Spirit. Samuel Rutherford, the Scotsman who wrote that marvelous book, The Loveliness of Christ, states, "If you would be a deep divine, I recommend to you the anointing." This anointing or the baptism of the Holy Spirit does not produce holiness of itself, though it can be a catalyst for that. Sanctification is a separate path and that has to be solidified whether you have or not have the baptism with the Holy Ghost. Samson was baptized with the Holy Ghost and did great exploits for God, yet his life was battered by uncleanness. We seek God for power but walk humbly before Him in a broken and contrite heart, a heart filled with love for Christ and His Church.

In dealing with the fragility of man and handling divine truths the sudden inflow of light such as during the Reformation always sees the reaction to error like a pendulum where truths propagated take a few generations to settle down to their pristine condition. Thus after a few hundred years, Athanasius thundered the doctrine of Trinity in AD 450, and what John Calvin put out was refined into the five points of Calvinism in the Council of Dort (1618-19) years after he died in 1564. Still, it was being refined further in the subsequent generations. This is the nature of truth even among the remnant before the Reformation since the times of the apostles. This pendulum of truth, which is given by God takes time since man always wants to take it to extremes on one side or the other. And it is so because of the effects of the sinfulness of sin in affecting man's faculties and interpretations. This is the same reaction we are seeing today in the violent reaction against the Pentecostal tongue's movement where godly fundamental Baptists and others have rejected the truths regarding the second work of grace in the Baptism of the Holy Spirit as given in the Scriptures and was believed over the centuries by many irrespective of their denominational affiliation.

To summarize this life in the Spirit; by Christ, we were saved (Col. 1:21, Eph. 2:4, 5), and in Christ, my old man died permanently (Rom. 6:6), and into Christ, I am grafted (Rom. 11:17,

Eph. 2:13), and I am now a new creature in Christ (2 Cor. 5:17), and in Christ, I am risen to new life and seated in the heavenlies (Eph. 2:6), and in Christ, is all riches (1 Cor. 1:30, Eph. 1:3). If in Christ is all fullness (Col. 2:9), and I am in Christ (Col. 3:3), and Christ is in me (Col. 1:27) then in the filling of the Holy Ghost, the Spirit enables me to do what Christ desires me to do [as unto Him] in power (Acts 1:8). It could be in our witness, it could be in praying, it could be in living, it could be in preaching, but it would be in life itself (Phili. 1:21). Jesus continued all night in prayer to God (Luke 6:12), the disciples could not stay awake for an hour to pray with Christ (Mark 14:37). After Pentecost, "prayer was made without ceasing of the church unto God" - Acts 12:5.

Some objections examined: There are a few passages that are taken from the Scriptures to justify the position that this baptism of the Holy Spirit happens to all at the point of regeneration. One such passage is, "For by one Spirit are we all baptized into one body, whether we be Jews or Gentiles, whether we be bond or free; and have been all made to drink into one Spirit." – 1 Cor. 12:13. This specific verse (within the context of the whole passage) deals with the mystical body of believers. This context is further explained in the next verse that "the body is not one member, but many." This is further expounded in stating the position of the Gentiles as, "That the Gentiles should be fellowheirs, and of the same body, and partakers of his promise in Christ by the gospel:" – Eph 3:6 and conveyed that this mystical body is to be unified in love. Paul begins in Ephesians 4 with the Spirit's work in one body (v4) and one baptism (v5), "From whom the whole body fitly joined together and compacted by that which every joint supplieth, according to the effectual working in the measure of every part, maketh increase of the body unto the edifying of itself in love." – Eph. 4:16. There is a vast difference contrast between what the Spirit does in this union with Christ to enjoin us to the body of believers in Christ which is different from what John the Baptist stated of what Jesus does in equipping His children for service. "he shall baptize you with the Holy Ghost, and with fire" – Matt. 3:11.

John R. Rice who speaks of the position of D. L. Moody and R. A. Torrey, who believed in this additional work of the Spirit, contrasts it with the Plymouth Brethren who denied this position regarding the baptism of the Holy Spirit. He writes, "There is a deadness in the Plymouth Brethren position about the Holy Spirit. If you simply tell people, 'You already have all there is; if you just obey the Lord, that is all you can do now to be useful,' then people do not wait on God nor seek nor pray for the mighty power of God for soul winning. That means there will be no great evangelists among people who hold very clearly to the teachings of Plymouth Brethren on the Holy Spirit."

Having the proper motive: We read, "ye have not, because ye ask not" (James 4:2); we also read, "Ye ask, and receive not, because ye ask amiss, that ye may consume it upon your lusts" (James 4:3). Seeking this enduement must be for the sole purpose that Christ might be revealed. We see that the Holy Ghost is given (for a specific purpose) to them that obey Him (Acts 5:32), with similarities seen in Christ's admonition to the disciples in John 14:15-16 that was tied to obedience for the power that they were to be given at Pentecost. Any motives of self-interest must be burned up at the altar of sacrifice. Our desire must be for all of Christ and for his Spirit to have all of us, not just for service but for all our daily living. Paul came to the place of this fullness where he lost his self-identity and embraced all of Christ where he was able to state, "For to me to live is Christ, and to die is gain." – Phili. 1:21. Not live for Christ or serve Christ or obey Christ but to live (life itself) is Christ. You don't earn the anointing, for it is a gift, but you must prepare your vessel to receive it by removing any hindrances. God fills clean vessels, and a faith that is tested with the fire of God will be rewarded with God's provision from above. I want to emphasize the truth that this **anointing is not for my benefit; it is for the kingdom of God and the glory of God** (Luke 11:2, 1 Cor. 1:29, 10:31). It is for God Himself, which excludes everything else, including myself and others (Rev. 4:11). Are you able to say, putting everything aside, "Oh Christ, to be all of thee and none of me, to be lost in thee, is my only desire"? If God does not fill you with power, will you still be joyful if He filled you with a pure life by the fire that burns your dross away? Can you pray with Robert Murray M'Cheyne, "Lord make me as holy as a pardoned sinner can be"? The baptism of fire is for purification, which is needed for the power of the Holy Ghost.

In John 16:13-14, "Howbeit when he, the Spirit of truth, is come, he will guide you into all truth: for he shall not speak of himself; but whatsoever he shall hear, that shall he speak: and he will shew you things to come. He shall glorify me: for he shall receive of mine, and shall shew it unto you," and in John 12:32, "And I, if I be lifted up from the earth, will draw all men unto me." It is not through our cleverness, exhortation, or ability that Christ will be revealed but through the Spirit. He alone can do that. And the enduement of power brings that revelation of Christ to those around us in a flood of blessing with power (the same word *dynamis* used in Philippians 3:10 regarding the resurrection power, and at Pentecost, among others that we have seen already), to have free course upon the word and cut down the hearts of men. Only the exchanged life (discussed earlier) can bring us to the place of total consecration towards God, where He can fill us and use us. D. L. Moody, after he was endued with power from on high, said, "I was all the time tugging and carrying water, but now I have a river that carries me." And once you have received this Baptism of the Holy Ghost and fire, you will never want to live without it, for the fullness of Christ is sweeter than all that the world could offer. To reiterate, this is not about reaching a state of sinless perfection. Neither is this for talking in "tongues" in the way it is promoted today, which was unknown to Christendom before the 1900s.

Are you driven to desperation to pray consistently, Lord, move me to grasp as Jacob did wrestling with the Angel, and prepare me to receive, or would all your labors be in word only where you are content with it, to burn up as wood, hay, and stubble in that great and terrible day (2 Cor. 3:6, 5:10). While we realize that the anointing is a gift where there is nothing that we can do to earn it, we do know that God requires that, as His steward, we are found faithful (1 Cor. 4:2), a vessel meet for the Master's use (2 Tim. 2:21). While we give our heart in total consecration to Christ in surrender, in the anointing we take on God's heart. Then we see as He sees, hear as He hears, feel as He feels, speak as He speaks, and so forth. It is a costly request. *A word of caution:* God will bring you to the place where you completely abandon your all to Him. It may be in the sorrow of the night or a simple act of faith, but in either case, God will strip you of anything that pertains to the flesh, so you can add no credibility to your flesh when God's work is done. "Upon man's flesh shall it not be poured" - Exo. 30:32. And remember, when God brings you into this experience, and you see great exploits done by His power, always look to God and **never let the outcome hide the Source from whom it flows**.

As in the days of Gideon, God puts His fire in the vessel and cleanses it by the baptism of the Holy Ghost and fire, and breaks the vessel of self, passion, and pride, where He shows Himself mighty, slaying the hearts of men, even a multitude that cannot be numbered, where everyone will know that it is of the Lord. I close with the promise that Jesus gave to all His children, "If ye then, being evil, know how to give good gifts unto your children: how much more shall your heavenly Father give the Holy Spirit to them that ask him?" – Luke 11:13. God is desirous for us to have this gift. He longs to have intimate fellowship with us, and this gift brings us into a closer union with Christ that is experiential and beyond just head knowledge (Eph. 3:19). But we realize that just as a child would not be ready to receive something of value until he comes of age, God will bring us to the place where we are made willing to be able to receive it. While we may get frustrated that God is not answering our request, the greater desire for us to have the fullness is on the part of God, and we must be willing to trust our heavenly Father when He says, "how much more" (v13) from that earthly example given of a father's heart to give good things to his children that ask. Our prayer as we ask, confess, and prepare to receive this anointing, is that God would grant us patience (James 1:3-4), as we are "made willing" by our loving heavenly Father. Praise be to His name.

Prayer

Much has been written on prayer from giants of the past, such as "Power through prayer" by E. M. Bounds, "The kneeling Christian" by an unknown Christian, and others. We realize that it is an inexhaustible topic and of tremendous importance. Yet the church fails to avail this means, which is to be her life and breath. Not just in saying prayers but in uttering costly prayers; to try and grasp that command to "Pray without ceasing." – 1 Thess. 5:17. That early church thrived on prayer where they stated, "But we will give ourselves continually to prayer, and to the ministry of the word." – Acts 6:4. There is a set order that is given on what they thought was important. Today we have reversed that order and, at times, completely eliminated the greater need for "continually to prayer." Not dry and barren prayers but thriving in prayer. Jesus "went out into a mountain to pray, and continued all night in prayer to God." - Luke 6:12. Think about the Son of God praying to His Father through the night before He chose His disciples, and yet we run churches with no consistent weekly nights of prayer. These disciples did not come to Jesus and ask Him to teach them to sing or preach. Instead, they said, "Lord, teach us to pray" - Luke 11:1. They saw something sacred far beyond what they had experienced, more than the miracles of Jesus calming the storm, walking on water, lepers being made whole, the blind receiving their sight, or the dead brought to life again. Gethsemane would have been too great for them to bear where Jesus had to go further away from His disciples to pray with such unction. The possibility of prayer is the possibility of God Himself, where He desires to hear and answer the impossible. But this is about seeking God Himself and not what He can provide for us, or maybe in meeting our needs such as health, finances, etc. Yet there are conditions that must be met, conditions of purity, sacrifice, heart yearnings after God for who He is rather than what He can do for us, and such.

Are our prayers in accordance with "Thy kingdom come, Thy will be done in earth, as it is in heaven" (Matt. 6:10), or is it more of "My will be done"? Do we pray from a heart of contentment with thanksgiving (Phili. 4:6)? Are we willing to allow the thorn in our flesh if that is more profitable for us (2 Cor. 12:7-10)? And praying when we are supposed to act according to the revealed teaching of Scripture is deceiving ourselves. God delights in answering prayers that are from a pure heart. After that grand passage where God says, "Call unto me, and I will answer thee, and show thee great and mighty things, which thou knowest not." – Jer. 33:3, God shows the need they have for repentance because He has hidden His face from the city (v5). We ought to pray by engaging our minds and giving thought to the underlying need. Most of our prayers never reach God; we rush into prayer, giving no thought to the sacredness of whom we are addressing. The hypocrites love to pray (Matt. 6:5), and so do the Pharisees (Luke 18:10-12), but they never get heard. When we think about prayers that reach heaven, we can take, for example, a baby that cries, which is the means he uses to tell that he needs his mother. The need can only be met by the source, which is his mom. Prayer is not uttered as a duty that must be done, but there is a point where we need to go beyond prayer and touch God. Thus, prayer is not the goal that we are after; instead, it is about reaching God, who is the real focus, and what He wants to do in our midst. Prayer is the means, but God is the one who can meet our needs.

Is God only limited to what He can provide for us materially? Are our petitions for success at a job or buying a home, etc., proof that our prayers are being answered though our lives don't show the nature of God reflected in us? Such thoughts may soothe the unbeliever when resting upon a supposed belief of faith in Christ, but such is the devotion of a person who's religious. A heathen speaks of devotion to his idol when offering puja or requesting help for his endeavors through a priest by doing religious ceremonies for his deity. And through the course of his life, when he is prosperous, he attributes it to his devotion to his false god. But the God who made us, being a good God, "he maketh his sun to rise on the evil and on the good, and sendeth rain on the just and on the unjust" – Matt. 5:45. While He delights to provide for His children for their physical needs, He is much more interested in a deeper need that man has, which is his spiritual need, and leads them into a life of holiness. And while his physical needs may be met, there are instances where they may not be met, like in the case of the rich man and Lazarus, who was a beggar (Luke 16).

The Pharisees prayed, but they reduced prayer to words and hypocrisy. But prayer is not about words and what we can put together. Jesus said, "But when ye pray, use not vain repetitions, as the heathen do: for they think that they shall be heard for their much speaking." – Matt. 6:7. Then the natural question to be asked is, "What is prayer?" Eight attributes are demanded in prayer.

- **First, prayer is an attitude toward God.** A heart attitude that you rely upon Him and submit to His Lordship. He is the Great Shepherd, and you are His sheep in absolute dependence upon Him. We see the times in the New Testament when they fell down and worshipped Christ. It was a posture of submission and needing help. Being prostrate on our faces before His presence, surrendering our rights, and wholly given over to Christ. We see the woman of Canaan in Matthew 15 who "came ... and worshipped him, saying, Lord, help me." Jesus commended her as having great faith when she said, "Truth, Lord: yet the dogs eat of the crumbs which fall from their masters' table." – Matt. 15:27.
- **Second, prayer is a covering.** Through prayer, we have access to the throne of God, who can help us. Prayer is not the end; instead, it brings us into contact with God. Sometimes we can think of Hebrews 4:16 (Let us therefore

come boldly unto the throne of grace, that we may obtain mercy, and find grace to help in time of need) as a sense of entitlement where it almost makes us arrogant. The picture is quite the opposite; the verse speaks of boldness as a child would have to his father without fear of condemnation but with confidence, being part of this love relationship without torment (Eph. 3:12, 17-19, 1 John 4:18). But it also has the effect of reverential fear, humility, and trembling before this great God whom we are privileged to call our heavenly Father. It speaks of mercy and grace, where the lost cannot enter into the holy of holies lest they be killed, but we who have been redeemed and washed in His blood are able to enter in knowing that we are accepted in Christ as His beloved. When Abraham was interceding for Sodom, his stance was one of humility when he said, "Behold now, I have taken upon me to speak unto the Lord, which am but dust and ashes:" – Gen. 18:27.

- **Third, prayer speaks of a relationship.** We read this paternal statement from our Beloved, "If ye then, being evil, know how to give good gifts unto your children, how much more shall your Father which is in heaven give good things to them that ask him?" – Matt. 7:11. The word "how much more" should cause us to pause and worship Him in adoration of a God who has given us such favors; favors to unlovable, undeserving, and wretched sinners, redeemed and called the children of God. And in enjoying and growing in this relationship, we also realize that God gives good things in His time and not as per our wants. We may desire something, thinking it is best, but God, who sees the end from the beginning, knows precisely when and how to give when we ask Him. Though God is "not willing that any should perish, but that all should come to repentance," the early church obeyed the Spirit when "the Spirit suffered them not" - Acts 16:7. Thus, we pray with Scriptural understanding to desire to know the mind of God, and the heart of God, where we can pray according to the will of God, so our prayers can be heard and answered.

- **Fourth, prayer is a cry.** There are areas that we are not privy to enter in knowing the depths that we can never attain as mortal flesh, but yet we are comforted to know that "Likewise the Spirit also helpeth our infirmities: for we know not what we should pray for as we ought: but the Spirit itself maketh intercession for us with groanings which cannot be uttered." – Rom. 8:26. It is a heart cry from the depth of our heart to the One who rules all things. Since repentance and faith are gifts from God, the fervent cry must be that the Spirit of God would not be grieved but use the word of God to have free course making effectual the truth of God to reveal the Person of Christ to the audience. And when such gifts are assured by the Spirit, the preacher, during the course of his sermon, can be moved by the Spirit to call sinners to "repent ye, and believe the gospel," knowing that the Spirit will illuminate their minds regarding the matter. He thunders with the authority of God "To day if ye will hear his voice, harden not your hearts" – Heb. 4:7. This makes prayer essential in the life of a church and God's people.

- **Fifth, prayer is a builder.** Through prayer, we grow in faith where God hears our cry and brings our gaze to behold Him and reveal to us a more profound knowledge of Himself (Heb. 12:2); through prayer, we learn the trustworthiness of God. In seasons of prayer with tears and searchings', we learn the heart of God. In prayer, there is the enjoyment of God. And through prayer, we desire Psalm 119:18 to "Open thou mine eyes, that I may behold wondrous things out of thy law."

- **Sixth, prayer is never satisfied.** Can a thirsty child be satisfied with a few drops of water? The Psalmist stated it well when he prayed, "As the hart panteth after the water brooks, so panteth my soul after thee, O God. My soul thirsteth for God, for the living God:" – Psa. 42:1-2.

Habakkuk learned the importance of resting in God in times of plenty or barrenness, where he was able to say, "Although the fig tree shall not blossom, neither shall fruit be in the vines; the labour of the olive shall fail, and the fields shall yield no meat; the flock shall be cut off from the fold, and there shall be no herd in the stalls: Yet I will rejoice in the Lord, I will joy in the God of my salvation." – Hab. 3:17-18.

- **Seven, prayer is a form of worship.** From the heart of prayer, we utter worship in secret to the God of heaven, who rewards us openly. It is the prayer of God's people from a pure heart, which is a sweet incense to the nostrils of God. "Who shall ascend into the hill of the Lord? or who shall stand in his holy place? He that hath clean hands, and a pure heart; who hath not lifted up his soul unto vanity, nor sworn deceitfully." – Psa. 24:3-4. As you are confronted with the greatness of God, you will come to grips with who He is and fall in adoration and worship towards Him before you bring your petitions before His throne.

- **Finally, prayer is a weapon.** We see that grand passage on the armor of God in Ephesians 6, where it ends after going through each of the weapons of the armor to fit it all together as it were with "Praying always with all prayer and supplication in the Spirit, and watching thereunto with all perseverance and supplication for all saints;" – Eph. 6:18. We see other instances of prayer such as; the storming of the throne of God, "the kingdom of heaven suffereth violence, and the violent take it by force." – Matt. 11:12; Jacob wrestling with God to be called Israel, "for as a prince hast thou power with God and with men, and hast prevailed." – Gen. 32:28; Moses interceding with God where God states, "Now therefore let me alone, that my wrath may wax hot against them, and that I may consume them: and I will make of thee a great nation." – Exo. 32:10. Abraham's intercessory request for Sodom to spare the city if there was found ten righteous in her (Gen. 18). There are glimpses in the Scriptures of the heavenly war that takes place when a saint kneels in prayer birthed in travail. It is spiritual warfare (Eph. 6:12). Though we may not see the physical breakthrough immediately, we still see the work of the knees moving through time and space and touching eternity. Why is prayer regarded as such strivings into heaven? It is not that God is not willing to answer; instead, it is because of the spiritual nature of it and the war in the heavens that we are up against (Matt. 17:21). Such was the case with Daniel. When Daniel prayed with mourning and fasting, it was immediately heard, "for from the first day that thou didst set thine heart to understand, and to chasten thyself before thy God, thy words were heard, and I am come for thy words." – Dan. 10:12. But the answer was hindered until God broke through, "But the prince of the kingdom of Persia withstood me one and twenty days: but, lo, Michael, one of the chief princes, came to help me; and I remained there with the kings of Persia. Now I am come to make thee understand what shall befall thy people in the latter days: for yet the vision is for many days." – Dan. 10:13-14. Such prayers move the hand of God to prevail against men, and David could testify that God prevailed like the breach of waters upon his enemies (2 Sam. 5:20).

Persevering in prayer has various pictures given from the Scriptural context. We can think of Jacob and the Angel, we can think of Hannah and her desperation for a man-child, we can think of Christ at Gethsemane "being in an agony he prayed more earnestly: and his sweat was as it were great drops of blood falling down to the ground" - Luke 22:44. Paul writing to the church at Galatia, "My little children, of whom I travail in birth again until Christ be formed in you" – Gal. 4:19. Such groans and utterances of prayer have the picture of persisting in prayer, one who has been impregnated with a great burden from the Lord. Costly prayers where there is no energy of the flesh to continue but moves into the realm of the Spirit until they break through. These return from their sacred striving with surety by the witness of the Spirit that the prayer has reached heaven, a faith to rise above unbelief and storm heaven (Matt. 11:12).

While we see all the blessings and the power of prayer, we realize that the communication method may vary. It could be groans, may have words, maybe tears, unutterable brokenness, etc. Such prayers are costly and not for the faint of heart. Prayer consumes us and pushes us to the place of prevailing with God until He comes. With such prayer comes the assurance by the Spirit and confidence of certainty that God will answer in the future for what we have prayed for. I am reminded of a certain historic revival, where during their seasons of prayer, they suddenly knew the previous night with the assurance that God was going to come the next day, and He did. And it is our privilege to burn out for God in getting to know God through prayer even if we need to walk halted upon our thigh for the rest of our lives (Gen. 32:31-32). In one sense, preaching is the culmination of the strength of prayer, prayers for God to work, the Spirit to be honored, His word to have free course, the lost awakened to their need, etc. The enduring result among the congregation should tell us of the effectiveness of what was prayed for.

John (Praying) Hyde was called the apostle of prayer. John Wilbur Chapman wrote to a friend about an encounter with Praying Hyde.

> I have learned some great lessons concerning prayer. At one of our missions in England, the audience was exceedingly small, but I received a note saying that an American missionary was going to beseech the Lord on behalf of our work. The man was known as Praying Hyde. Almost immediately, the tide changed. Crowds began to pack the hall, and many accepted Christ as their Saviour.

Meeting Mr. Hyde later, I said, "Brother, I want you to pray for me personally." He came to my room, turned the key in the door, and dropped to his knees. He waited five minutes without a single syllable coming from his lips. I felt hot tears as they began running down my face. Although he had said nothing, I knew I was in the presence of God. Then with upturned face and with eyes streaming, he said, "O God!" And was still again. When he seemed to sense that he was in full communion with the Lord, there came from the depths of his heart petitions such as I had never heard. I rose from my knees to know what real prayer was!

It was found by a medical doctor, during his final years on earth, that his heart had shifted from its natural position on the left side of his chest to a place over on the right. His travailing in prayer had taken its toll upon this man of God. Yes, God answers the prayer of faith of a little child, but God also wants us to grow and be partakers of meat and pray costly prayers that cost us something, our health, our livelihood, and our life itself, if need be. Americanized Christianity wants to retire with a fat salary and see how they can build their next mansion on earth, but God is looking for the blood of the martyrs, which is the seed of His church in this generation through apostles of prayer.

The Office of the Holy Spirit

At an age where the work of the blessed Spirit of God is undermined and pushed aside, there is a great need to ask the question, who is the Holy Spirit? This needs to be more than just a statement that He is the third Person of the Trinity and part of the Godhead. The Holy Spirit is a Person just as Jesus is a Person. Jesus, in robing Himself with humanity, was limited in being able to be in many places at once as the Son of man. The Spirit of God who has been given to indwell us brings us to that Person of Christ, being God Himself dwelling inside of us. Here are some characteristics of the Spirit of God. He is a Person (John 15:26), He is equal with God

(Matthew 28:19, 1 John 5:7), He is the Spirit of truth (John 16:13), He wrote the word of God (2 Peter 1:21), He is the Spirit of wisdom, understanding, counsel, might and knowledge (Exo. 31:3, Isa. 11:2, Dan. 5:14), He can be grieved (Gen. 6:3, Eph. 4:30, 1 Thess. 5:19), He was involved in Creation in the beginning (Gen. 1:2), He is sovereign in His ways (Acts 13:2, 16:6, 8:29), He draws people to the Person of Christ by Divine illumination, penetrating hearts (Matt. 16:17, John 6:44, 16:7-11, Acts 2:37), He is sovereign in His gifts (1 Cor. 12:4-11), He is sovereign in the fruits that He produces (Gal. 5:22-23), He convicts of sin (John 16:8), we can have His companionship (Gal. 5:16, 25), He endues (anoints) people with power (Judg. 6:34, 14:6, Isa. 61:1, Zech. 4:6, Matt. 3:11, Acts 2:4, 4:8, 31, 10:38, 13:9), God judges those who grieve Him (Isa. 63:10, Acts 5:1-11, 1 Cor. 3:16-17), blasphemy of Him is the unpardonable sin (Matt. 12:31-32), He uses and empowers the word (1 Cor. 2:4, 3:6, 4:20, 1 Thess. 1:5, Eph. 6:17), He produces faith (Rom. 10:17, Gal. 3:2-3), He leads us in intercession (Rom. 8:26), He bears witness of our sonship (Rom. 8:16, 1 John 5:6).

Though much more can be said and has been discussed earlier, the need to reiterate the importance of certain offices exclusive to the blessed Spirit of God arises again. It was the Spirit who directed that early church, "As they ministered to the Lord, and fasted, the Holy Ghost said, Separate me Barnabas and Saul for the work whereunto I have called them." – Acts 13:2, it was the Spirit that forbade them from preaching the gospel in certain areas, "Now when they had gone throughout Phrygia and the region of Galatia, and were forbidden of the Holy Ghost to preach the word in Asia" – Acts 16:6, while at times He gave specific instructions, "Then the Spirit said unto Philip, Go near, and join thyself to this chariot." – Acts 8:29, for the gospel to go into Africa. It is the blasphemy of the Holy Ghost that Jesus stated as the unpardonable sin (Matt. 12:32), and the sinning against Him caused the death of Ananias and Saphira in final judgment (Acts 5). In the life of Christ, one can see the event after Christ's baptism, "And immediately the Spirit driveth him into the wilderness." – Mark 1:12. We see a similar

IF MY PEOPLE

event in the early life of Samson "And the Spirit of the Lord began to move him at times in the camp of Dan between Zorah and Eshtaol." – Judg. 13:25. "When the enemy shall come in like a flood, the Spirit of the Lord shall lift up a standard against him." – Isa. 59:19.

In the context of His work and office, Americanized Christianity has the wrong starting point; it comes from the premise that a lost man in himself has the ability to see their need if he can be convinced and can be moved to make a decision for Christ. But God declares, "The Lord looked down from heaven upon the children of men, to see if there were any that did understand, and seek God. They are all gone aside, they are all together become filthy: there is none that doeth good, no, not one." – Psa. 14:2-3; The lost seek after "a god" but not "the God," for he will gladly have a golden calf rather than the living God to fill their void. God declares, "But the natural man receiveth not the things of the Spirit of God: for they are foolishness unto him: neither can he know them, because they are spiritually discerned." – 1 Cor. 2:14; God declares to be saved as "With men it is impossible, but not with God: for with God all things are possible." – Mark 10:27. Impossible since man does not have the capacity in himself to work up faith to believe; God declares that he has to be awakened to his need because he is dead, "And you, being dead in your sins and the uncircumcision of your flesh, hath he quickened together with him, having forgiven you all trespasses" – Col. 2:13; God declares that the Holy Spirit has to operate to open his blinded eyes because "In whom the god of this world hath blinded the minds of them which believe not, lest the light of the glorious gospel of Christ, who is the image of God, should shine unto them." – 2 Cor. 4:4, only then and after then is where the command is to be made to repent and believe the gospel. We can have light by the word of God (Psa. 119:105, 130), but it will be as a philosophy of man or even something helpful in its application. But when the Spirit opens the eyes and gives understanding, then the reality of what is said is seen. Immediately, you are ushered into the supernatural where the truth becomes that

226

life that you can partake of (1 Cor. 2:4-5, 1 Thess. 1:5). This was what Paul stated as his commission from God, "To open their eyes, and to turn them from darkness to light, and from the power of Satan unto God, that they may receive forgiveness of sins, and inheritance among them which are sanctified by faith that is in me." – Acts 26:18. And this would not be by the eloquence or ability of the apostle Paul who stated, "And my speech and my preaching was not with enticing words of man's wisdom, but in demonstration of the Spirit and of power: That your faith should not stand in the wisdom of men, but in the power of God." – 1 Cor. 2:4-5.

A vital prayer would be that the Holy Spirit would not be grieved to work in our midst, and we deal with sin and put things away that will hinder Him, and desire Him to come and give the gift of repentance and faith to those who are blinded by sin. To summarize this, we must realize that the preparation and preaching of a sermon comprise many dimensions and are executed by various offices that God has ordained.

- The truth of the letter as light is one dimension *(Scriptures)*. "The entrance of thy words giveth light; it giveth understanding unto the simple." – Psa. 119:130
- The preparation of the truth by the preacher is another dimension *(prayer, word, Spirit, discerning the heart of Christ)*. "Study to shew thyself approved unto God, a workman that needeth not to be ashamed, rightly dividing the word of truth." – 2 Tim. 2:15. "Howbeit when he, the Spirit of truth, is come, he will guide you into all truth: for he shall not speak of himself; but whatsoever he shall hear, that shall he speak: and he will shew you things to come." – John 16:13
- The word coming in power where it is made alive in effectual calling is another dimension *(Spirit)*. "For our gospel came not unto you in word only, but also in power, and in the Holy Ghost, and in much assurance; as ye know what manner of men we were among you for your sake." – 1 Thess. 1:5

- The hearer given sight is another dimension *(Spirit)*. "Finally, brethren, pray for us, that the word of the Lord may have free course, and be glorified, even as it is with you:" - 2 Thess. 3:1
- The hearer receiving understanding is another dimension *(Spirit)*. "John answered and said, A man can receive nothing, except it be given him from heaven." – John 3:27
- Godly sorrow to repentance is another dimension *(Spirit)*. "And when he is come, he will reprove the world of sin, and of righteousness, and of judgment:" – John 16:8, "In meekness instructing those that oppose themselves; if God peradventure will give them repentance to the acknowledging of the truth;" - 2 Tim. 2:25
- Faith given to believe is another dimension *(Spirit)*. "Jesus answered and said unto them, This is the work of God, that ye believe on him whom he hath sent." – John 6:29
- Christ being made all the more lovely is another dimension *(Spirit)*. Jesus said, "No man can come to me, except the Father which hath sent me draw him: and I will raise him up at the last day." – John 6:44, "But it is good for me to draw near to God" – Psa. 73:28.
- A new heart given in regeneration is another dimension *(Spirit)*. "A new heart also will I give you, and a new spirit will I put within you: and I will take away the stony heart out of your flesh, and I will give you an heart of flesh." – Eze. 36:26
- The will of man that moves in obedience is the natural outflow of the new heart *(hearer)*. "Even so faith, if it hath not works, is dead, being alone." – James 2:17

In all this, we start seeing **the need for holy supplication for the Spirit to come and work in our midst**, knowing that "All is vain unless the Spirit of the Holy One comes down;" (George Askins). Preaching is laying your all on the altar, seeing God's fire consume you, and hearing God speak, by the Spirit through the word, to those who hear where it moves them to where God is. Not the power of words but the power of God.

While a general call of the gospel is there to all who believe, the effectual working will show itself on those who have godly sorrow to repentance to salvation (2 Cor. 7:10). **And convincing by the witness of the word to the conscience must be followed by the witness of the Spirit to its truth** (1 Thess. 1:5) and ignoring that would be plucking unripe fruits (Matt. 23:15). It is not our ability to convince that matters, instead it is for God's office to convict. Only the Holy Ghost can do that. Some may question this, but what are the fruits of these "decisions" that multitudes have made for salvation without getting to the Person of salvation? Yes, there are a few, blessed by God to open their blinded eyes, who saw their need and came under conviction and are, by the drawing of the Spirit, regenerated, but what about the majority multitude who have become proselytes and will die and go to hell because we have moved them to mental assent. Christianity in the past gave hope. A mother who had an abusive husband, after conversion, has one who is sober and loving, and children who did not have a bite to eat for weeks now have their table filled with food instead of their dad wasting it on drink and pleasure. But today, we see broken homes because the parents claimed to have "made a decision" but lived like the devil and split homes and hell wide open. They have believed and been baptized but are still "in the gall of bitterness, and in the bond of iniquity." – Acts 8:23. I am convinced that we are producing more lost people who think they are going to heaven than lost people who know they are going to hell. I am grieved by the ruin that superficial fundamentalism leaves in its path.

I am afraid we have excluded the Spirit long enough that He has left us where God is fighting against us (Isa. 63:10), and we are given over to our own devices. Everywhere I turn, it is instruction, instruction, instruction, but where is life? where is the conviction of sin that the sinner comes in tears and brokenness before God? where is the manifest presence of God where the people are visibly moved to silence as they gaze upon Him, where a Spirit of holiness descends upon the congregation? **Everything we have in our services is geared to exclude Him**, our invitations that are pre-canned to get the best results or "decisions," our scheduled "revival" meetings, our sinner's prayer, our decision cards, our assurance based on the word of God and not needing the inward witness of the Spirit, Bible colleges teaching their students on how to get your point across using whatever human methods possible instead of treading into sacred depths such as travailing in prayer, weeping, fasting, companionship with the Spirit and so forth. We added so many frills to the gospel with the sinners' prayer, Roman's road, altar calls, and such that the essence of the gospel and what it is supposed to do is lost in the weeds. Why do we need the Holy Spirit? I see no reason why He should be needed from what is being propagated and followed in practice. You can take a ministry that's been preaching from the Bible for decades and be dead and cold. Such was that Laodicean church. You can take the message by that Puritan Jonathan Edwards, Sinners in the hands of an angry God, and read it or preach it, but you won't get the same results where men are holding on to the pews and crying to God for mercy; why? Because there's a missing element, He is called the Holy Spirit. They realized that they needed not only the word but also life, which can be given only by the Holy Spirit to the word. Without the Spirit, the word becomes just an opinion. And your college degree is not going to help you with that. Sometimes I've sat in meetings grieved, in essence, "waiting for the Holy Spirit to be honored." **When is He honored?** When we put down our flesh or any displays of it in our services; when more seek him in prayer before the service than after the service; when we emphasize holiness rather than make way for sinfulness; when we desire God for Himself rather than what He can give; when we long after God more than heaven itself; when we desire obscurity rather than to be known of men. Fire is the most attractive element we see in the natural world, and when we lose the fire of God, we have to attract the lost with what the world finds attractive, shaving cream, magic tricks, and theatricals. I am not against people reaching out in God-honoring ways, but if we desire to bring prominence to worldly methods and substitute the hard work of prayer, preaching the reproach of the gospel, and persevering in the Spirit, then that speaks of the bankruptcy of the church.

Irrespective of the camp that one belonged to historically, in the time of the evangelical revival and other times, it was understood by Arminians and Calvinists that regeneration was an operation of the Holy Ghost and not just based on a person's understanding of the word alone. **The epicenter of all true religious experiences of being born of God is the transaction of sinfulness to holiness in their innermost being. From such a transaction comes the desire to live a holy life.** Those in the past who believed and preached in the power of the Spirit by implication of the Spirit's work affected the heart since only He can go beyond the mind and into the heart. But to preach while ignoring the office of the Holy Spirit will only affect the mind and never penetrate the heart, producing an intellectual proselyte. It will give them a factual Christ but not the living One. The great challenge for the Arminian is to realize the role of the Spirit, and just as much to the Calvinist to obey the command to go ye into all the world to preach the gospel, calling to repent and believe the gospel, with the Spirit being the center of our actions, not in word only but in demonstration of His power (1 Cor. 2:4).

While there have been excesses by those who have claimed works of the "Spirit" and have caused many to go astray, our responsibility is to try the spirits and not be fearful of what God intended for His church (1 John 4:1). John Owen stated, "The sin of the Old Testament was against the Father, the sin of the New Testament was against His Son, and the sin of the church today is against His Holy Spirit." Dear brethren, Is not this the greatest need of our day? We have the most resources ever available to the Christian church, but we are the most bankrupt in power; we have countless preaching from many sources until they come out of our nostrils, but our pulpits are powerless with no authority; we have services but no ability to make an impact in the community; we have special efforts but no sustaining movements of God that build faith, leaving a lasting impression of God in our midst; we have our denominations, but we are unable to stop the tide of sin that is sweeping our land, or the course of our young people to forsake the God of their youth. What was done in secret is now done openly and celebrated as good! The laws of the land that are passed which promote great wickedness do not show the strength of darkness; instead, it shows the absence of light. We have the world, the flesh, and the devil chopping up the church, where the victorious Christian living is seen as a farce. And singing we serve the God of the impossible is not going to cut it. What we need is this power, and we can't work it up because "power belongeth unto God" – Psa. 62:11. We must be honest to recognize our lack and pray for the need that the **Spirit can only meet**. We need...

- **Conviction of sin:** Those during preaching suddenly awakened and made aware of their awful standing before God, bowed down and crying out for mercy, those backslidden becoming aware of their wickedness and prostrating themselves in humility and submission, being overcome by the fear of God. We have not seen such scenes, which have been common in historic revivals; we can pray for that. (1 Chr. 13:12, Job 40:4-5, Luke 3:10, 12, 14, Acts 2:37, 16:30-31)
- **The manifest presence of Christ:** Being overcome with fear like Jacob, a terror of realizing the implication of the holiness of God, being afraid of approaching God with unclean hands, filled with groans and shouts of joy in enraptured worship and a spirit of stillness that pervades the congregation. We have not seen such moving of God; we can pray for that. (Gen. 28:16-17, 1 Kings 19:11-13, Isa. 6:1-5, Luke 5:8, Rev. 1:17)
- **Spirit of repentance:** The sinner who sees the greatness of his sin having the spirit of godly sorrow that leadeth to repentance, those who have played the prodigal forsaking

their idols and coming as one unworthy to be called a servant let alone a son, cries of woe is me, I am undone. We have not seen such deep work of the Spirit; we can pray for that. (Acts 19:18-19, 2 Cor. 7:10, 2 Thess. 3:1)

- **The genuine act of regeneration:** Those who have moved from death unto life knowing their standing in Christ by their testimony of the witness of the Spirit in their hearts, those who can cry out "Abba, Father" in seeing their lives instantly transformed and strongholds broken knowing they are made one with the Creator and adopted into the family of God. We have not seen such scenes of hordes of sinners swept into the kingdom of God without altar calls or coaxing with sentimental songs and such; we can pray for that. (Mark 5:15, Acts 2:41-47, 4:4)

- **Heaven-sent revival:** Whole communities affected by God in the midst of His people, those in mockery saying, "Where is their God?" are silenced as they are made aware of the reality of the living God, scenes of the terror of the Lord and the great grace and witnessing power that is given, similar to what was experienced in the book of Acts, God making bare His arm and His enemies are scattered. We have only read of such moving of God in the past and have not seen that in our generation; we can pray for that (Psa. 68:1, Isa. 64:1, Acts 4:31-33, 5:1-11, 19:20). *Sidenote:* While the term "revival" has been often used and abused, we realize that it is to signify the work of God in relation to "an outpouring" that affects large communities and nations. There are various ways of God that we see that have a more subdued effect and affect a smaller group of people or individuals, such as "stirrings" and "times of refreshing," which are unique in themselves and can (at times) flow into rivers of revival into a community and affect nations.

- **Intercession:** We saw earlier of the office given to the Spirit to bear witness of who Christ is and guide us into truth (John 16:13). We see Moses standing upon the mount when Israel was fighting Amalek, the picture of Aaron and Hur holding up his hands, and what happened in Moses's hands being lifted or being let down, showed by Israel winning or losing the battle. Similarly, for people to be convinced of the truth that if we don't pray, it will not be the same in the services where we are made to see the desperate value that prayer has. The Spirit's role in teaching us to pray (persistence and prevailing in prayer) and the danger of the lack of it — seeing prayer as the lifeblood of a church. We need His intercession, for we know not what we should pray for as we ought. We have not understood terms such as, "for as a prince hast thou power with God and with men, and hast prevailed." – Gen. 32:28, "the kingdom of heaven suffereth violence, and the violent take it by force." – Matt. 11:12; we can pray for that. (Exo. 17:8-16, Matt. 21:13, John 16:13, Rom. 8:26, James 4:2, 5:17)

- **God of the word:** There is a grave danger when we substitute the Person of Christ (the essential Word in John 1:1, the Lord Jesus Christ) for the words of Christ (the written word of God). The word of God is to point us to the Person of Christ and is not meant to be an end in itself. Anything can unintentionally become an idol. Prayer, Bible reading, ministry, etc., were given as a means to commune with God, who is personal, but we can focus on the means of grace (that we can see) and forget the God who gave it (whom we don't see). He becomes impersonal, just someone who excites our thought life. Jesus said, "And I, if I be lifted up from the earth, will draw all men unto me" – John 12:32. And only the Spirit can bring us to that Person in all His beauty. Even in the matter of salvation, I am concerned that we have focused on the superficial with an intellectual agreement to truth, holding to a passage of Scriptures and decisions rather than the Person of Christ being revealed in supernatural illumination (Matt. 16:17). The word of God is able to make us wise unto salvation (2 Tim. 3:15), but it is not salvation for salvation is a Person (Luke 2:28-32, John 10:9). He did not point to the door of eternal life; He is that door (John 10:9). He did not come to bring us manna from heaven; He is that heavenly food that we partake of and receive life from His death (John 6:53-58). A picture that ought to be remembered in our communion services (Luke 22:19-20, 1 Cor. 11:24-26). The law is a schoolmaster (Gal. 3:24-25), which brings us to Christ, with Christ being the essential Word to whom we are pointed by the written word. The essential Word was always there, having no beginning nor end, even when there was no written word. The ark of the covenant in 1 Samuel 4 did not help the Israelites in battle because God was not in their midst though the ark had the word of God and other artifacts in it. The word of God without the Spirit of God cannot regenerate anyone. The word of God can only have free course to break hardened hearts by the aul of the Spirit; to have that high view of God. We can pray for that. (Eze. 36:26, Matt. 16:17, John 3:8, Acts 2:37, Eph. 6:12, 2 Thess. 3:1)

"Without me ye can do nothing" - John 15:5. This matter of abiding in Christ is not just about depending upon God by praying, being truthful to the word of God, living holy lives, and trying to yield to the Spirit, etc. We can do all that and still not see God's power manifested in our midst. While we do need to be fully convinced of the reality of those truths and do them, there's one more element that is needed. It is desiring the Person of Christ Himself to be there by the power of the Holy Spirit.

Abiding in Christ

What does it mean to pray without ceasing and to nurture and cultivate God's presence? In the realm of the spiritual, we should look at the Christian life as lived on two parallel streams. The one stream is where the interaction with the world, the daily duties of life, the enjoyment of God's blessings, the place of spiritual warfare, and such take place. The other stream is to create a hidden cloister in the inner man who is completely isolated from the other. This hidden sanctum is to be in constant communion with Christ, praying without ceasing, abiding in Christ by leaning on His breast, given to gazing on Him, and attentive to His voice. The great longing in this parallel stream is that God would always have an unhindered abode (John 14:23) so that, "he would grant you, according to the riches of his glory, to be strengthened with might by his Spirit in the inner man" - Eph. 3:16. This is the place where we can experientially know the depth, height, and breadth of the love of God (v17-19). This parallel stream only has access from the inside to the outside stream and not the other way around.

Abiding is a continual resting (loving heart-surrender) in what is already true of our position, that we have been engrafted into the Vine by God, He is the Husbandman, faithful is He that calleth who also will do it, and nothing can separate us from the love of God. In reckoning such truths, we rest on His ability to feed us as we yield our will, desire, and life to Him daily, to realize His strength in replacing our weaknesses; our champion of the Cross who routed His enemies and made a shew of them openly (Col. 2:14-15).

Jesus never lost communion with His heavenly Father though he was busy meeting the needs of the people. His example shows us the way for needing to compartmentalize our lives into this inner sanctum which is in constant pull towards God. The branch that realizes it utter impotency to sustain life of its own is in the proper place to realize the need it has to abide in the Vine so nourishment can flow from the Vine to the branches. Jesus said, "I am the vine, ye are the branches: He that abideth in me, and I in him, the same bringeth forth much fruit: for without me ye can do nothing." – John 15:5. Even in the picture of a branch we have the innermost spongy tissue called the pith which is fragile but is crucial for storing and transporting the nutrients that flow from the roots to the branches. Our inner sanctum must be guarded at all costs and anything that hinders must be put away. Only the blessed Spirit of God can shine the light of truth inward so we can confess, forsake, and receive cleansing, keeping the channel free from sin. "Faithful is he that calleth you, who also will do it." – 1 Thess. 5:24. While the enduement of power is external, for service, abiding in Christ is internal, intimacy with Christ. It is the ability to have an unbroken fellowship with God.

Hear Hudson Taylor as he shares regarding abiding in Christ in a letter to his sister, "But how to get faith strengthened? Not by striving after faith, but by resting on the Faithful One. As I read I saw it all! 'If we believe not, He abideth faithful.' I looked to Jesus and saw (and when I saw, oh, how joy flowed!) that He had said, 'I will never leave you.' 'Ah, there is rest!' I thought. I have striven in vain to rest in Him. I'll strive no more."

There is much more that can be said regarding this but something for us to consider; It is not that God cannot reach the lost without us or find His fulfillment in his creation through the lives of those whom He has redeemed, being self-sufficient he has no lack and He is in need of nothing. Rather, He has made a willing restraint to find enjoyment through us for the glory of His Father, and this is fulfilled by abiding in Him. What a glorious Christ, may we in worship adore Him and in humility live in light of such love. "As the Father hath loved me, so have I loved you: continue ye in my love." - John 15:9.

Evangelism

The danger of realizing the truths of such far-reaching consequences can bring us to a place of sterility where we can have a skewed view of God's sovereignty and man's responsibility, which can paralyze us in either direction. While diving deep into the riches of the word of God, we must come to the place regarding the souls of men that God's sovereignty is God's business, but we are given truths upon truths of our responsibility in this matter, which we ought to obey. "And he [Jesus] said unto them, Go ye into all the world, and preach the gospel to every creature." – Mark 16:15

(emphasis mine), "And of some have compassion, making a difference: And others save with fear, pulling them out of the fire; hating even the garment spotted by the flesh." – Jude 1:22-23, "And the Spirit and the bride say, Come. And let him that heareth say, Come. And let him that is athirst come. And whosoever will, let him take the water of life freely." – Rev. 22:17. The spontaneous response of the woman who met Christ at the well "left her waterpot, and went her way into the city, and saith to the men, Come, see a man, which told me all things that ever I did: is not this the Christ?" – John 4:28-29.

The hymn, **Jesus! what a Friend for sinners,** by **J. Wilbur Chapman,** speaks of the heart of Christ for the lost and His sustaining grace through life itself.

> Jesus! what a friend for sinners!
> Jesus! Lover of my soul;
> Friends may fail me, foes assail me,
> He, my Saviour, makes me whole.
>
> > *Refrain:*
> > Hallelujah! what a Saviour!
> > Hallelujah! what a friend!
> > Saving, helping, keeping, loving,
> > He is with me to the end.
>
> Jesus! what a strength in weakness!
> Let me hide myself in Him;
> Tempted, tried, and sometimes failing,
> He, my Strength, my vict'ry wins.
>
> Jesus! what a help in sorrow!
> While the billows o'er me roll,
> Even when my heart is breaking,
> He, my comfort, helps my soul.

Jesus! what a guide and keeper!
While the tempest still is high,
Storms about me, night o'ertakes me,
He, my pilot, hears my cry

Jesus! I do now receive Him,
More than all in Him I find;
He hath granted me forgiveness,
I am His, and He is mine.

public domain

We see the example of the apostle Paul, who traveled great distances and gives us a glimpse of his labors to spread the gospel to every creature, "in labours more abundant, in stripes above measure, in prisons more frequent, in deaths oft. Of the Jews five times received I forty stripes save one. Thrice was I beaten with rods, once was I stoned, thrice I suffered shipwreck, a night and a day I have been in the deep; In journeyings often, in perils of waters, in perils of robbers, in perils by mine own countrymen, in perils by the heathen, in perils in the city, in perils in the wilderness, in perils in the sea, in perils among false brethren; In weariness and painfulness, in watchings often, in hunger and thirst, in fastings often, in cold and nakedness. Beside those things that are without, that which cometh upon me daily, the care of all the churches." – 2 Cor. 11:23-28. We see his great burden for Israel to the point of wishing himself accursed if that would be profitable for the saving of their souls (Rom. 9:1-3) and goes on to state, "Brethren, my heart's desire and prayer to God for Israel is, that they might be saved." – Rom. 10:1. If we claim to be filled with the Spirit of God, we would be weeping, fasting, and in tears burdened about lost souls and their eternal damnation, to go into the highways and hedges compelling them to come in (Luke 14:23) for they are white already unto harvest (John 4:35) while praying for more laborers (Matt. 9:37-38). To do what we can while applying the truths already mentioned to pull those out of the fire. The reality of the danger the sinner is in compels us to preach to flee from the wrath that is come.

The response of the sinner who's awakened and rejects God and thus condemns himself to damnation should cause us to shudder for the responsibility of man and call men everywhere to repent (Acts 17:30). The urgency that tomorrow may not be theirs should have us cry out, "To day if ye will hear his voice, harden not your hearts" – Heb. 4:7, and "behold, now is the accepted time; behold, now is the day of salvation" - 2 Cor. 6:2. In all this, it hinges on the Spirit and the word to awaken the sinner by the prayer, pleading, and travail of those who proclaim. True evangelism springs from the heart that has been broken before God, one that has been touched with the fire from the altar, to go to a lost world, to fall into the ground and die (Isa. 6:6-8, John 12:24-26). And the dependence is on God and not on the outcome and response of man. We plead knowing God's heart that He "is longsuffering to us-ward, not willing that any should perish, but that all should come to repentance." - 2 Peter 3:9.

When we think about the vessels God used, we are reminded of the ways that God has used women in the past for the propagation of the gospel. Though some may question them, they have still been in accordance with Scripture, such as 1 Corinthians 14:34-35 and 1 Timothy 2:11-12. God forbids women to teach from the perspective of usurping authority over the man or by preaching to bring men into subjection under their influence. In the context of what God gave, it has been misused by men and abused by women. While women are not called to be Pastors, as in leading the flock, God has used them in marvelous ways for propagating the gospel. They sang like Annie Davies in the Welsh Revival, shared testimonies and saw the gospel go forward like Mary Peckham, prayed like Peggy and Christine Smith in the Hebrides Revival, displayed undaunted strength like Ann for her husband Adoniram Judson, who were missionaries to Burma, taught children in raising them for the glory of God like Susanna Wesley, and many others. These had a common thread of holiness, humility, and submission in desiring God to work through them, not to be leaders over men but to be willing servants for Christ. We fondly remember missionaries such as Amy Carmichael, Corrie ten Boom, and Gladys Aylward; and those whom God used during the early years of the Salvation Army; or like Aquila and his wife Priscilla, who took Apollos and expounded unto him the way of God more perfectly (Acts 18:26). In all this there is no controversy.

All who were filled with the Spirit of God were great soul-winners. Not just getting numbers by counting "decisions," but seeing the sinner born anew in the work of regeneration and displaying it by a changed life. You can think of the early church, missionary movements like the Moravians, or ordinary men and women whom God has used, such as Samuel Chadwick, Amy Carmichael, Charles Haddon Spurgeon, D. L. Moody, Dr. Martyn Lloyd-Jones, David Brainerd, R. A. Torrey, General William Booth, Asahel Nettleton, and a multitude of others; they had an urgency in the pulpit or in their area of ministry to preach the gospel, for the sinner to repent and come to saving faith in Jesus Christ, relying on God to do the work that He promised to do. Think about Robert Murray M'Cheyne. James A. Stewart states, "He was a human skeleton when he died at about twenty-nine years of age. He wept in the vestry before he ever went to his pulpit. Hardly a morning and hardly an evening would pass that he did not break down in weeping, weeping over lost souls going to hell and over the poor spiritual condition of his congregation." He was not looking to his retirement fund but burned bright for His Savior and lit other hearts on fire even until this day. Here is the soul-yearning cry of David Brainerd, "Oh that I were a flaming fire in the service of my God."

The foundation of evangelism is God. When Jesus said for His disciples to tarry (Acts 1:4-5), He knew that just the facts of Christ were not enough; they were with Jesus for over three years, they learned the word from the Word, they saw lepers made whole, they saw His transfiguration, they saw the crucifixion, they witnessed His resurrection. They had been given the Holy Ghost prior, but still, it was not enough; they had to endued with power from on high. We must fully embrace the truth that without Him, this enduement of power, we can accomplish nothing of eternal value. Not our programs, not our four steps to salvation, not our sinner's prayer, and such. In asking for the old paths, we must realize that we must exalt Christ. The gospel is not primarily for man's betterment but for God's glory. To have a proper burden for evangelism, we must come to the place that the problem of man is not that he will be sent to hell; **the problem with man is that he has to face the holiness of God one day in its full force with the nakedness of sin upon him** and be cast into hell. The premise that heaven is the goal of the gospel is misrepresenting Christ. It is the reality of God and man's nature, repentance, salvation from sin, submission to Christ, and seeing the changed life that is promised; these must be at our forefront. We must put away all views that bring the gospel to the happiness of man, which is a fringe benefit and not the primary end. Presenting the goodness of God and how we have responded in rebellion to this good God, our present deplorable condition in utter depravity must be foundational in evangelism.

Two people fled the City of Destruction in Bunyan's Pilgrim's Progress. We see Christian and Pliable. Christian has that large burden on his back while Pliable goes along for the ride and continues for a while because of the hope of a "desirable place." When like the seed on stony ground and affliction came in the Slough of Despond, Pliable turned back and returned to the City of Destruction. He was never convicted of sin to desire to be rid of it. He showed no sorrow for sin. We have many who come to Christ for going to heaven but have never been burdened by their sin or desire to repent from it but are given the false hope that they can take Christ to go to heaven while having never felt the weight of their sin on their back. We sing "my burden of sin is gone," but have they felt it as a burden on their back in the first place?

Seeing one profess faith must be followed up with how their lives reflect it, in seeing its lack, to kindly guide them and seek the Lord until He is found instead of giving a false peace and assurance that will not stand the test of time and eternity. This numbering of decisions, coercing the audience with sad songs, can elevate man where the Spirit can be grieved and quenched. Pleading with people must be from the perspective of the danger they are in as an enemy of God, their trampling on the blood of Christ of this good God, and echo God's call of "I have no pleasure in the death of the wicked; but that the wicked turn from his way and live" – Eze. 33:11, instead of portraying an impotent God who yearns after their favor. Oswald Chambers stated, "There is nothing attractive about the gospel to the natural man; the only man who finds the gospel attractive is the man who is convicted of sin." If we are preaching a gospel that the world finds attractive, then the offense of the cross has been removed. "But we preach Christ crucified, unto the Jews a stumblingblock, and unto the Greeks foolishness; But unto them which are called, both Jews and Greeks, Christ the power of God, and the wisdom of God." – 1 Cor. 1:23-24.

There is a grave danger in taking incidentals that God has used in times of revival and assigning value to them for every generation. We see the time when Moses raised the serpent of brass for the people to look upon it and live (Num. 21). But we see in 2 Kings 18 where Hezekiah had to destroy the same brasen serpent that Moses had made, for Israel sinned against God and offered incense to it. Such is the darkness of man's heart. While there may have been incidental times when the term "decisions" may have been used in a real sense of that term, which is **a spontaneous response to God's call from the affected heart**, there is always the temptation to follow the method or terminology for convenience's sake. "My sheep hear my voice," and the decision or spontaneous response is "they follow me" (John 10:27). When Saul fell to the earth and heard, "I am Jesus whom thou persecutest," the spontaneous response was, "Lord, what wilt thou have me to do?" (Acts 9:1-6). And any incidental usage of terms carried to another generation must be rejected and thought through for every generation. As with Lazarus, we who have been made alive remove

243

the stone, which is a hindrance, through prayer where the voice of God can be heard by the dead. And once resurrected by God, the responsibility of the church is to remove, as it were, the grave clothes under the guidance of the Spirit. God has given the church many means of grace for helping with this, prayer, preaching, Scriptures, Lord's supper, the believer's baptism, attending worship, giving, trials, tears, and such for maturing the believer to fully embrace his union with Christ. While many of these means of grace apply to one's personal devotional life, corporate growth in a church that is aflame can truly be a beacon of hope for those living in darkness and for the nourishment of the believer to bring him or her to maturity from desiring the sincere milk of the word (1 Pet. 2:1-3) to desiring the meat of the word (Heb. 5:12, 6:1-2).

Discipleship

One of the areas where we have a great need is the matter of discipling a new believer. This, I realize, is hard work, but Jesus said, "Go ye therefore, and teach all nations, baptizing them in the name of the Father, and of the Son, and of the Holy Ghost: Teaching them to observe all things whatsoever I have commanded you: and, lo, I am with you always, even unto the end of the world. Amen." – Matt. 28:19-20. We realize that this teaching is not only in a corporate setting of a church service but also in one-on-one to build up those who are young in the faith. To help them partake of the riches of Christ, in a personal way, by investing in their spiritual growth and having accountability for their lives before God and before man. While God does the saving and keeping, we also see that God holds man accountable for the new life he has been given, just as Israel was required in their accountability towards God, who brought them with a strong arm from the clutches of Egypt and nurtured them and carried them through, all the days of old. "I will mention the lovingkindnesses of the LORD, and the praises of the LORD, according to all that the LORD hath bestowed on us, and the great goodness toward the house of Israel, which he hath bestowed on them according to his mercies, and according to the multitude of his lovingkindnesses. For he said, Surely they are my people, children that will not lie: so he was their Saviour. In all their affliction he was afflicted, and the angel of his presence saved them: in his love and in his pity he redeemed them; and he bare them, and carried them all the days of old. But they rebelled, and vexed his holy Spirit: therefore he was turned to be their enemy, and he fought against them." – Isa. 63:7-10. We know that salvation is by grace alone, through faith alone, in Christ alone, for the glory of God alone; we also realize that those born of God will show by their lives the characteristics of their new nature and are called to obedience. "That ye may be blameless and harmless, the sons of God, without rebuke, in the midst of a crooked and perverse nation, among whom ye shine as lights in the world" – Phili. 2:15. In Ephesians 4, after speaking of the renewed mind in verse 23, we come to the next verse, which states what the nature of the new man is, "the new man, which after God is created in righteousness and true holiness" (v24). The outflow of the new man will be from what he was created on the inside; righteousness and holiness.

In living the Christian life, faith is one of the agents that is often mentioned. Verses such as, "without faith it is impossible to please him" – Heb. 11:6, the grand hall of faith in Hebrews chapter 11, "building up yourselves on your most holy faith" – Jude 1:20, and a host of others. Jesus spoke of the faith as a mustard seed. "And the Lord said, If ye had faith as a grain of mustard seed, ye might say unto this sycamine tree, Be thou plucked up by the root, and be thou planted in the sea; and it should obey you." – Luke 17:6. When considering the magnitude of this statement and the statement of moving mountains (Matt. 17:20) they seem almost an impossibility of having such faith. But realizing that faith is a gift of the Spirit (1 Cor. 12:8-10) and a fruit of the Spirit (Gal. 5:22-23) causes us to realize that it is not what we can work up ourselves but rather the Spirit-filled life which can enable us to have faith that will ask according to the will of the Father and see God move in ways that would be impossible for us to do. Thus, living by faith is the work of God in the obedient man (Gal. 3:3, Rom. 10:17, 2 Peter 1:4-7).

This work by the Spirit can be accomplished when we, One, Remove the hindrances (Matt. 13:58, 1 Thess. 5:19, Eph. 4:30). Second, Study His word with the intent of pursuing God (Rom. 10:17, 2 Tim. 3:16-17). Third, Desire His mind and His way (abide in him, John 14:23, 15:5, Phili. 2:5-8, Jude 1:20). Four, Obey the Spirit (1 Peter 1:22, Heb. 12:2, 2 Peter 1:4-7). By doing such, we will "Walk in the Spirit, and ye shall not fulfil the lust of the flesh." – Gal. 5:16, through the Spirit be able to mortify the deeds of the flesh (Rom. 8:13, 1 Cor. 9:27), and "grow in grace, and in the knowledge of our Lord and Saviour Jesus Christ." - 2 Peter 3:18. Progress will be made when we live the exchanged life, in light of this, which we saw earlier. And such faith will produce substance where it will be proven by the outcome of what it does. By having a proper view of God, removing the hindrances, and walking in the Spirit, we can begin to cultivate the presence of God.

In all this, we see God's part in persevering us to the end. Still, we also see with equal force the responsibility of man *(the new man who has been redeemed by the blood of the Lamb)* that is often forgotten or overlooked in Americanized Christianity.

- **God's part (Sovereignty of God):** Able to keep you (Acts 15:11, Jude 1:24-25, Rom. 8:38-39, Phili. 1:6, 2:13, Heb. 4:14-16, 12:6-8), cannot be plucked (John 6:37, 10:27-29), calleth will also do it (1 Thess. 5:24).
- **Our part (Responsibility of man):** Stand fast (1 Cor. 16:13, Gal. 5:1, Phili. 1:27, 29, 4:1, 1 Thess. 3:8), hold fast (Heb. 3:6, 14, 4:14, Rev. 2:10, 25, 3:11), endureth to the end (Matt. 10:22, 32-33, Matt. 25, Luke 9:62, James 1:12, 2:18, 26), endure hardness (2 Tim. 2:3-4), work out your salvation (1 Cor. 3:16-17, Phili. 2:12-13, 1 Peter 1:13-16), punishment of the branch that was natural (Matt. 7:21-23, Rom. 11:18-22), call to persevere (Luke 13:24-27, Heb. 2:1-3, 3:12-15, 4:1, 11, 6:11, 15, 10:26, 38-39, 12:15, 25, 28, 1 John 5:13, Rev. 3:2), call to warfare (1 Tim. 6:12, James 4:7, Eph. 6:11-

13), desire sound doctrine (2 Tim. 2:15, 3:16-17, Titus 1:9, 2:1, 2 Peter 1:4-8).

A sobering verse is given of Israel who tempted God in the wilderness in Psalm 106:15, "And he gave them their request; but sent leanness into their soul." We are reminded of the warnings to quench not, grieve not, and such (Eph. 4:30, 1 Thess. 5:19, Heb. 3:8) "Teaching us that, denying ungodliness and worldly lusts, we should live soberly, righteously, and godly, in this present world;" - Titus 2:12. Sadly, we are preaching a man-centered gospel where we have no responsibility on our part regarding what it means to follow Him.

The early Christians didn't think that; identifying with Christ in baptism was a death sentence and showed that they had believed; they went to their graves while being steadfast in their faith. We see baptism as symbolizing our old man who had died and our death with him on the Cross, our willingness to follow Christ to the end, even to our grave, and the new life that is ours through resurrection life in Jesus Christ. This was set forth by our Lord, who was baptized to show us this truth of the death and resurrection life He was here for and what was to be true of His followers. Such significance was to be emphasized and imprinted where those early Christians could follow the imagery of their position in Christ after their conversion through baptism. Baptism is more than just passive obedience; it is active participation. These people did not live flippantly and had the attitude of "once saved, always saved," where they could deny Christ and go on with life. Their baptism was the outward flow of their inward work that they believed. It was the fruit of saving faith and having no alternatives. They did not have any attitude of flippancy when they were about to be thrown to the lions or watch their newborn baby being torn limb to limb by wild beasts, or like the Waldensians where the fathers were made to wear the heads of their children suspended on their necks on the way to their death. They realized that it was non-negotiable in this matter of following Christ until the very end. It was allegiance to Christ above all else.

And they could say with the apostle Paul, "I have fought a good fight, I have finished my course, I have kept the faith:" – 2 Tim. 4:7. Americanized Christianity has raised a whole generation that calls the name of Christ but does not live the name of Christ but calls themselves "Christians" because of a childhood "decision" that neither changed them nor kept them.

Earnestly Contend for the Faith

When confronted by his brothers in challenging Goliath, David declared, "Is there not a cause?" – 1 Sam. 17:29. There was a reason David was there in obedience to his father, and there was a reason that David's heart burned within him when he heard the uncircumcised Philistine mock the living God. Our need for contending for the faith must be for the very reason that the various topics have been discussed prior. Such is the nature of the human heart, where it tends to go the easy way and forsake the old paths. "Thus saith the Lord, Stand ye in the ways, and see, and ask for the old paths, where is the good way, and walk therein, and ye shall find rest for your souls. But they said, We will not walk therein." – Jer. 6:16. "and there arose another generation after them, which knew not the Lord, nor yet the works which he had done for Israel." – Judg. 2:10; it was not that they did not know the past, they did not see God work the way He did during Joshua's day, and they went apostate. In Jude 1:3, we see the exhortation to "earnestly contend for the faith which was once delivered unto the saints." The faith was once delivered but preserved for every generation by God Himself, and it is the great responsibility of each generation to ensure that the purity of the gospel is preserved. We cannot ride on the glories of the past. It is easy for the leaven of falsehood to destroy God's truth in one generation if we don't purge it from our midst. We contend because we love Christ. And in loving Christ, when His truth is slighted and despised and changed, love for Christ brings about a holy hatred to reject that which is evil and pursue that which is good (Psa. 101:3).

Every movement has the potential and generally moves to a place of compromise, at most times, in the same or next generation. We see that in the succession of kings in the life of Israel and the church at Sardis, where God called her to repentance. To "Be watchful, and strengthen the things which remain, that are ready to die: for I have not found thy works perfect before God." – Rev. 3:2. Though he rebuked the church at Ephesus for leaving their first love, He commended them by saying, "I know thy works, and thy labour, and thy patience, and how thou canst not bear them which are evil: and thou hast tried them which say they are apostles, and are not, and hast found them liars:" – Rev. 2:2. They were trying those who said they were apostles, rejecting them, and warning their sheep of the wolves. Those early Christians were able to contrast false teachings with the message they preached. Today we have such a blurring of the lines in pseudo-Christianity that looks like the truth but lacks the essential life that the true gospel brings. "Having a form of godliness, but denying the power thereof: from such turn away." - 2 Tim. 3:5. Paul writes, "Now we command you, brethren, in the name of our Lord Jesus Christ, that ye withdraw yourselves from every brother that walketh disorderly, and not after the tradition which he received of us." – 2 Thess. 3:6. He named names to protect the flock who may be swept unawares by their deceptive words, "For Demas hath forsaken me, having loved this present world, and is departed unto Thessalonica... Alexander the coppersmith did me much evil: the Lord reward him according to his works." – 2 Tim. 4:10, 14. And much more forcefully, "But though we, or an angel from heaven, preach any other gospel unto you than that which we have preached unto you, let him be accursed. As we said before, so say I now again, if any man preach any other gospel unto you than that ye have received, let him be accursed." – Gal. 1:8-9. To "mark them which cause divisions and offences contrary to the doctrine which ye have learned; and avoid them." – Rom. 16:17. "(For many walk, of whom I have told you often, and now tell you even weeping, that they are the enemies of the cross of Christ: Whose end is destruction, whose God is their

belly, and whose glory is in their shame, who mind earthly things.)"
- Phili. 3:18-19. We ought to be contending.

Though contending is to be done in righteous anger (see Acts
17:16-17), and we don't apologize for defending the truth, it must
be done with the right attitude of humility and not for proving
personal pride. "Wherefore, my beloved brethren, let every man be
swift to hear, slow to speak, slow to wrath:" - James 1:19. It must
also be done with sorrow and brokenness. Samuel weeping for Saul,
Jeremiah having a yoke upon his neck weeping over Judah, Jesus
weeping over Jerusalem, etc. Think of the social upheaval that we
have today in the area of gender and identity. God created us as
male and female; is that a conviction we bear? If it is, then it is non-
negotiable. Our culture is reprogramming us for acceptance of evil
by using terms such as "unconscious bias, micro-iniquity (in the
name of equality for sexes)" and trying to normalize the (sinful)
behavior. Someone says they want to use a pronoun instead of their
name; while you can agree to call them by their name, you cannot
agree to call them by their pronoun. By calling them by their
pronoun, you agree to their sinful lifestyle or identification of
themselves in rebellion against God, and you are not only agreeing
but promoting it. It is similar if you worked in a gambling place,
porn store, or a saloon, where you are agreeing and promoting
things that are evil and destroying lives, "normalizing" sin or calling
evil (man's rebellion against His Creator) as good and calling good
(what truth is, and God-given) as evil. The homosexual movement
is the offspring of the evil one and must be confronted as such.
When we talk about the sins of a nation that fills up the measure of
God's wrath (1 Thess. 2:16), we realize that there are sins that take
what God has given, such as reason, self-awareness, inquisitive
thinking, and such, which differentiates us from animals (having
been created in the image of God), where a man can use that to
defy God with it. An atheist may defy God, but by the very nature
that he can think otherwise is because God created him with the
ability to reason, and in his lost condition, he rejects God though
God gave him the mind in the first place. Some sins destroy the

fundamental representation of God's image, who we are, our body, soul, and spirit (1 Cor. 6:16, 18). While we can think of tattoos, body piercings, and such, the danger the homosexual and transgender movement brings us is in the way the fundamental definition of how God created us is being challenged, accepted, and promoted as a nation. And God's curse is upon those who are in willful rebellion against Him (Psa. 7:11, 9:17, 1 Cor. 6:9-10). Jesus said, "I tell you, Nay: but, except ye repent, ye shall all likewise perish." - Luke 13:3.

We contend not only in the matter of the truth but also in the way we represent ourselves in dress and what we allow to influence us, such as in the matter of music. Christian contemporary music, which emulates the spirit of this world, undermines the high view of God, no matter how scriptural it may be. There is nothing neutral in this world, and what comes from the abundance of man's heart is evil (Jer. 17:9). What comes from God is good, and there is always a battle of the kingdoms. God is not neutral when He spoke of the strange woman "with the attire of an harlot" – Prov. 7:10. To align ourselves in a proper understanding of the holiness of God should affect the way we see things that affect our bodies and our minds. We are to "Prove all things; hold fast that which is good. Abstain from all appearance of evil." - 1 Thess. 5:21-22. James is direct when he states, "Ye adulterers and adulteresses, know ye not that the friendship of the world is enmity with God? whosoever therefore will be a friend of the world is the enemy of God." - James 4:4. Even the world knows what they promote; Little Richard in 1978 said, "Rock 'n' roll doesn't glorify God. You can't drink out of God's cup and the devil's cup at the same time. I was one of the pioneers of that music, one of the builders. I know what the blocks are made of because I built them."

This is not new since we are not ignorant of Satan's devices (2 Cor. 2:11). Satan can transform himself into an angel of light (2 Cor. 11:14) with so-called ministers of righteousness (2 Cor. 11:15). I shudder when I read the description of Lucifer and the power that he commands in his hierarchy of demons (Isa. 14:9-16, Eze. 28:12-

19, Eph. 2:2, 6:12), and he is not playing games. Generations in the past dealt with witchcraft, rock/sensual music, free love, forbidden sex, yoga, and rebellion against authority. Now, this generation is dealing with homosexuality and gender identity (with such prominence) in addition to everything else. We need to realize Satan's hand in destroying the sanctity of marriage using means of evil. It has already overrun the church because the church has been too blind to see it for what it is, and they are trying to address it as flesh and blood. The reason for this is that where light ceases, darkness abounds. If you don't speak the truth in love and tell the truth when necessary, or if you stay silent and accept it in the name of "reaching them," they won't know that it is wrong since they are not willing to change but would like to change you by their lifestyle and their boisterous propaganda. We will be found partakers of their evil deeds. We see the sad state of Lot when those angels came and saw that he had vexed his righteous soul. We know that God's truth (The law of God) always supersedes man's law. When they disagree, we ought to obey God rather than men (Acts 5:29). Though we don't take up arms in rebellion, and we submit to the government, we lawfully dissent where they disagree. How can we stay silent and not break down in brokenness and tears seeing men blaspheme what God gave as a covenant of grace in the rainbow and have taken it for their rebellion of sexuality and wave it in the face of Almighty God? There is a sobering statement that is mentioned where God "wondered" why there were no intercessors (Isa. 59:16) and that there was no one He found who would make up the hedge that He should not destroy it (Eze. 22:30). **An intercessor is someone who stands between a people who don't know their danger and a holy God, knowing that justice and judgment must prevail**.

We contend because "truth is fallen in the street, and equity cannot enter." – Isa. 59:14. Contending must be done with the thought not only of preserving the gospel for the current and future generations, to present a chaste virgin unto Christ, but it must also be for the supreme goal of loving the Lord Jesus Christ with all our hearts, soul, and mind. To see the doctrine of devils as dethroning Christ and not join with those who preach another gospel or another christ, be it Roman Catholicism, Mormon, JWs, Judaism, apostates under the guise of "Christianity," or other religions; "But though we, or an angel from heaven, preach any other gospel unto you than that which we have preached unto you, let him be accursed. As we said before, so say I now again, If any man preach any other gospel unto you than that ye have received, let him be accursed." – Gal. 1:8-9. "Neither is there salvation in any other: for there is none other name under heaven given among men, whereby we must be saved." – Acts 4:12. For the Jews or the gentiles, there is only one way of redemption, and it is through Jesus Christ. Jesus said, "He that is not with me is against me: and he that gathereth not with me scattereth." - Luke 11:23, there is a cut-off, and there is no middle ground. We contend in humility carrying the banner of truth for the world to know what truth is (1 Tim. 3:15). We see a world burning around us with gender, racial, and social issues that seem to swallow the church and false teachings that abound. The time for the church is not to cower over in a corner giving an uncertain sound, with an attitude of "me, mine, and that's fine," instead the time is now for her to rise up bearing His reproach and of some having compassion enough, to tell the truth, and making a difference. "Awake, awake; put on thy strength, O Zion; put on thy beautiful garments, O Jerusalem, the holy city: for henceforth there shall no more come into thee the uncircumcised and the unclean." – Isa. 52:1.

The Glory of God in Service

When thinking about the word "glory," when it is associated with God, it has various ways it is outlined in Biblical usage. When we consider some of the terms, we quickly come to the exclusivity of the Person of God to whom only this can be given. No one else could share in this, for He alone is the owner and rightful recipient of it. Here are just five of them. **Honour:** something of incalculable value that deserves praise to be given for its greatness of it. Who else can receive this except God? All we have is corruption, and what we produce fails and falters, but what God has done is always perfect and "very good" as per His standard of perfection (Gen. 1). **Splendour:** something that cannot be equaled in its majesty and beauty. Who can have any glimpse of even meeting this except God, whose splendorous attributes permeate everything He does and we are part of? His attribute of holiness permeates in heaven where the seraphims cover their faces and cry, "Holy, holy, holy, is the Lord of hosts: the whole earth is full of his glory" - Isa. 6:3, His attribute of omnipresence which permeates in His essential presence (Jer. 23:24), His attribute of self-existence which permeates in the trustworthiness of His handiwork (Psa. 19:1). **Riches:** the value that God places, which is very different from what man places value on. From the richness of His love to the riches in Jesus Christ that have been imparted to His children, how can we compare or hope to even place anything we can do; or think we should receive from the One who has given such graces that are priceless? "Thanks be unto God for his unspeakable gift" (2 Cor. 9:15). **Reverence:** response of a humble heart to behold One of great value to give Him due respect. And can we show reverence to anyone less than God Himself in the truest sense of that word? This is not just respect but also worship due unto deity in the form of worship and adoration. Only God is worthy of that, not angels (Rev. 22:8-9), saints, or man (Job 15:14-16, 25:4). We see the many instances of the Theophanies of Christ in the Old Testament where such worship was given to Him (Gen. 18:1-3, Exo. 3:2-6, 24:8-11, Josh. 5:13-15, Dan. 10:5-10). **Abundance:** beyond human comprehension of vastness. Who can be seen as having abundance but God to whom the nations of the earth are as a drop in the bucket, and meted out heaven with the span, and telleth the number of the stars and calleth them all by their names (Isa. 40:12-17, Psa. 147:4)? How can One who created all things willingly become subject to His laws of Creation? But in Christ, we see the greater riches and abundance of His ability to constrain Himself to mortal flesh and walk among men as God in human flesh. What a glorious Christ. In seeing, from just a few, of all that entails the word glory, who else must this belong to but God? And one who desires glory for himself is treading on the height of foolishness and something that he is grossly undeserving of. We see this sobering statement from God, "To whom then will ye liken God? or what likeness will ye compare unto him?" – Isa. 40:18.

Though we have seen the glory of God exhibited in regeneration, in the victorious Christian life, and such, when we think about what is at stake, we come to the place of asking ourselves if I am operating purely for God to be glorified by who I am and what I do or do I desire the praise of man, which is but a vapor. Moses pleaded with God based on God's covenant to "remember" in Exodus 32:12-14, which was not for getting his way by blaming God or making God "owe" something. It was for having the purest motive of the glory of God alone, for God to remember His promise since it had God's sacred covenant in it. As a minister, if I am content because it was a good sermon or it impressed the people, and it was prayed for and such; while we may have sought God for Him to be glorified, it will have the hidden motive of the glory of man (our old nature in Adam). But the purest motive is for God to work because He is worthy of the glory (1 Cor. 1:29). And such motive must be mingled with the sorrow of the heart that it will not be given if He does not come through in power and be in the midst of us. We see this in the response of Moses to God, "And he said unto him, If thy presence go not with me, carry us not up hence." – Exo. 33:15. Basically stating that they were not going to go one step further unless God came with them. In essence, **there is nothing of value when God is not in it** (Heb. 11:26); this must be a point of conviction that we live or die by. Every prayer that is uttered for God to work should be for the purest motive of God Himself, whose glory is at stake. Not in the sense of what Adam can do to glorify God, but what God the Holy Spirit can do to glorify God the Father and lift up God the Son. We saw earlier regarding bringing the cross to bear upon our selfish motives in the topic of the exchanged life, which can help with this. Though much can be said about "Whether therefore ye eat, or drink, or whatsoever ye do, do all to the glory of God." - 1 Cor. 10:31, we must stop here.

The Church Aflame

In Ecclesiastes 4:12, we read that "a threefold cord is not quickly broken." What is the life of a church, what is the life of the Spirit that flows within the church, and how does the representation of the Bride of Christ relate to her preparation for her Groom? We are called the Bride of Christ (Eph. 5:25-27), and those redeemed, blood-bought saints are to live in expectation of the coming day when she will behold her Beloved. And she purifies herself, making ready for Him (Rev. 19:7). When we think about the truth that Christ died for His church and gave Himself for her, we come to the sober realization that He is coming for a chaste Bride. So how do we, as individuals and collectively prepare ourselves for Him?

We begin with a question, why do we go to church? If we realized in our hearts that we are going there to meet God, not the Americanized version of a god but the Biblical God who is high and lifted up. We say we go to worship, to pray, to fellowship, to sing, but if we have the view that we are going there to enter into the holy of holies, how would that affect our services? If the singing, praying, and preaching are all preparing the Bride to make herself ready to meet her beloved Groom, how would we conduct the "order of service"? If, when entering into the sanctuary, we still our hearts to hear His voice and we yearn after Him just as the Shulamite woman did in the Song of Solomon, how would our heart preparation be for such an event? Would "awe" describe our encounter with the holy One? Instead, if the people have to be entertained in church, just like they partake of the world's pleasures, what does that indicate? It indicates the deadness of those who come or those in the pulpit.

There is much talk about end-time prophecy, and the church is split between historical, pre-trib, post-trib, mid-trib, spiritual, and all the other persuasions. And they all seem to have their own reasoning for why their interpretation is accurate and others are wrong. Irrespective of what those entail, can the church ask God to prepare them for what's ahead, so we might go through them and be found faithful? I am reminded of the time on January 25, 1736, when John Wesley wrote of his encounter with the Moravians. He was on the ship with them where they were in one of their services, fervently worshipping God. He wrote, "In the midst of the Psalm wherewith their service began, the sea broke over, split the main-sail in pieces, covered the ship and poured in between the decks, as if the great deep had already swallowed us up. A terrible screaming began among the English. The Germans calmly sung on. I asked one of them afterwards; 'Were you not afraid?' He answered, 'I thank God, no.' I asked: 'But were not your women and children afraid?' He replied mildly: 'No, our women and children are not afraid to die.'" The storm was boisterous, but the Moravians kept praising God. Finally, the storm subsided." **Dear brethren, can we face what's ahead of us? if it is certain persecution that we are called to, to seal our testimony in blood?** Is Christianity in America prepared for that instead of building their hope on something that may never happen in their generation?

The overwhelming desire to present a pure Bride rest upon the heart of a Pastor. He is considered the friend of the Groom. John the Baptist speaks of the purpose of why He came. "He that hath the bride is the bridegroom: but the friend of the bridegroom, which standeth and heareth him, rejoiceth greatly because of the bridegroom's voice: this my joy therefore is fulfilled." - John 3:29. And the Pastor is to consider this task of being an under-shepherd as something far greater value than preaching three times a week and visiting the members. A friend who helps prepare the Bride is one, who would remove the hindrances that may cause her to become polluted, he would warn of the dangers that may harm her, he would pray for knowing the heart of the Groom who has given His love letter for her, the word of God, and speak kindly to her on how to prepare to meet her soon-coming Lord. His focus is on the

Groom's desire though it may inconvenience the Bride with truths that she has to reckon with (Heb. 13:17). We see another picture with Abraham's servant fetching Rebekah for Isaac. He realizes that the attraction of the Bride must always be toward her Bridegroom and not toward himself, or else he would play the harlot. The Pastor would be careful to put down any idolizing of men by the people. And he is ever so careful to make sure that those regenerated show credible proof of God's work in seeing the nature of the Groom imparted to her. And those desiring to join the church are to be met, discipled, and prayed upon multiple times, even to the point of stating, "Lord, they are showing credible evidence of regeneration, but we don't know their hearts, we love Thee and desire a pure Bride for Thee. Lord help us." Those early apostles asked something similar before Pentecost in Acts 1:24-25.

Our motivation must come from the heart of Christ's view of what He promises to accomplish with regard to the individual and the church. "The Lord will perfect that which concerneth me: thy mercy, O Lord, endureth for ever: forsake not the works of thine own hands." – Psa. 138:8, "Faithful is he that calleth you, who also will do it." - 1 Thess. 5:24, "Being confident of this very thing, that he which hath begun a good work in you will perform it until the day of Jesus Christ:" – Phili. 1:6, "Now unto him that is able to keep you from falling, and to present you faultless before the presence of his glory with exceeding joy" - Jude 1:24. "And the Lord make you to increase and abound in love one toward another, and toward all men, even as we do toward you: To the end he may stablish your hearts unblameable in holiness before God, even our Father, at the coming of our Lord Jesus Christ with all his saints." - 1 Thess. 3:12-13. How precious are these promises, and to know that the work of God in a church will be undergirded, moved, and perfected by Him. We see in 1 Corinthians 3:9, "For we are labourers together with God: ye are God's husbandry, ye are God's building." We can go in faith with anticipation that if we can get a small group of like-minded people united in truth, we can start praying for a kindling of that fire from God. In time we pray for God to expand the circle larger and larger until the whole church is enclosed, to remove the hindrances through the week, and live for the glory of God. And during such times of prayer, spiritual truth gets imparted to those who come; even through seasons of dryness, there is anticipation, the Spirit is honored, and the work of God is done in the life of the church where she is glorious. Those of the redeemed come knowing that the desire of God will be fulfilled in the assembling of themselves together. A place where God is pleased to draw near, the fellowship of the saints that breeds holiness, and a place of great spiritual vitality. God may even use such expressions of love to provoke jealousy among other churches to seek the Lord in spirit and in truth.

Oh! may we find the hidden gems of tenderhearted Davids in our congregations who are yearning after God in secret and tie their hearts together with God, teach them the hidden treasures of prayer, spiritual warfare, and going on with God. These are unknown men and women who, in their humility, seek the face of their heavenly Father and love Him for all that He is, One who is altogether lovely. May they be as burning coals of fire to spur the desire of God among our midst.

Have you ever wondered why the heavens rejoice when a sinner repents (Luke 15:7)? If we remember the times when the phrase "the glory of the Lord" is mentioned, we can get a small glimpse into something of the nature of this event. We see it manifested in unlikely places like the wilderness (Exo. 24:16-17), in the tabernacle (Exo. 40:34-35), in the temple (2 Chr. 7:1-3), and we also see it departing from the land (Eze. 10:18-19). We see the last time it filled the house of God (Eze. 44:4) around BC 574, and we don't see it anymore until Luke 2:9, "And, lo, the angel of the Lord came upon them, and the glory of the Lord shone round about them: and they were sore afraid." This same glory was manifested when the Holy Spirit came upon Mary in Luke 1:35 to birth the Christ child upon that virgin womb. But when a sinner is regenerated, the same Holy Spirit in His grand work of regeneration displays the glory of God

259

in an unlikely place, the heart of man. Here the sinner is cleansed, his sins blotted out, and he is declared righteous (Acts 3:19, Rom. 8:32-34, Col. 2:13-14). And what is a greater miracle than Emmanuel, which being interpreted is God with us (Matt. 1:23)? If there is something greater, it is God IN us, Christ in you, the hope of glory (Col. 1:27). Can we even fathom the statement that we are the habitation of God? His tabernacle where He dwells, His holy place (John 14:23, Eph. 2:22)? His temple not made with hands (1 Cor. 6:19)? And so, we see the rejoicing in heaven when this glory of the Lord is shown to unworthy sinners speaking of the goodness of God and His abundant mercy. And such is the desire of Christ who nourisheth and cherishes His church (Eph. 5:29) to display this glory in a congregation that is desirous of Him.

Some may think that such encounters with God as a dread. On the contrary, in Psalm 16:11, we read that "in thy presence is fulness of joy; at thy right hand there are pleasures for evermore," and in Psalm 73:28, we read, "But it is good for me to draw near to God." The greeting of the angels to the Shepherds in Luke 2:10 was, "behold, I bring you good tidings of great joy, which shall be to all people." Jesus said, "These things have I spoken unto you, that my joy might remain in you, and that your joy might be full." – John 15:11. There was great joy in that city in Acts 8 when God was working in their midst (v8). To that early church, "Whom having not seen, ye love; in whom, though now ye see him not, yet believing, ye rejoice with joy unspeakable and full of glory:" - 1 Peter 1:8. *Sidenote:* One of the fruits that the Spirit produces is joy (Gal. 5:22-23). We are trying to work up a lot of joy without Christ and the time needed to seek His presence, thinking that it will be drudgery, but how wrong we are. Happiness and joy are not the same. Happiness is a state of the mind, while joy is a state of the heart. Americanized Christianity cannot produce joy, but it can work up a lot of happiness that is temporal, leaving the sheep just as empty as when they walked into the door of the sanctuary. While God wants us to be happy people because of our position in Christ, joy is from within that is produced as a fruit of the Spirit (Gal. 5:22) and abides even in times of difficulty. The happiness of the world is from without that needs something to be constantly given to us to keep us in that state like a drug. Happiness can be taken away, whereas joy can be like a stream of water flowing calmly amidst the storm. A lost person cannot experience joy because his heart is dead, and so he tries to find happiness through emotions in what he experiences. A saved person can have joy (Gal. 5:22), which can produce happiness irrespective of the circumstances and not the other way around. There is the general state of happiness that comes about with good things that are universal, like the mother and her newborn baby. The times "happy" is mentioned in the New Testament are always tied to the will of God, whether they were free (Rom. 14:22) or suffering for righteousness' sake (1 Peter 3:14).

Such is the desire of Christ for His church, and we should take great comfort when thinking about the matter of revival. We know that God wants to revive His church more than us, and when we repent and pray, we can corporately and individually cry out to Him from our hearts. But also, we can cry out in confidence, after removing the hindrances, ask God to prepare us and bring us to the place for receiving His times of refreshing from the presence of the Lord. The psalmist in Psalm 80, not knowing how else to seek Him, cries out to God three times, "Turn us again." What a glorious Christ who can do just that!

In Closing

As we conclude these areas of vital importance, I am reminded, "For we wrestle not against flesh and blood, but against principalities, against powers, against the rulers of the darkness of this world, against spiritual wickedness in high places." – Eph. 6:12. And this battle is not only for lost souls but for the very life of this nation that we love. In the book **Is America committing Suicide** by **Austin L. Sorenson**, the author recalls the most common reasons for the fall of the Roman Empire as attributed to Gibbon *(the English Historian: 1737-1794)*

1. The rapid increase in divorce and the undermining of the sanctity of the home.
2. The spiraling rise of taxes and extravagant spending.
3. The mounting craze for pleasure and the brutalization of sports.
4. The building of gigantic armaments and the failure to realize that the real enemy lay within the gates of the empire, in the moral decay of its people.
5. The decay of religion and the fading of faith into a mere form, leaving the people without a guide.

I believe that the fifth reason stated above (the word religion used here *in relation to* truth and not a "system" of religion) is the key to all the other areas where a nation perishes from the judgment of God. We see this forcefully displayed in the nation of Israel, where when they were faithful to God, the nation prospered; when they rebelled against Him, they reaped the consequences of their sin in a myriad of ways until they were finally destroyed and sent into exile. Though America has not replaced Israel, the light that America has been given and the blessings that have come from the kind hand of God have been far greater than what the Old Testament Israel had, and much shall be required. When Jesus spoke to the chief priests and Pharisees of His day regarding His people who rejected Him, "Therefore say I unto you, The kingdom of God shall be taken from you, and given to a nation bringing forth the fruits thereof." – Matt. 21:43. But He states the price to be paid for any nation (even in the context of the gentile church) that is blessed by God for this purpose, "And whosoever shall fall on this stone shall be broken: but on whomsoever it shall fall, it will grind him to powder" (v44). We can choose to deny it, but America was blessed by God (through many godly people) for its desire in her early days for holiness and to spread the gospel, where God sent massive Awakenings, Missionary movements, and printing press movements to spread the gospel across the globe, and additionally showering her with abundance. And when we turn around and mock God, **we are on dangerous ground, and God will crush us**.

While we "come boldly unto the throne of grace, that we may obtain mercy, and find grace to help in time of need" – Heb. 4:16, we are also comforted with the truth that the sacrifice of Christ and the veil that was rent has allowed us to be sprinkled with the blood of Christ. In Him, we have access, but He is still the same God of the Old Testament that we are approaching in obedience and reverential fear, the God who dwelt among His people in Shekinah glory. Someone might say in anger to "Judge not" – Matt. 7:1, or get defensive and say, "who do you think you are?" But that is a smokescreen to hide our iniquity. God hates hypocritical judgment, but He always desires justice and judgment that brings us to evaluate our sinfulness in light of His holiness and what He has said, "For if we would judge ourselves, we should not be judged." - 1 Cor. 11:31. "To do justice and judgment is more acceptable to the Lord than sacrifice." – Prov. 21:3. "Thus saith the Lord, Keep ye judgment, and do justice: for my salvation is near to come, and my righteousness to be revealed." – Isa. 56:1. And "the time is come that judgment must begin at the house of God" - 1 Peter 4:17.

In addition to what has been shared in this topic of Found Wanting, we can cover much more on separation from the world unto Christ, missions, packaging so great salvation into a set of cookie-cutter methods, our equating of blessing with financial prosperity rather than the manifest presence of the eternal God in our midst, willing to overlook the sin in the camp, and a church that has lost her voice, etc. **The temptation is always there to find the surface-level behaviors and try to fix them**, but that will be dealing with the fruits and not the root of the issue. The topics discussed here are just the manifestation of the underlying roots that have been ingrained into us. But such deeper streams of corruption must be repented of, for such is the depravity of the human heart to take what is good, and while being well-intentioned, one can embrace things in their lives where it hides the face of Christ. A farmer doesn't expect a harvest if he has not done the toil of plowing, breaking up the fallow ground, clearing weeds and things detrimental to the seed, fertilizing, watering, and such. We are trying to marry the American lifestyle to Biblical Christianity, which does not work. Such was the condition of that Laodicean church where Christ said, "Because thou sayest, I am rich, and increased with goods, and have need of nothing; and knowest not that thou art wretched, and miserable, and poor, and blind, and naked:" – Rev. 3:17. I was found wanting in my own life when coming to grips with the reality of where we are as Americanized Christianity which is detrimental to the faith that pleaseth God (Heb. 11:6).

Paul, writing to the church at Thessalonica, says, "Finally, brethren, pray for us, that the word of the Lord may have free course, and be glorified, even as it is with you:" – 2 Thess. 3:1, "For the kingdom of God is not in word, but in power." – 1 Cor. 4:20. "Who also hath made us able ministers of the new testament; not of the letter, but of the spirit: for the letter killeth, but the spirit giveth life." - 2 Cor. 3:6. Samson "wist not that the Lord was departed from him," David, in his confession, wept, "Cast me not away from thy presence; and take not thy holy spirit from me." Jesus warned the church in Revelation 2:5 to deal with the root of the issue, "Remember therefore **from whence thou art fallen, and repent, and do the first works**; or else I will come unto thee quickly, and will remove thy candlestick out of his place, except thou repent" *(emphasis mine)*. Matthew Henry commenting on that verse, states, "If the presence of Christ's grace and Spirit be slighted, we may expect the presence of his displeasure. He will come in a way of judgment, and that suddenly and surprisingly, upon impenitent churches and sinners; he will unchurch them, take away his gospel, his ministers, and his ordinances from them, and what will the churches or the angels of the churches do when the gospel is removed?"

In all these topics, one may contend that they are making the gospel easy for the modern man who has no time to go into depth with his busy schedule. But the New Testament was written for those who were illiterate, slaves, and rulers of their day. Sincerity can never be an excuse for truth. Many are sincere but are sincerely wrong; we must go back to what God conveys about Himself, His ways, and the result of His work, seen not only in the Scriptures but also in church history. I am not asking for more than what the Scriptures reveal, and I am not trying to make it harder than what God demands. Still, maybe the answer is not in how hard this seems to be from a human perspective and instead fix our sights on what God promises to do. Such would allow for realizing the simplicity of the gospel given by the outworking of the Spirit of God (2 Cor. 11:3) without all the frills. **There is a vast difference between the simplicity of the Gospel as opposed to the shallowness of the American gospel.** If we cannot run a church without the frills, then the frills have become our idols. It is the supremacy of Christ Himself displayed in earthen vessels. If we are faithful to why Jesus came even though it is foolishness to the lost man, God will be faithful to shed light on a darkened heart; instead of that if we make the gospel attractive by making it about heaven or happiness and not deal with the root issues of the heart of man, the wages of sin and the Adamic nature of sin itself, we grieve the Spirit of God and produce proselytes. The early church had nothing, but they had God, and truth flowed. Today the American church has everything except God.

The gospel has not changed because man's problem of sin has not changed, and only God has the answer, and it is by His way, and anyone touching to steady the ark is not pleasing God. Americanized Christianity has put its unclean hands to steady the ark by using the light of the conscience instead of getting to the light of the Spirit, by calling for human decisions, by substituting with the natural human faith instead of that saving faith which is a gift from God, by reciting the sinner's prayer, by convincing using intellectual arguments and leading into an intellectual assent, by counting its converts who are still in their sin and having no desire to change, by promising heaven instead of submission to Christ and

265

His teachings. And God's curse is upon it. We are just fooling ourselves if we think that the God who rejected the apple of His eye because of their sin will somehow overlook our sin and not judge us. It is almost blasphemous to say it, but we must give the blessed Holy Spirit His rightful place. The gospel cannot stay true by simplifying its message, but rather the true gospel shines in the possibility of the God of the message who can work in human hearts (Luke 18:27). Our responsibility is to be faithful to the One who has called us and sent us into the highways and hedges to compel them to come in. Someone may say that it is a hard thing to require such things as being awakened, repentance, believe, and others. **Dear friend, what puts our greater dependence upon God and drives us to our knees?** Is it not in desiring the Spirit to work, the things that are impossible with men? It is easy to convince someone and say "believe," though they love their sin. It is hard work to say that we must pray earnestly to see the Spirit awaken them, bring them to godly sorrow, and bear witness in their heart, yet it is a work that will last through time and eternity. Why must we linger at the place where we can get results, but they are still in their damnable estate? Must we not run to Christ, fall on our face before Him, and desire the Father to send forth His blessed Spirit to convict, regenerate, and bear witness?

Beloved, God gave us more than John 3:16. He gave us truths upon truths and deep riches from His heart so we can enjoy Him on earth and in eternity forever. He has given us "wholesome words, even the words of our Lord Jesus Christ, and to the doctrine which is according to godliness" – 1 Tim. 6:3. In the book of Acts, there is no mention of the word love; does that mean we don't love when reaching out? The book of John does not mention the word faith; does that mean we don't need faith? We understand that we look at the whole counsel of God's word to understand the proper view of God and what is truly involved in regeneration and in being a follower of Jesus Christ. In the harmony of the gospels by the Spirit, the gospel of John is generally dated to have been written last, which brings us to the consideration that the earlier books dealt with topics such as repentance in detail, and John does not see the need to repeat them again. To the church in Sardis in Revelation 3, God's requirement was not to do their best, be accepted in the community, and have a name for themselves in their city, but to be perfect before Him "Be watchful, and strengthen the things which remain, that are ready to die: for I have not found thy works perfect before God" (v2). Jesus said, "Be ye therefore perfect, even as your Father which is in heaven is perfect." – Matt. 5:48. To represent salvation by one verse in the Scripture for getting quick results is to deny and be unfaithful to the revealed truth of God, the sinfulness of sin, the heart of men, and the nature of God.

Understanding the gravity of what it means to tread into sacred waters where there are such frightful consequences on what we are called to do should bring us to our knees and acquire a new meaning to what Jesus said, "I am the vine, ye are the branches: He that abideth in me, and I in him, the same bringeth forth much fruit: for without me ye can do nothing." – John 15:5.

In considering these varied topics, we do well to remember the hymn, **Let All Mortal Flesh Keep Silence** by **G. Moultrie**.

> Let all mortal flesh keep silence
> and with fear and trembling stand;
> ponder nothing earthly-minded,
> for with blessing in his hand
> Christ, our God, to earth descending,
> comes our homage to command.
>
> King of kings, yet born of Mary,
> as of old on earth he stood,
> Lord of lords in human likeness,
> in the body and the blood
> he will give to all the faithful
> his own self for heav'nly food.

Rank on rank the host of heaven
spreads its vanguard on the way
as the Light from Light, descending
from the realms of endless day,
comes the pow'rs of hell to vanquish
as the darkness clears away.

At his feet the six-winged seraph,
cherubim with sleepless eye,
veil their faces to the presence
as with ceaseless voice they cry:
"Alleluia, alleluia!
Alleluia, Lord Most High!"

public domain

Historical Agreement on Crucial Doctrines

Though we don't base our theology on the sayings of men, there is wisdom when we align ourselves to the word of God to investigate the lives of those whom God has used, irrespective of their school of thought. Not because they agree on every point of doctrine but on their high view of God and the reality of His hand upon them in the ways God used them. Below are a few quotes regarding some of the crucial topics that plague us today with our low view of God, which is sure to impact our view of Christ Himself.

On Repentance:

I give it as my deliberate conviction, founded on twenty-five years of ministerial observation, that the Christian profession of today owes its lack of vital godliness, its want of practical piety, its absence from the prayer meeting, its miserable semblance of missionary life, very largely to the fact that old-fashioned repentance is so little preached. You can't put a big house on a little foundation. And no small part of such preaching comes from a class of modern evangelists who desiring more for their own glory to count a great number of converts than to lay deep foundations, reduce the conditions of salvation by one-half and make the other half but some intellectual trick of the mind rather than a radical spiritual change of the heart. Like Simon Magus, they believe indeed, but 'their heart not being right in the sight of God, they have no part nor lot in this matter. They are yet in the gall of bitterness and in the bond of iniquity.' Such converts know but little and care less about a system of doctrine. They are prayerless, lifeless, and to all steady church work reprobate (**B.H. Carroll**)

Repentance is not penance; it is not penitence, it is a change of mind about sin, and self, and the Savior, turning with a broken and contrite heart from sin and self to the Savior. It is not just a change of opinion; it is a change of one's inner attitude; it is willing not only that God should take away sins by forgiving them, but being willing to put them away by forsaking them… There is nothing meritorious about repentance, or about faith, or about prayer. They just bring us in contact with God; that's what gives them value. And the step must be followed by the walk; we must bring forth fruits meet for repentance (**Vance Havner**)

Just now, some professedly Christian teachers are misleading many by saying that 'repentance is only a change of mind.' It is true that the original word does convey the idea of a change of mind, but the whole teaching of Scripture concerning the repentance which is not to be repented of is that it is a much more radical and complete change than is implied by our common phrase about changing one's mind. The repentance that does not include sincere sorrow for sin is not the saving grace that is wrought by the Holy Spirit. God-given repentance makes men grieve in their inmost souls over the sin they have committed and works in them a gracious hatred of evil in every shape and form. We cannot find a better definition of repentance than the one many of us learned at our mother's knee: 'Repentance is to leave the sin we loved before, and show that we in earnest grieve by doing so no more' (**Charles Haddon Spurgeon**)

On Faith:

... let no man deceive his own soul. It is diligently to be noted, the faith which bringeth not forth repentance, and love, and all good works, is not that right living faith, but a dead and devilish one. For, even the devils believe that Christ was born of a virgin: that he wrought all kinds of miracles, declaring himself very God: that, for our sakes, he suffered a most painful death, to redeem us from death everlasting; that he rose again the third day: that he ascended into heaven, and sitteth at the right hand of the Father and at the end of the world shall come again to judge both the quick and dead. These articles of our faith the devils believe, and so they believe all that is written in the Old and New Testament. And yet for all this faith, they be but devils. They remain still in their damnable estate, lacking the very true Christian faith. **(John Wesley)**

Saving faith is not a conclusion drawn from facts presented; saving faith is a gift of God to a penitent man or woman." "The difference between faith as it is found in the New Testament and faith as it is found now is that faith in the New Testament actually produced something - there was a confirmation of it." "Do you realize that your faith is a gift from God? You should look upon your faith as a miracle. It is the ability God gives lost men and women to trust and obey our Saviour and Lord... And Jesus is the author of our faith." "The man of faith can go into the wilderness and get on his knees and command heaven - God is in that. The man who dare to stand and let his preaching cost him something - God is in that. The Christian who is willing to put himself in a place where he must get the answer from God and God alone - the Lord is in that! **(A. W. Tozer)**

Faith is very far from being a mere conviction of the truth of God's Word or a conclusion drawn from certain promises. It is the ear which has heard God say what He will do and the eye which has seen Him doing it. Therefore, where there is true faith, it is impossible for the answer not to come. We must do this one thing that He asks of us as we pray: "Believe that ye have received." He will see to it that He does the thing He has promised: "Ye shall have them." **(Andrew Murray)**

On Unction or Enduement of Power for Service:

In the Christian system unction is the anointing of the Holy Ghost, separating unto God's work and qualifying for it. This unction is the one divine enablement by which the preacher accomplishes the peculiar and saving ends of preaching. Without this unction there are no true spiritual results accomplished; the results and forces in preaching do not rise above the results of unsanctified speech. Without unction the former is as potent as the pulpit… This unction is not an inalienable gift. It is a conditional gift, and its presence is perpetuated and increased by the same process by which it was at first secured; by unceasing prayer to God, by impassioned desires after God, by estimating it, by seeking it with tireless ardor, by deeming all else loss and failure without it. **(E. M. Bounds)**

When Ignatius was on trial at Rome, he was asked by the Emperor, "What is the meaning of your name, Theophorus?" (God-bearer). He promptly replied, "He who has Christ in his breast." And all Christians are God-bearers, whether they realize it or not. The unspeakably glorious mystery of an in-dwelling Holy Ghost is the possession of even the weakest and most failing child of God. The mistake has often been made of looking upon the incoming of the Holy Spirit as an experience subsequent to conversion, as an arbitrary bestowment rather than a necessary vitality. But the Scriptures plainly teach that the Holy Spirit is a universal gift to all believers, one without which they cannot be believers at all. At the same time, we recognize the fact that to possess the Holy Spirit is one thing, but to be filled with the Spirit is quite another. Before Pentecost, the Holy Ghost had been given to the disciples. Christ had breathed upon them and said, "Receive ye the Holy Ghost." But Pentecost made an unspeakable difference to them. The visible tongues of fire were only emblems of what had passed within. What new creatures they then became! How their gross conception of Christ's kingdom was purged away, and how they were raised from earthliness to spirituality! Their intellects were flooded with Divine light, their souls throbbed with Divine sympathies, and their tongues spoke so wonderfully of the things of God, and all who had known them previously were amazed, saying, "What meaneth this?" They were all raised to a new altitude; a new energy and force possessed them. Each one became strong as an iron pillar, "the weakest as David, and the strong as the angel of the Lord." They met together as the sincere but timid and partially enlightened followers of Christ, but they left the upper room full of light, and power, and love. They were now filled with the Holy Ghost as an all-illuminating, all-strengthening, all-sanctifying presence. The baptism of fire has consumed their inner depravity, subsidized all their faculties, and filled to the full each capacity with Divine energy and life... Almost all prominent Christian workers, whose labours have been pre-eminently owned of God, bear witness to the reception of a distinct blessing which they received subsequent to conversion, and which inaugurated a new era in their spiritual life. (**Thomas Cook**)

I have read many books on the ministry of the Holy Spirit in which it was dogmatically stated that the promised baptism predicted by John the Baptist and by our Lord, i.e., "the promise of the Father" has nothing to do with power for Christian witness. This seems incredible. One is startled more when he realizes that such a statement comes from men of deep spiritual maturity. As a young convert, I respected my elders in their teaching that the baptism mentioned by John the Baptist was fulfilled in the incorporation of the believers into the body of Christ, according to 1 Corinthians 12:13. I accepted their teaching, as these men were spiritual, safe, and sane Bible scholars. They had an unequalled comprehensive grasp of the contents of the word from Genesis to Revelation, which has enabled me to maintain a balanced Christian life. Yet, as I continued to study the word for myself on my knees, I was astounded to see that my conclusions on this matter differed from theirs. This pained me considerably, as I held these teachers and writers in high esteem. My seeking the truth from the word for myself arose from my desperate need of spiritual power in witnessing to my new-found Lord. More and more, the Scriptures quoted above encouraged me to believe that there was a mighty spiritual experience awaiting me which could be called "A baptism of power" or "the fullness of the Holy Ghost." God met my need and heart hunger in a very blessed way, for which I praise Him. After thirty years, without bias of any particular Bible school or theological seminary background to color my thinking, it is still my definite conviction that "the promise of the Father" is a baptism of supernatural power. **(James A. Stewart)**

Maintaining Biblical Faith

While not discounting the work that God has done despite our frailty in human flesh, the call of God is to study to shew thyself approved unto God (2 Tim. 2:15), to earnestly contend for the faith which was once delivered unto the saints (Jude 1:3), to ask for the old paths (Jer. 6:16). We are to have a view that is worthy of Him, the God of the Bible. In Matthew 23:3, Jesus stated, "All therefore whatsoever they bid you observe, that observe and do; but do not ye after their works: for they say, and do not." The need to learn from where God brought me and His daily sustenance reminds me of the need I have to draw nigh to God constantly. The Psalmist said, "As the hart panteth after the water brooks, so panteth my soul after thee, O God. My soul thirsteth for God, for the living God" – Psa. 42:1-2. I have to be constantly aware of the temptation of using the word of God as an end and never getting to the God of the word. We hear, "God said it, and that settles it," but have you plowed through and found the God who said it? That's where faith begins. The word of God was not given to excite us intellectually but to change us as we read and obey the God of the word. Satan knows the word of God better than any of us and can quote it better than we can, tempting the Lord with it in Matthew 4; Christ used the Scriptures to reveal the nature of the God of the word and His preeminence in His life. If Solomon, in all his encounters with God and the overwhelming blessings of God in wisdom, wealth, and earthly goods, could still be turned away from his God and follow other gods; we must be sober regarding the greatness of the wretchedness of one's own heart that continually draws us back to turn to the mire of sin. But God, who is rich in mercy and grace, is well able to keep us from sin and in continual victory by His triumphant victory on the cross and resurrection. In learning truths that were true for every generation, these are some areas that can help in "Casting down imaginations, and every high thing that exalteth itself against the knowledge of God, and bringing into captivity every thought to the obedience of Christ;" – 2 Cor. 10:5. I realize that the battle against the regenerate man is the battle for the mind. The mind influences the heart and affects our perceptions of the truth, causing the will to follow in its ways. The other great danger is becoming critical of what is seen as practiced and becoming prideful of what God has done personally. In keeping all this in mind, the first area I needed to be watchful of was the area of pride.

Pride says, "look at me," "I don't need God," or "I know better than God." Pride is about replacing God with self, to become our own god (Gen. 3:5); pride is about wanting to live outside of God in whom we live, move, and have our being (Acts 17:28); everything has been received, what is there for us to have pride in? (1 Cor. 4:7). How dangerous and damming pride is because God brought us into this world and gave us everything, and to turn around and say those statements is beyond abominable. I see that not only do we need Him, but we are alive because of Him; I am here because of Him; He upholds all things, including our very breath, "that in all things he might have the preeminence." – Col. 1:18. A constant looking to Christ will allow us to walk in humility while realizing that we are here for Him (Rev. 4:11). True humility does not look around, in an effort to compare or contrast, instead it looks up to the greatness of God and in godly reverence eclipses itself to be lost in Him, realizing one's own insignificance and smallness. Like a grain of sand against the infinitude and majesty of the Universe. God is not here to make you look good, but we are here for bringing glory to God (1 Cor. 10:31); and "when ye shall have done all those things which are commanded you, say, We are unprofitable servants: we have done that which was our duty to do" - Luke 17:10. Oh! to live

275

in complete awareness and influence of Christ in and by whom I exist and to be completely unaware and uninfluenced by self.

While being gracious to others and receiving truths of what God desires to do through the preaching of His word, I don't look for ways to find fault but instead discern what is being said and ensure that the truths preached are worthy of Christ. We realize that the responsibility lies with us like the Bereans did, who did not blindly receive the words of the apostle Paul but made sure it was what God had said, and they were called more noble (Acts 17:11). We must do the same with the songs that are sung. We have some weird renditions that have entered our hymns and brought down our needed high view of God. When seeing God as someone who is touched with the feeling of our infirmities, His concern for the lost, and those to whom He ministered from the poorest to the wealthiest and expressed human emotions like tears and sorrow, we must ensure that our view of God always humbles us to ask in humility, "What is man, that thou art mindful of him? or the son of man that thou visitest him?" – Heb. 2:6. Anything that exalts man and puts the focus on him must be rejected. Instead, we have hymn verses such as, when I get to heaven, Christ will gird Himself and serve us with sweet manna all around; or when He takes me by my hand and leads me through the promised land; or God is watching from heaven hoping that man will accept His Son, and for the angel to go sound the horn because man has made the right choice so they can now start building his mansion. Not only is it wholly unscriptural and sentimental, but it also has absolutely no bearing on who God is. We'll be stunned and awed by His majesty, and our only response would be to fall down and worship Him. The joy of the Lord is much greater and more fulfilling than satisfying what our fallen minds can produce. Similarly, reading some of the books from today's authors that are sentimental, man-centered, and appease the carnal man, only brings me to the more assured conclusion that they are serving another god and not the God of the Bible.

We have to realize that it must be a purposeful intent to follow after Christ, to ensure the truths heard are not blindly accepted without bringing to the place of trying the spirits. "Beloved, believe not every spirit, but try the spirits whether they are of God: because many false prophets are gone out into the world." – 1 John 4:1. The Scriptures are to be the sole foundation and authority for faith and practice. Where one may disagree, I have to reject it and align myself with the Scriptures, **not just the text of the Scripture but the spirit of its teachings as illuminated by the Spirit**. As sincere as men may be in preaching the truth, they are still men who have a fallen nature. Yes, we submit to authority with a glad heart, hold the arms of those in leadership like Aaron and Hur did to Moses (Exo. 17), pray with them, weep with them, see the work of God go forward, have the common bond of unity, but in all this realizing that our personal accountability to God does not diminish nor is it acceptable to be living by another person's convictions. We must all stand before God and give an account for the deeds done in our body by ourselves (2 Cor. 5:10), and we cannot blame our Bible colleges or our teachers, or someone else for our skewed views of God. God is no respecter of persons when calling into account regarding what we did with the light we have been given (Col. 3:25, Rev. 2:21-23).

The judgment seat of Christ for the believer would be the most terrifying encounter when we stand before a holy God and see our works burned up as wood, hay, and stubble. It would be such agony that God has to wipe away all tears from our eyes (Rev. 21:4). Can you imagine standing next to the apostle Paul or Ann Judson and waiting for your turn to give an account of your life before God? Ann Judson, who was the first female missionary sent from America, went through deep sorrow and suffering in Burma, with her husband in prison, losing all her children, and died there. At one time found herself unable to nurse the little one. Tormented by its pitiful cries, Ann took her baby up and down the streets of the city, pleading for mercy and for milk: "You women who have babies, have mercy on my baby and nurse her!" When I see my life in relation to how people have lived in the past, how they broke through the ranks of the enemy and did exploits and bore in their body the marks of the Lord Jesus; they had the same Bible, they had the same God, but their results were very different; when I stand before His all-blazing eye of holiness I am not expecting to hear "Well done, thou good and faithful servant."

Peter says to "add" to your faith (2 Peter 1:5-8), it is personal, and the responsibility is on us to plunge deep into Christ and learn of Him desiring Himself. It says to put on the whole armor of God (Eph. 6:10-18); it is a personal action of putting on and fighting the good fight of faith. We are to earnestly contend for the faith (Jude 1:3) and judge righteous judgment in humility and without hypocrisy (John 7:24). We are to not only protect our inner sanctum but hate even the garment spotted by the flesh (Jude 1:23). It is a constant evaluation that I must do consistently regarding my standing before God. We see this in Christian living, where if God is seen as someone whose primary focus is being there for us, our prayers and needs are always seen as something God must take care of. This is the Americanized Christianity mindset since we have everything at our fingertips; credit cards if we need money, a variety of food of the same kind, fast food on every corner, etc., and it can bleed into our perspective of God as well. Instead, suppose we see it the way it was supposed to be seen from an eastern point of view, where we are the ones who need God, and it causes us to realize our absolute dependence upon Him. In that case, it will show in our attitude in walking humbly before Him desiring His favors. And whether God grants us our desire or not, we realize the need to follow close after Him knowing that without Him, we can do nothing (John 15:5).

Christ is the desire of heaven, but is He the desire of the American church? If He is, we would desire holiness, repentance, solemn assembly, putting down our flesh, the joy that springs from God, and removing all the frills we have added to make our services appealing to the lost. Americanized Christianity has desired Christ for what He can do for them rather than for who He is. What if there is no heaven? Will they still come to Christ? Will they accept all of who He is and what He demands, obey all His teachings, and embrace the entirety of what He has given in the Old and New Testaments? And only a regenerated heart can do that, and it will prove itself by doing it, affecting the will of man in his obedience to the truth. As of writing this in 2022, I can sincerely state that I don't see heaven as the motivator when I face death. Instead, it is the longing and desire to meet my Beloved, my Savior, my Lord.

We boast of financial blessings, crowds, and comfort, but can we say, "Lord, we don't want the crowds, nor the money, but we what you," irrespective of everything else? I am grieved and annoyed by the begging that goes on. We speak of God as our great provider and that "I have been young, and now am old; yet have I not seen the righteous forsaken, nor his seed begging bread." – Psa. 37:25 and turn around and pressure people with threatening's such as "I rather have God's blessing with my 90% than God's curse with my 100%" In a large meeting, I heard a statement that sickened me, "Think Jesus is coming and passing the plates for the offering." Isn't this an act of faith that those who "preach the gospel should live of the gospel" - 1 Cor. 9:14? Yes, He uses human instruments to make provision for His saints, but is that by the impression of the Holy Spirit or the coaxing for preplanned goals? The God of the Bible is our great reward and is well able to take care of His children, as He did for George Mueller. God loveth a cheerful giver as an act of worship. An example is seen in Exodus 36, where the people gave too much and had to be restrained.

In trying to discern what is being taught, read, or received as an inflow of "truth," **we must ask a few questions.** Do the teachings bring me to a high view of God? does it elevate man and his self-ability? Does the Holy Ghost bear witness through the entire counsel of the word of God? is the Person of Christ revealed, and does it cause me to yearn for a life of holiness? We must consistently seek after Christ in our personal devotional life. We must also

279

realize that we will always have ebbs and flows when following Christ, living in the world, dealing with the flesh, and resisting the devil. Still, we must ask God in all things to undergird us, for He is the Vine, and we are the branches (John 15:5), and in our flesh lieth no good thing (Rom. 7:18). Expect the supernatural in those professing regeneration that flows from within, and not just accepting a decision, see if they can show credible evidence of the Spirit. But in stating this, I quickly add to this by saying, don't expect perfect repentance, though you should expect repentance; don't expect a complete change to perfection, though you should expect an immediate change in varying degrees; don't expect a faultless love, though you should expect love that yearns after God; and so forth. And where the authority strays away from Christ against truth and our conscience, we realize their authority comes from God. In usurping Christ's authority, they have forfeited that authority themselves. **We must never be a slave to another man's conscience**.

In saying all this, we are to ensure that we do all things in charity (1 Cor. 13), realizing that charity "Rejoiceth not in iniquity, but rejoiceth in the truth" – 1 Cor. 13:6. We are not to have a divisive spirit or sow discord among the brethren, which God calls an abomination (Prov. 6:16, 19); we must walk in humility and in the fear of the Lord (Eccl. 12:13). Not have hatred but love "Hatred stirreth up strifes: but love covereth all sins." – Prov. 10:12. We must be willing to ask forgiveness and make restitution where possible (James 5:16) with "clean hands, and a pure heart; who hath not lifted up his soul unto vanity, nor sworn deceitfully" (Psa. 24:1-4). We must put down pride, "Only by pride cometh contention" – Prov. 13:10. "But he giveth more grace. Wherefore he saith, God resisteth the proud, but giveth grace unto the humble." – James 4:6. "He hath shewed thee, O man, what is good; and what doth the Lord require of thee, but to do justly, and to love mercy, and to walk humbly with thy God?" – Micah 6:8. "If it be possible, as much as lieth in you, live peaceably with all men." – Rom. 12:18. "Follow peace with all men, and holiness, without which no man shall see the Lord:" – Heb. 12:14.

Maintaining Biblical faith can only be concluded by bringing light to a crucial topic one must be aware of. As with any move of God, such as the 1904 Welsh Revival, there is always a time of flowing and a time of eventual subsiding of revival blessing. During such times, there is a great need for two things. One is the need to put down the manifestations of the flesh and counterfeits that Satan brings during and after the revival. This would also entail surrounding oneself with godly men whom God can raise having the Spirit of discernment. Two, the need for those called by God who must disciple those affected by the revival to be grounded in the word of God. There is a great need for the focus of the people to stay in the word of God and desire to continue to find the God of the word by the Holy Spirit. Though manifestations may be seen during a revival, there is always a difference to be discerned if it attracts attention to the one going through it or if it brings awe and glory to God. Anything that gives temporal display without the depth of a holy life and a desire to seek the God of the Bible needs to be put down and carefully weeded out from what God has for His people. What we need today is a revival of truth, of holiness, not a revival of manifestation or emotions, though they may follow in the workings of the Spirit. John states, "Beloved, believe not every spirit, but try the spirits whether they are of God: because many false prophets are gone out into the world." – 1 John 4:1. And this exhortation is relevant whether during this time of barrenness or during seasons of refreshing from heaven that has lasting effects. The application of the word of God that flows through revival power by the Spirit needs to be established as the lifelong journey of one's walk with God, which is critical for preventing any disillusionment of those touched by a visitation from God.

THE POURING FORTH

Prayer, Not America's Greatest Need

This topic may seem contradictory to what has been said prior or even seen around us in emphasizing prayer, but a particular order must be followed if we are to follow God's way. There is a vast difference between the God of the Bible and our view of who God is. We have strayed so far away as Bible believers that we need to come to the place of seeing the difference between the God of the Bible and what we have portrayed of Him and repent of our unworthy views of God. God has no obligation to correct His view about Himself, for He has already given that in His word, and unless He intervenes in an act of mercy, we will continue this downward trend. David went through three years of famine before he asked God and found the cause as the breach that Saul did against the Gibeonites (2 Sam. 21). Only after he changed course God was intreated for the land. The most fearful place to be is when God lets us alone to follow our own ways. "Ephraim is joined to idols: let him alone." – Hos. 4:17. You cannot build a house from a broken foundation that is unsteady. **We must deal with the root instead of trying to trim the fruits**. We must put away the corruption, repair and build the altar, put the wood in order, sacrifice and place the bullock, expect the supernatural, **and only then** call upon God for the fire to fall (1 Kings 18:30-38).

In the time of Nehemiah, they had to first put away and acknowledge the sins of the people as their own sins in taking personal accountability before they sought the face of God for times of refreshing. "And said, I beseech thee, O Lord God of heaven, the great and terrible God, that keepeth covenant and mercy for them that love him and observe his commandments: Let thine ear now be attentive, and thine eyes open, that thou mayest hear the prayer of thy servant, which I pray before thee now, day and night, for the children of Israel thy servants, and confess the sins of the children of Israel, which we have sinned against thee: both I and my father's house have sinned. We have dealt very corruptly against thee, and have not kept the commandments, nor the statutes, nor the judgments, which thou commandedst thy servant Moses." – Neh. 1:5-7. Nehemiah had not personally sinned in that fashion, but he realized that unless there was a corporate confession, God was not going to hear (repeated in chapter 9). We must have personal and corporate repentance. We see this in the time of Solomon when they were as one in their response (2 Chr. 5:13), similar to when the day of Pentecost was fully come, they were all in one accord in one place (Acts 2:1). Israel's greatest danger was not from her enemies surrounding her but from allowing sin to overcome her. In sinning against God, they incurred the wrath and judgment of Almighty God; and who could save them when He became their enemy? Consider this from Jeremiah about God, "He hath bent his bow like an enemy: he stood with his right hand as an adversary, and slew all that were pleasant to the eye in the tabernacle of the daughter of Zion: he poured out his fury like fire. The Lord was as an enemy: he hath swallowed up Israel, he hath swallowed up all her palaces: he hath destroyed his strong holds, and hath increased in the daughter of Judah mourning and lamentation." – Lam. 2:4-5. Samson was given over to his sin where he wist not that the Lord was departed from him. Gideon, who knew how God had worked in the past, asked the right question, "Oh my Lord, if the Lord be with us, why then is all this befallen us? and where be all his miracles which our fathers told us of, saying, Did not the Lord bring us up from Egypt? but now the Lord hath forsaken us, and delivered us into the hands of the Midianites." – Judg. 6:13.

We hear much about the promises of God who hears and answers prayer, ask and it shall be given (Matt. 7:7), call unto me, and I will answer thee (Jer. 33:3), faith to move mountains (Matt. 17:20), and so forth, but though those promises are true the desperate need we have is to acquaint ourselves with the God who answers by fire before we exercise His promises. And it is true today with His church as well. "For unto whomsoever much is given, of him shall be much required: and to whom men have committed much, of him they will ask the more." – Luke 12:48. God desires purity of heart and unity of motive. Everything lives or dies on Truth (Matt. 21:44), and for something to be a conviction, it must be upheld for truth's sake and not because of the opinions of men or personal preferences or likes and dislikes.

Praying for revival without obedience is an abomination. Revival is God coming down, but preparation for God to come down has various areas that must be dealt with. There is breaking up our fallow ground; there is obedience to known truth; there is putting away of hindrances and things that promote a low view of God; there is the remembrance of God in renewing our vows before Him; there is the praying for the Spirit of discernment, and so forth. It is easy to say we need to pray for revival, or we are praying for revival, but if we don't do anything to prepare for it, there is no reason for God to send it. It is like saying, send us rain for our thirst, but we are full of the pleasures of Egypt and have no vessel that is clean to receive it. I believe the appropriate response to a church that states they are praying for revival would be, how are you preparing to receive it? I hear of children praying for their parents not to get divorced. Still, I am grieved that neither party wants to repent, humble themselves, have deep-seated roots of bitterness, and are unwilling to put things away, but they encourage their children to pray for the other party, saying that God will answer their prayers. What a travesty and blindness where the child blames God when their parent divorces and marries another.

285

To summarize, asking people to pray or teaching them to pray is the wrong starting point, for it is trying to fix the fruit while ignoring the root issue. The root issue is our need to humble ourselves, repair the breach, and deal with an angry God whose frown is upon us, where He and His Spirit have left us and is fighting against us (Deut. 31, Josh. 24:20, Psa. 66:18, 80:4, Isa. 29:13, 63:10). "Hear the word of the Lord, ye children of Israel: **for the Lord hath a controversy with the inhabitants of the land**, because there is no truth, nor mercy, nor knowledge of God in the land." – Hos. 4:1 *(emphasis mine)*. And God says, "when ye spread forth your hands, I will hide mine eyes from you: yea, when ye make many prayers, I will not hear: your hands are full of blood. Wash you, make you clean; put away the evil of your doings from before mine eyes; cease to do evil; Learn to do well; seek judgment, relieve the oppressed, judge the fatherless, plead for the widow. Come now, and let us reason together, saith the Lord: though your sins be as scarlet, they shall be as white as snow; though they be red like crimson, they shall be as wool." – Isa. 1:15-18. It is after we repent and put things in order that God cleanses and makes us white as snow. And prayer for God to work is no substitute for repentance. As H. A. Ironside stated regarding Christ knocking at the door of His church in Revelation 3:20, "the door is unlatched only by repentance; it can be opened in no other way. So long as there is pride and arrogancy He remains outside."

We need to candidly put in writing that which has offended God, materials that portray an inadequate view of God, confess it before God and man, repent of them, and put them away permanently. In repentance, there may be a need for church discipline to put away members or leadership of the church who are after their belly or a hindrance to the cause of seeking God, with a desire for them to repent and be restored to the fellowship. Judgment must begin in the house of God (1 Peter 4:17), and the Great Commission cannot be fulfilled without the proper foundation. It is the great omission that is the danger we are faced with today in Americanized Christianity. We need prayer, yes, but prayer is not an excuse for obedience; we need mercy, yes, and thousand times yes, but mercy cannot be used as an excuse to continue in sin and not take personal responsibility in forsaking sin, and only those who forsake their wicked ways will receive mercy (Isa. 55:7). We have sown to the wind and are now reaping the whirlwind (Hos. 8:7). We have been guilty of making the word of God to fit our doctrine, leaving the God of the word out, being satisfied with what He said, and not plowing through and getting to His manifest presence and meeting the God of the word.

Of the church at Sardis Jesus said, "I know thy works, that thou hast a name that thou livest, and art dead" – Rev. 3:1. Unless we repent, we are just a "gerbil on a wheel," with much activity and no progress. Beloved brethren, can you not read the victory of Christ in the book of Acts on that early church that had nothing but God Himself and honestly state that we are "turning the world upside down" in this generation? Can you not sense the heart of Christ that is grieving over His Bride, who is staggering around as a cripple trying to hold on to her crutches?

A Glimmer of Hope

If what I read and study in the Scriptures about apostolic Christianity is true, then I can't but come to the conclusion that we're in trouble following an American pseudo-Christianity, and we are a nation under Divine judgment. Yes, we are in deep darkness, and the light seems to have almost been extinguished, but America has been in similar depths of sin in her past. Think of this recollection from J. Edwin Orr.

"Not many people realize that in the wake of the American Revolution (following 1775-1783), there was a moral slump. Drunkenness became epidemic. Out of a population of five million, 300,000 were confirmed drunkards; they were burying fifteen thousand of them each year. Profanity was of the most shocking kind. For the first time in the history of the American settlement, women were afraid to go out at night for fear of assault. Bank robberies were a daily occurrence. The Chief Justice of the United States, John Marshall, wrote to the Bishop of Virginia, James Madison, that the church 'was too far gone ever to be redeemed.' Voltaire averred, and Tom Paine echoed, 'Christianity will be forgotten in thirty years.' Take the liberal arts colleges at that time. A poll taken at Harvard had discovered not one believer in the whole student body. They took a poll at Princeton, a much more evangelical place, where they discovered only two believers in the student body and only five that did not belong to the filthy speech movement of that day. Students rioted. They held a mock communion at Williams College, and they put on anti-Christian plays at Dartmouth. They burned down the Nassau Hall at Princeton. They forced the resignation of the president of Harvard. They took a Bible out of a local Presbyterian church in New Jersey, and they burnt it in a public bonfire. Christians were so few on campus in the 1790s that they met in secret, like a communist cell, and kept their minutes in code so that no one would know."

Did the people quote that they are in the last days and give up on seeking after God, or did they say in unbelief that revival is not possible? From such darkness came the gracious movement that God sent, known as the Second Great Awakening. And God has sent many more since then to a people who humble themselves in repentance, forsake their sin, and seek the One who can make bare His arm. A people set apart and waiting for Him, a heart prepared, and a people aware of the need for God to come. In Malachi 3:1, we see the place of preparation and the place of delighting in the Lord Himself, and then, "the Lord, whom ye seek, shall suddenly come." "Let God arise, let his enemies be scattered: let them also that hate him flee before him." – Psa. 68:1. We rejoice in the goodness of God, but that should not blind us to our need to face the reality of a God who has His frown upon us, whose hand is against us, for we have quenched His blessed Spirit. We see it evidenced in the apathy and coldness prevailing around us, the church unable to stem the tide of wickedness, and the many news we hear of men in the ministry falling into gross sins. "Or despisest thou the riches of his goodness and forbearance and longsuffering; not knowing that the goodness of God leadeth thee to repentance?" – Rom. 2:4.

We see the promise of God to "pour water upon him that is thirsty, and floods upon the dry ground" – Isa. 44:3. Though this promise is true at an individual level, we can also see it from the perspective of a corporate body of believers. The inner circle of the thirsty is the church that realizes her desperate need for God to pour water, for she is very dry. And as we see the dryness within the church, we also recognize that this dryness prevails around the church, community, and nation. We also realize that the barren condition of the world reflects the state of the church, which lacks in giving that life-giving water to the world. And as God pours water upon the thirsty church, it overflows as a flood around her, impacting the community and the nation in a torrent of blessing. The book of Jonah is a beautiful picture of God's heart to restore not only a rebellious nation that was a heathen but a rebellious prophet as well, to show mercy where no mercy was deserved.

We see the great upheavals of evil that America is going through, and people question asking, "where is God?" or "If He is in control and is good, then why did He allow this to happen?" During such times, we must remind ourselves that we live in a sin-cursed world because we have rejected God; and we told God that we don't need Him in America; we want to promote wickedness and call evil as good, and when He leaves us to our own devices, we reap what we sow. Mankind is willing to submit and flourish in the natural laws that God created, such as gravity, seasons, and such, but is unwilling to submit when it pertains to themselves regarding what God says they must live by. By rejecting God, we are destroying ourselves, for our rights come from God. Thomas

Jefferson, the 3rd president of the United States and Drafter and Signer of the Declaration of Independence, said, "God who gave us life gave us liberty. And can the liberties of a nation be thought secure when we have removed their only firm basis, a conviction in the minds of the people that these liberties are of the gift of God? That they are not to be violated but with His wrath? Indeed, I tremble for my country when I reflect that God is just; that His justice cannot sleep forever..." And the church must take the mantle to be that intercessor to plead with God that in wrath He might remember mercy (Hab. 3:2). Not so that we can continue sinning, but so we can seek God for an outpouring of His Spirit who is the only source who can heal our land. The lost will not seek God, for they know not God. It must be by those who are called by His name. We must realize that it is not that the nation has rejected God; it is the churches that have rejected God, and the state of our nation is just a fruit of what the churches have done. It is time for the church to evaluate where she is and take responsibility for the sins of the land, for she is the one who will be held accountable by God for being the light amidst darkness as the pillar and ground of the truth (1 Tim. 3:15). And before she fulfills her mandate to spread the gospel, she must ensure that the gospel she preaches is that which was once delivered unto the saints. If we have a wrong foundation, the fruit will inevitably be corrupted.

"Draw nigh to God, and he will draw nigh to you. Cleanse your hands, ye sinners; and purify your hearts, ye double minded. Be afflicted, and mourn, and weep: let your laughter be turned to mourning, and your joy to heaviness. Humble yourselves in the sight of the Lord, and he shall lift you up." – James 4:8-10. "Therefore also now, saith the Lord, turn ye even to me with all your heart, and with fasting, and with weeping, and with mourning: And rend your heart, and not your garments, and turn unto the Lord your God: for he is gracious and merciful, slow to anger, and of great kindness, and repenteth him of the evil. Who knoweth if he will return and repent, and leave a blessing behind him; even a meat offering and a drink offering unto the Lord your God? Blow the trumpet in Zion, sanctify a fast, call a solemn assembly:" - Joel 2:12-15. We see this solemn assembly repeated many times in the life of Israel. But we see a clear example in the life of king Josiah. There are a few characteristics that one can observe when we read 2 Kings 22 and 23. There was obedience to known truth, there was a reckoning of the reality of God's displeasure, there was an asking of the Lord for His mercies, there was an evaluation and a covenant made before the Lord, and there was a putting away in destroying the idolators and idols with thoroughness to make sure nothing was missed. In addition, there was obedience in desiring God's way of worship by what He had said, there was a heartfelt seeking and spending the time needed for it, and there was healing in the refreshing they received from the Lord. Finally, there was great rejoicing in God's goodness and the building up of faith. All this was done as a corporate body with everyone involved.

One Accord

I need to elaborate on this before we go further regarding those who come together, see the need, and desire the work of God in their midst and the nation. When we talk about meeting in one accord, the surface-level thought may be in the matter of coming together and praying. But this is much deeper than that. Some fundamental truths have to be upheld.

One, we cannot yoke up with unbelievers in coming together. This seems basic, but we cannot join hands with Mormons, Catholics, Unitarians, and those who don't believe in the fundamentals of the faith and desire God to work. Some could justify the tendency to compromise in order to get a larger number of people to seek the Lord. But God does not look for numbers; He looks for truth and calling unto Him out of a pure heart. God desires a few who have united on truth than a thousand joined by falsehood. **Unity at the expense of truth is the unity of demons** (1 Sam. 15:22). We see the explicit command in 2 Corinthians 6:14-15, "Be ye not unequally yoked together with unbelievers: for what fellowship hath righteousness with unrighteousness? and what communion hath light with darkness? And what concord hath Christ with Belial? or what part hath he that believeth with an infidel?" and the command to come out from among them and be ye separate. We see further warnings in 2 John 1:9-11. It is imperative that this is the starting point. If there is no adherence to this, we are confronted with that searching question, "Can two walk together, except they be agreed?" – Amos 3:3. How can you pray to the God of the Bible with someone who rejects the deity of Jesus Christ? It is impossible. While we join on the essentials of our faith, we must also have the same starting point on sin and what offends a holy God, the nature of genuine regeneration, and such.

Two, we must uphold the expectation of what we are coming together for. One may have the hope of churches filled with people, others may be interested in seeing many "decisions" being made, and still, others may be purely emotional. There must be a calling into account what the gathering of "one accord" is for. We see this picture in Joshua 3, where the priests came together bearing that ark to the edge of the river Jordan and, when they dipped their feet, saw the miracle happen. Before Pentecost, Peter had to deal with sorting out the matter of Matthias and the unity that they exhibited in the decisions that were made. I like the account Duncan Campbell gave recounting the Lewis Awakening of what they came together for, which I believe is a good guide for helping in these matters.

The praying men and women of Barvas had four governing principles that they adhered to: *(Compiled from the book, The Lewis Awakening by Duncan Campbell)*

1. They themselves must be rightly related to God, and in this connection, the reading of Psalm 24 at one of their prayer meetings brought them down in the presence of the Lord, where hearts were searched, and vows renewed.

2. They were possessed of the conviction that God, being a covenant-keeping God, must keep His covenant engagements. Had He not promised to "pour water upon him that is thirsty, and floods upon the dry ground"? Here was something that for them existed in the field of possibility; why were they not actually experiencing it? But they came at length to the place where, with one of old, they could cry "Our God – is able – and He will."

3. They must be prepared for God to work in His own way and not according to their programme – God was sovereign and must act according to His sovereign purpose – but ever keeping in mind that, while God is sovereign in the affairs of men, His sovereignty does not relieve men of responsibility. "God is a God of revival, but man is the human agent through whom revival is possible."

4. There must be a manifestation of God, demonstrating the reality of the Divine in operation, when men would be forced to say, "This is the Lord's doing; it is marvellous in our eyes."

God uses the weakness of men that have been put to death on the cross and are raised to walk in resurrection life. Though the men God used in history were varied in theology from schools of thought such as Calvinists and Arminians, they had five distinct areas *(in addition to the absolute authority of the word of God and the fundamentals of the faith that they united upon)* they were certain about to the point of conviction.

- One: The high view of God
- Two: The proper view of self
- Three: The Person and Work of the Holy Spirit
- Four: Regeneration as being born of God, proven by the outcome
- Five: The place of intercession

Thus, you could have Dr. Martyn Lloyd-Jones commend A. W. Tozer; George Whitefield, and John Wesley, who worked together during the Evangelical Revival; General William Booth participating in the meetings during the 1904 Welsh Revival; J. C. Ryle inviting D. L. Moody to hold a campaign in Liverpool; Leonard Ravenhill praying with Duncan Campbell; Dr. Lee Robertson recommending Ian Paisley for holding special meetings in Tennessee, and many others. We realize that the body is one but many members who need each other in order to thrive. "That there should be no schism in the body; but that the members should have the same care one for another. And whether one member suffer, all the members suffer with it; or one member be honoured, all the members rejoice with it. Now ye are the body of Christ, and members in particular." – 1 Cor. 12:25-27. I am reminded of Christ's intercessory prayer in John 17:20-21, "Neither pray I for these alone, but for them also which shall believe on me through their word; That they all may be one; as thou, Father, art in me, and I in thee, that they also may be one in us: that the world may believe that thou hast sent me."

The Heart of God

There are certain areas we dread to walk lest when we dare peer into them, we become liars, for it is impossible to accurately tell of things that are too sacred for us to dwell in, where God alone owns supreme sway. But we see glimpses of what God has revealed, hear of what God has said, and lay our hands upon our mouths and declare, "God forbid: yea, let God be true, but every man a liar" – Rom. 3:4. Did not God declare in Ezekiel 33:11, "I have no pleasure in the death of the wicked; but that the wicked turn from his way and live: turn ye, turn ye from your evil ways"? And in Micah 7:18, "Who is a God like unto thee, that pardoneth iniquity, and passeth by the transgression of the remnant of his heritage? he retaineth not his anger for ever, because he delighteth in mercy." We serve a good God, a God of mercy, but it must be on His terms and not what we can come up with in building a new cart for placing the Ark (2 Sam. 6). In seeking mercy, we see something unfathomable in His response to the children of Israel, who acknowledged their sin and put away the strange gods from among them and served the Lord. We see this rare glimpse of God's heart where we read, "and his soul was grieved for the misery of Israel" – Judg. 10:16. If the grief of man could be unutterable at times, how much greater is the grief of God? We see God's call to Israel to repent through the prophets that He sent. The prophet Hosea was told to marry a harlot and showed Israel's whoredom with other gods; after such dealings, we see something that we cannot go too much further into, "How shall I give thee up, Ephraim? how shall I deliver thee, Israel? how shall I make thee as Admah? how shall I set thee as Zeboim? mine heart is turned within me, my repentings are kindled together." – Hos. 11:8. God's heart in distress for the misery of His people and the judgment that is to come upon them. Sometimes it was seen as shadows in His prophets like Jeremiah who was called as a "weeping prophet." We see similar glimpses at Gethsemane "And being in an agony he prayed more earnestly: and his sweat was as it were great drops of blood falling down to the ground." – Luke 22:44. There we see that the more sin blinded us and bound us, and eventually destroy us, it affected God's innermost being in what He was facing, in shedding His own blood for our iniquities. That prophetic passage in Isaiah 53 speaks of such depths that we cannot comprehend how much it cost God; when we read, "it pleased the Lord to bruise him" (v10), God the Father forsook His Son that Christ cried out with a loud voice, "My God, my God, why hast thou forsaken me?" - Matt. 27:46.

If heaven is as brass, and God sought for a man to stand in the gap lest He destroys the land (Eze. 22:30), we need to realize that it is not just alignment with the truth that is going to matter. It is that, but we must also be aligned with God by taking on His heart. And pray for intercessors that God would raise them up to reach the ear of heaven. Dear reader, can we not see the need for us to heed the warning that God gives us to bring us back to Him to return unto the Lord? He desires mercy and not destruction; for us to repent.

Heeding the Warning

Suppose someone says that many have preached in prior years on the coming destruction. And today, we see various judgments of God prevalent in our land, such as giving us over to uncleanness, acceptance of lies, withdrawal of His manifest presence, wide acceptance of shallow forms of evangelism, having a form of godliness, a nation in decline, heaven is as brass, and our prayers fall by the wayside, and such (Rom. 1:18-32). However, though we have seen such, we have not seen judgments such as what Sodom experienced. Suppose that is our attitude towards the increasing wickedness in America. What should we consider? There is a **cry of sin that reaches heaven**. And when it gets filled to the brim, God will intervene with Divine justice unto destruction or with Divine mercy to send an outpouring. The cry of sin came from the blood of Abel (Gen. 4:10), from the days of Noah (Gen. 6:13), from Sodom and Gomorrah (Gen. 18:20-21), from the Amorites (Gen. 15:16), from Nineveh (Jonah 1:2), to whom God showed mercy when they repented of sin and evil (Jonah 3:5-9), from Israel in Canaan who polluted the land with blood (Psa. 106:35-40), from the Jews in the New Testament where Jesus said that the blood of all the prophets would be required from that generation (Luke 11:50-51), and it was fulfilled in AD 70 when Titus plundered Jerusalem and utterly destroyed it, and from the Jews during the time of the apostle Paul (1 Thess. 2:16). If the warnings from the past have not been heeded in America and we have continued our downward trend, how much closer are we then to the judgment of

God? and if we repent of our ways would we see mercy extended in Divine intervention?

Sentimental Christianity portrays a "Christ" of emotional acceptance and not the Christ of Truth, a god of convenience and not the God who demands everything of us. Are we willing to put away anything that robs the proper view of God, our sinner's prayers, our pre-canned meetings, cookie-cutter methods, shallow evangelism with shallow fruits, repent from the lack of all-night weekly corporate prayer, materials that need to be thrown away and burned up which promote a sentimental Christianity? We must deal with what God hates; pride, spiritual blindness, our cliché statements, unwillingness to see our true condition, and unbelief that questions if God is still able to work as He did in the book of Acts. We must repent from our denominational arrogance, pride in our achievements and academic degrees, self-deceit, and rebellion against the Spirit by our actions which is similar to the sin of witchcraft, and stubbornness of being set in our ways which are as iniquity and idolatry. We must be honest before God that all the trimmings that we have added to the pure unadulterated word have been due to our unbelief to portray by our actions that God works only in the way that "we have prescribed for Him." To pray for revival without forsaking and putting away its hindrances is madness. "Sow to yourselves in righteousness, reap in mercy; break up your fallow ground: for it is time to seek the Lord, till he come and rain righteousness upon you." – Hos. 10:12. "Repent ye therefore, and be converted, that your sins may be blotted out, when the times of refreshing shall come from the presence of the Lord." – Acts 3:19.

Dear brethren, the sin of Achan must be put to death; the breach made in Shittim must be stopped as Phinehas, the son of Eleazar did when he thrust the javelin through the man of Israel and the Midianitish woman through her belly; it was then that the plague was stayed (Num. 25). God, who is the author of our salvation and loved the church and gave Himself for her, has every right to dictate the terms. Grace does not shield us from God when we take for granted the magnitude of meeting with God. Instead, grace in the New Testament brings us into a closer relationship with God, the veil having rent, much more intimately than He was revealed in Abraham's day, who rejoiced the day of His coming (John 8:56); God's judgment of sin has not changed. While He has been longsuffering toward us, we don't know how long He will suffer (Gen. 6:3, 2 Peter 3:9). When that cry of sin comes unto the Lord, God's judgment will fall (Gen. 4:10, 6:13, 18:20-21, Jonah 1:2, Matt. 23:32, 37-38, 1 Thess. 2:16, 1 John 5:16). For Lot, it was the presence of ten righteous; I wonder how much is needed for America before God will pour out His judgment upon us, seeing the lack thereof. If we are not part of the solution, then we are part of the problem. Given below are some truths that have been a help to me in rethinking the God of the Bible, who is the same God we serve today.

1. Realize the serious nature of what God has said about Himself. (Isa. 40:25-31, 46:5, 9-10, 57:15, Mal. 3:6, Rev. 1:8)
   a. The uniqueness of God and the inability of man to comprehend, and the impossibility of man to be able to wrap his mind around this glorious Being.
2. Recognize what God has said about man. (Psa. 14:1-3, 51:5, 103:14, Job 15:14-16, 25:4-6, Eph. 2:1)
   a. Not just what he does against God, but who he is, its root, and where all his actions come from. Sinner from head to toe, by nature and by choice, dead, and unable and unwilling to do good that is acceptable to God.
3. Rethink the awfulness of sin in relation to a holy God. (Psa. 7:11, 9:17, Isa. 5:14, 6:1-5, Matt. 12:31-32, 21:12-13, Matt. 23, Luke 16:19-31, 1 Cor. 3:17, Acts 5:1-11, Rev. 14:19-20, 21:8)
   a. Divorcing and rejecting all other beliefs (including current inadequate teachings in Christendom),

religions, and philosophies. Realizing that the God
of the Bible judges' sin even unto death.

b.   Be desirous to be led by the Spirit through the word
alone and consider God's dealing in the Old and
New Testament. He has given us so many clouds of
witnesses in the providential guidance of His church
in history, those who have contended for the purity
of the gospel.

A prayerful discourse on these crucial topics could be done to
bring the people to an accurate understanding of God, man, and
the need to be rightly related to Him, not just for salvation but for
seeking His face. Dear brethren, God is still God, and He hates sin
just as He ever hated sin, for He changes not (Mal. 3:6); it is time
for us to repent, to put away the evil in our midst, and wholly turn
to the Lord before we pray. Being humble means being honest. "If
my people, which are called by my name, shall **humble
themselves**, ..." – 2 Chr. 7:14 *(emphasis mine)*. **This is what we
have need of in the American church**. Unless we humble
ourselves, the rest of the verse does not apply. We see a parallel
passage in James 4:8-10, where James speaks of drawing nigh to
God (v8) but quickly goes on to give the requirements for doing that
in verses 8-10. Exhortations are given to cleanse your hands of sin,
purify your hearts, not be wavering, be afflicted, mourn, weep, and
finally **humble yourselves**, so He can lift us up (He draws nigh
to us). This is the time to [Lord] "turn ye even to me with all your
heart, and with fasting, and with weeping, and with mourning: And
rend your heart, and not your garments, and turn unto the Lord
your God" – Joel 2:12-13. Our prayers will not be heard if we don't
follow God's order of how this is to happen. As we humble ourselves
in fasting and mourning from a broken and contrite heart, we can
then pray to seek His face and turn from our wicked ways
(determined not to go back to it).

In that grand declaration of David's confessional prayer (Psa.
51), v1-11 deals with confessing his sin and humbling himself; in

v12-13, he asks for restoration for making an impact on sinners around him; continues to sing God's righteousness and shewing forth God's praise in v14-15; continues to God's standard for restoration and cleansing in identifying his own need for God's favor and protection upon him in v16-19. It is easy to quote 1 John 1:9, but unless we humbly repent, there is nothing to go forward with. God's condition remains the same, "Let the priests, the ministers of the Lord, weep between the porch and the altar, and let them say, Spare thy people, O Lord, and give not thine heritage to reproach, that the heathen should rule over them: wherefore should they say among the people, Where is their God?" – Joel 2:17. Blaming God for not answering our prayers, pointing the finger, looking at politicians or the White House will not help. Acknowledgment of wrong does not mean conviction of sin. Getting caught or feeling remorse because you have done wrong does not mean conviction of sin by the Spirit. Saul said, "I have sinned" (1 Sam. 15:24) but it was not the same as when David said, "I have sinned" (2 Sam. 12:13). True conviction is evident when we take action against our sin in repentance. In 2 Corinthians 7:10, they felt godly sorrow and it led to repentance, but what did that repentance produce? It produced seven outcomes against the wrongdoing (v11): carefulness (diligence), clearing of yourselves (self-examination), indignation (against how far they have strayed from God), fear (of God's displeasure), vehement desire (a sense of urgency), zeal (unceasing energy in pursuing the cause), and revenge (against the wrong to make it right before God)!

Again, God is not looking for the lost to seek His face; He is looking for His remnant, where one man with God is a majority. "For the eyes of the Lord run to and fro throughout the whole earth, to shew himself strong in the behalf of them whose heart is perfect toward him." – 2 Chr. 16:9.

It is now well past October 2021, over many years after my dad entered into his rest. I am often reminded that my rest is in heaven. We are not here to live long, retire in wealth, and expect a long life of ease and comfort. If travailing for God in this journey brings us to an early grave, let it be so, for He is worthy of all by our living or dying. Looking back and echoing with the Psalmist, "But as for me, my feet were almost gone; my steps had well nigh slipped." – Psa. 73:2, I can say that God, in His goodness, led me all the way. In faithfulness, He doth continue to guide me in this journey of faith; and my heart, with worship and adoration, cries out in enraptured love, "Abba, Father." I think of the chief end of man as stated in Westminster's shorter catechism, "Man's chief end is to glorify God, and to enjoy Him forever," but if there was only one verse we had in all of the Scriptures that we were left with, to me, it sums up in, "Thou art worthy, O Lord, to receive glory and honour and power: for thou hast created all things, and for thy pleasure they are and were created." – Rev. 4:11. We were created for Him to bring Him pleasure, and everything else flows out from that union with Christ. And what is the essence of life itself of a regenerated man? By living, you display the truth of God; by living the crucified life, you portray the glory of God; by sealing your testimony in blood, you honor God Himself.

A good prayer to meditate upon is the prayer of Daniel in Daniel 9:3-19. He begins by humbling himself in sackcloth and ashes, acknowledging their sins, repenting from the heart, remembering the holiness of God and God's hatred toward sin, and finally ends with five heart-rending cries for God's response to hear, forgive, hearken, do, and not delay (defer not). And it was "for thine own sake, O my God: for thy city and thy people are called by thy name" (v19). There are precious and glorious promises from God given to us for our healing, but only if we repent of our ways and let Him break us; then He will bind us up.

"Turn us again, O God, and cause thy face to shine; and we shall be saved." – Psa. 80:3, "Let us search and try our ways, and turn again to the Lord" – Lam. 3:40, "Come, and let us return unto the Lord: for he hath torn, and he will heal us; he hath smitten, and he will bind us up." – Hos. 6:1.

About the Author

Jabez Abraham is the founder and president of Desiring Revival Ministries, dedicated to advancing the cause of revival and making God known to all generations and nations. The ministry began with a divine call in 2005, burdening him with the need for genuine revival among God's people and an awakening in the nation. Since then, God has nurtured this burden, instilling a desire for believers to return to a vibrant and authentic Biblical Christianity, as depicted in the book of Acts.

Soli Deo Gloria

www.ingramcontent.com/pod-product-compliance
Lightning Source LLC
Chambersburg PA
CBHW030909120626
46554CB00001B/80